CiTY·SMaRT™
GUIDEBOOK

San Antonio

Second Edition

Erik Ketcherside

John Muir Publications
Santa Fe, New Mexico

John Muir Publications, P.O. Box 613, Santa Fe, New Mexico 87504

Printed in the United States of America.
Second edition. First printing August 1999.

ISBN: 1-56261-489-4
ISSN: 1095-0710

Editors: Ellen Cavalli, Sarah Baldwin, Nancy Gillan
Graphics Editor: Heather Pool
Production: Rebecca Cook
Design: Janine Lehmann
Cover design: Suzanne Rush
Typesetter: Melissa Tandysh
Map production: Julie Felton
Printer: Publishers Press
Front cover photo: © Robb Helfrick—Mission San Jose
Back cover photo: © Andre Jenny/International Stock—River Walk

Distributed to the book trade by
Publishers Group West
Berkeley, California

CONTENTS

See San Antonio the City•Smart™ Way　　　　　　　　**v**

1 Welcome to San Antonio　　　　　　　　**1**
Getting to Know San Antonio 2 • A Brief History of San Antonio 5 • San Antonio Time Line 10 • The People of San Antonio 12 • When to Visit 15 • Calendar of Events 17 • Dressing in San Antonio 20 • Business and Economy 21 • Schools 22

2 Getting Around San Antonio　　　　　　　　**23**
City Layout 23 • Public Transportation 25 • Driving in San Antonio 30 • Biking in San Antonio 32 • San Antonio International Airport 32 • Train Service 35 • Regional Bus Service 35

3 Where to Stay　　　　　　　　**36**
Downtown 37 • Northeast 50 • Northwest 52 • South 56

4 Where to Eat　　　　　　　　**58**
Restaurants by Food Type 59 • Downtown 60 • Northeast 66 • Northwest 76 • South 84

5 Sights and Attractions　　　　　　　　**86**
Downtown 86 • Northeast 100 • Northwest 106 • South 108

6 Museums and Galleries　　　　　　　　**111**
Art Museums 111 • Science and History Museums 113 • Military Museums 116 • Galleries 117

7 Kids' Stuff　　　　　　　　**122**
Animals and the Great Outdoors 122 • Music and Entertainment 126 • Museums and Libraries 127 • Stores Kids Love 129 • Theme Parks 130

8 Parks, Gardens, and Recreation Areas　　　　　　　　**132**

9 Shopping　　　　　　　　**141**
Shopping Districts 141 • Notable Bookstores and Newsstands 145 • Other Notable Stores 146 • Department Stores 149 • Shopping Malls 150 • Factory Outlet Centers 153

10 Sports and Recreation　　　　　　　　**154**
Professional Sports 154 • Recreation 158

11 Performing Arts　　　　　　　　**168**
Theater 168 • Classical Music and Opera 170 • Dance 171 • Concert Venues 173

12 Nightlife　　　　　　　　**180**
Dance Clubs 180 • Jazz Clubs 182 • Blues Clubs 184 • Rock Clubs 185 • Country and Western Clubs 185 • Tejano, Salsa, and Latin Clubs 186 • Other Clubs 188 • Pubs and Bars 190 • Comedy Clubs 191 • Poetry Spots 191 • Movie Houses of Note 192

13 Day Trips from San Antonio   195

Lyndon B. Johnson National Historical Park 195 • Enchanted Rock State Park and Fredericksburg 197 • Hill Country Magic Tour and Hill Country Escape 199 • Lady Bird Johnson Wildflower Center and Austin 199 • San Marcos 200 • Laredo, Texas, and Nuevo Laredo, Mexico 201 • Brackettville 202 • Space Center Houston 203

Appendix: City•Smart Basics   205

Emergency Phone Numbers 205 • Hospitals and Emergency Medical Centers 205 • Recorded Information 205 • Visitor Information 206 • Disabled Access Information 206 • City Tours 206 • Car Rental 206 • Post Offices 206 • Resources for New Residents 208 • Multicultural Resources 208 • Babysitting/ Child Care 208 • City Media 209 • Bookstores 209

MAP CONTENTS

Greater San Antonio Zones   vi

3 Where to Stay
Downtown San Antonio   38
Greater San Antonio   48

4 Where to Eat
Downtown San Antonio   61
Greater San Antonio   68

5 Sights and Attractions
Downtown San Antonio   87
River Walk   90
Greater San Antonio   102
Mission Trail   109

13 Day Trips from San Antonio
San Antonio Region   196

See San Antonio the CiTY·SMaRT™ Way

The Guide for San Antonio Natives, New Residents, and Visitors

In *City•Smart Guidebook: San Antonio*, local author Erik Ketcherside tells it like it is. Residents will learn things they never knew about their city, new residents will get an insider's view of their new hometown, and visitors will be guided to the very best San Antonio has to offer—whether they're on a weekend getaway or staying a week or more.

Opinionated Recommendations Save You Time and Money

From shopping to nightlife to museums, the author isn't afraid to tell you what he likes and dislikes. You'll learn the great and the not-so-great things about San Antonio's sights, restaurants, and accommodations. So you can decide what's worth your time and what's not; which hotel is worth the splurge and which is the best choice for budget travelers.

Easy-to-Use Format Makes Planning Your Trip a Cinch

City•Smart Guidebook: San Antonio is user-friendly—you'll quickly find exactly what you're looking for. Chapters are organized by travelers' interests or needs, from Where to Stay and Where to Eat, to Sights and Attractions, Kids' Stuff, Sports and Recreation, and even Day Trips from San Antonio.

Includes Maps and Quick Location-Finding Features

Every listing in this book is accompanied by a geographic zone designation (see the following pages for zone details) that helps you immediately find each location. Staying in Alamo Heights and wondering about nearby sights and restaurants? Look for the "Northeast" label at the end of the listings and you'll know that statue or café is not far away. Or maybe you'd like to explore the King William Historic District. The listing in the Sights and Attractions chapter gives you the street boundaries as well as a "Downtown" label, so you'll know where to look for it.

All That and Fun to Read, Too!

Every City•Smart chapter includes fun-to-read (and fun-to-use) tips to help you get more out of San Antonio, city trivia (did you know that San Antonio is the headquarters of Columbia 300, one of the world's largest manufacturers of bowling balls?), and illuminating sidebars (to learn how to order Mexican food, for example, see page 72).

SAN ANTONIO ZONES

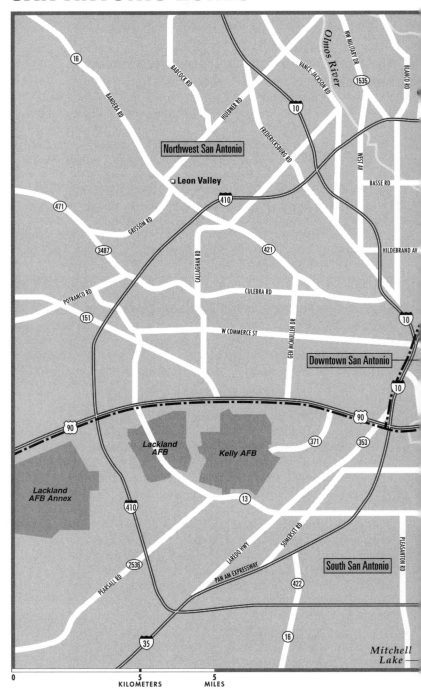

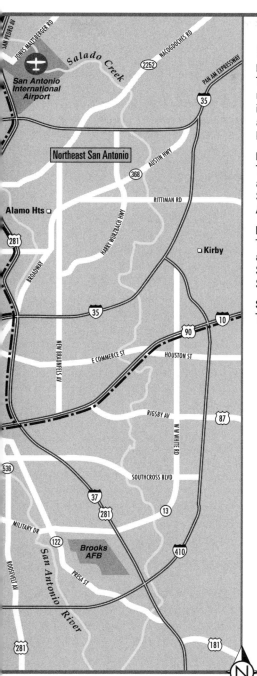

SAN ANTONIO ZONES

Downtown (DT)
The area bordered by a rough rectangle of highways including I-10, I-35, U.S. 90 and U.S. 281; includes the River Walk.

Northeast (NE)
The area east of U.S. 281 and north of U.S. 90; includes San Antonio International Airport.

Northwest (NW)
The area west of U.S. 281 and north of U.S. 90; includes Six Flags Fiesta Texas and Sea World.

South (S)
The area south of U.S. 90.

1

WELCOME TO SAN ANTONIO

San Antonio is a city with a cornerstone firmly set in irony. Its most renowned landmark, the Alamo, was an abandoned church that became the unlikely site of an ill-advised land battle between a scruffy band of American settlers and the Mexican government that invited them onto its territory. Today the inaccurately restored Alamo is fervently revered as "the Cradle of Texas Liberty."

Every spring, normal city functions take a back seat to Fiesta—a boisterous South Texas Mardi Gras that once commemorated the bloody aftermath of the Alamo siege, the Battle of San Jacinto. The descendants of the opposing sides in both the Alamo and San Jacinto battles— Texans (or "Texians") and Mexicans—are eager co-celebrants, seemingly oblivious to the strife that brought about their merrymaking. That remarkably comfortable Tex-Mex blend is reflected in most facets of San Antonio life.

San Antonio is a colorful city, maybe in part because of the frequent drabness of the landscape around it. Since live oak and mesquite trees and prickly pear cactus don't change their wardrobes with the seasons (which also don't change much), San Antonians wash their community in the colors that ran dry just as Mother Nature finished up the bluebonnets and Indian paintbrush. On porches and in kitchen windows all around town hang *ristras*—strings of glistening blood-red and emerald-green chiles (peppers, for Yankees). Downtown, in the touristy/traditional marketplace called El Mercado, are fat, frilly piñatas—icons of everything from cargo-laden donkeys to Elvis, with as many colors on their fragile exteriors as inside their candy-gorged shells. If you happen to visit during Fiesta, you'll lament your good fortune if you make it back to your hotel without a *cascarón*—a confetti-filled eggshell—exploding in a rainbow cloud above your head.

The shops, eateries, and romantic ambience along El Paseo del Rio (the River Walk), sheltered from the city traffic just a few stairs above, have earned San Antonio the title of "America's Venice." The River Walk is the most popular tourist attraction in the state—quite an accomplishment for a public works project necessitated by disastrous floods. Take a cruise on the San Antonio River's manmade downtown detour and you'll pass beneath the Mission Bridge, where the city's ecclesiastical history is recounted in rainbow tile mosaics, while on each side of your barge the River Walk's trees are draped in Christmas lights much of the year.

So float the river, stroll through the missions, stand quietly in the Alamo, and laugh under the *cascarones*. Take in all the colors. The confetti will eventually wash out of your hair, but your memories of San Antonio will be vivid forever.

Getting to Know San Antonio

San Antonio is big—a rough circle over 20 miles in diameter. What's called the San Antonio metropolitan area would be, in many other states, a metropolitan area and a county. But here it's all San Antonio, the eighth-largest city in the United States, with a population of nearly 1.1 million.

San Antonio lies in Bexar (pronounced "bear") County. South of town the land is flat and devoted to agriculture. East is industrial. West is military. Northwest, roads undulate into the Texas Hill Country, famous for its hunting and its ranches (some of them truly Texas-sized) with the trademark longhorns, remarkable scenery, and idiosyncratic wildlife such as armadillos and roadrunners. To the northeast is more agriculture and (eventually) Austin.

Running through town is San Antonio's wet gold—a stream rather ostentatiously dubbed the San Antonio River. It meanders through the center of the city among the sidewalks, bridges, and fountains of Texas's most popular tourist destination, El Paseo del Rio—the River Walk.

San Antonio is surrounded by the military—with several army and air

If you plan to spend time hanging around the River Walk, call the Paseo del Rio Association (210/227-4262) before your trip and request a copy of *Rio, The Official Magazine of the River Walk*. It includes events calendars and discount coupons to River Walk merchants and restaurants.

force bases nearby. Unlike in Alamo days, today they're all friendly forces. To the northeast is Randolph Air Force Base (AFB) and, closer in, Fort Sam Houston, the city's oldest military installation and home of the Fifth Army. Southeast is Brooks AFB. Lackland AFB is to the southwest, as is Kelly AFB, which is undergoing a painful process of closure and privatization. And in the far northwest is the old Camp Bullis Army Reservation.

Neighborhoods in San Antonio

As San Antonio grows northward, new neighborhoods have little of the character that blesses the areas primarily around downtown. The most notable and historical of these are described below.

San Antonio's heart, downtown, with its history of cattle drives and commerce, is almost entirely given over to tourists today. Major businesses still locate there, some in beautifully restored high-rises, but most residents have gone elsewhere. There are exceptions: Houston Street's decade-dark windows now look out on a rebounding residential/arts center; and select—and expensive—apartments overlook the River Walk. But come 5 p.m., most San Antonians who work downtown head north, leaving the city center to visitors.

South of downtown and within a stone-skipping distance of the river, the King William District is an official historic district and a don't-miss destination for house gawkers. The area was settled in the second half of the last century by German immigrants who referred to it as the "Little Rhine." The houses are mostly Victorian, surrounded by enormous live oaks and the occasional palm. Most of these residences have been well maintained, and some have been turned into topflight bed-and-breakfasts. Visit the headquarters of the San Antonio Conservation Society on King William Street, and take the 25-block neighborhood walking tour—it's well worth the effort.

On the other side of Alamo Street from King William, Southtown has gained local attention in recent years as a center for progressive arts and culture. Much of this attention results from the presence of the Blue Star Arts Complex, an industrial complex transformed into galleries, studios, and a theater. Though still largely in need of renovation, Southtown is a good destination for an artsy walk, with the obligatory stops in local coffee shops and bistros.

Just east of downtown is Dignowity Park, a historic neighborhood named for a nineteenth-century Czechoslovakian physician who settled there. Anthony Dignowity's immense "Harmony House" is long gone—replaced by a city park—and the neighborhood surrounding it has sadly crumbled. But in the mid-1800s, Dignowity Park was the city's first tony neighborhood outside of the city center. While not as well-preserved as the younger King William District, some of Dignowity's history and dignity remain. The largely African American neighborhood looks forward to the continuing renovation of the St. Paul Square business district in the shade of the Alamodome and Sunset Station, once a center for black-owned enterprises.

East of San Pedro Avenue and north of downtown, historic Monte Vista is roughly contemporary with but not quite as well maintained as King William. The oldest houses in the neighborhood are 1890s-vintage, and a few are showing their age—the surrounding neighborhoods even more so. But some of the buildings are truly impressive, and every year a few more are restored. South of Monte Vista toward downtown is Tobin Hill, a similar neighborhood that was home to San Antonio architect Atlee Ayres, who designed Municipal Auditorium, the Tower Life Building, and his own massive two-story stone house at 201 Belknap Place.

West of U.S. 281 and north of downtown, Olmos Park is a 1920s–30s neighborhood named for nearby Olmos Creek, which was a major contributor to the floods earlier this century and created the Olmos Basin. Many of the houses are quite lovely, and the Olmos Pharmacy, whose old-time soda fountain advertises the world's best milk shakes, is worth a visit. Also of note: Best-selling UFO abductee and San Antonio resident Whitley Strieber had his first close encounter in the basin.

In Fort Sam Houston, the enlisted persons' housing holds no particular charm, but some of the late-1800s officers' homes (now private residences) approach castle status. The neighborhood around them, between I-35 and Broadway just northeast of downtown, has fallen into disrepair. But if you're paying a visit to Fort Sam and its museums anyway, drive around the fringes of the base first for a look.

Also northeast of downtown, adjacent to Fort Sam Houston, Terrell Hills is home to the prestigious San Antonio Country Club and the kind of folk who can afford to be members there. Large, beautiful homes on large, beautiful lots date from the 1930s–50s. The area was named for Dr. Frederick Terrell, whose family farm developed into the neighborhood.

Geronimo in San Antonio, 1886

Fort Sam Houston

East of U.S. 281 and south of Loop 410, Alamo Heights is a wealthy city-within-a-city. Its zip code designation—78209—has led people to refer (sometimes derisively) to its residents as "09ers." With some of the most expensive real estate in San Antonio, the plots currently most prized are found in the Lincoln Heights area around the trendy new Quarry Market mall, Quarry Golf Club, and the new Alamo Heights United Methodist Church. The latter is so enormous that it was instantly christened the "Methodome." The oldest Alamo Heights houses date from the 1890s, and 09ers take pride in maintaining their homes, yards, trendy shops, and air of exclusivity (they even have their own school district).

West of U.S. 281 and south of Loop 1604, the two rambling neighborhoods of Hill Country Village and Hollywood Park double as nature preserves. Residents aren't crazy about sightseers, but go anyway—particularly just before dusk. Enormous yards contain beautiful, sometimes quirky houses and large herds of free-roaming deer. Some manses have elegant landscaping surrounded by chicken-wire fences to keep the very tame mascots from munching the shrubs. Despite their snacking, the fauna are prized by Villagers and Parkers, so speed limits are very low and enthusiastically enforced.

A Brief History of San Antonio

In the late 1600s, threatened by French encroachment from the east in Louisiana, Spanish settlers began venturing north from their base in what is now Mexico. On June 13, 1691 (the feast day of St. Anthony of Padua), one group of settlers happened across a set of springs and a stream flanked by villages of peaceful Indians. The Payaya tribe had named the river Yanaguana (yah-nah-GWAH-nah), meaning "clear water." But the Spaniards named it for the saint whose day brought them to it: San Antonio.

Though the Spaniards recognized the charm of the area, it was hardly a discovery. Thousands of years before the Spanish "discovered" the springs, the land around them was already a bustling center of activity. Native Americans had been using the land around San Antonio as a trading and recreation area as early as 9000 B.C. At least five different tribes, including the Payaya, the Coahuiltecas, and the Comanches, came together around the springs in the seventeenth century. The Payaya established residence in the river/spring area, and it was they whom the Spaniards set out to Christianize in the 1700s.

Over the next few decades, Spanish Catholics—primarily Spanish Canary Islanders—took over the territory agriculturally and spiritually. In 1718 the Spanish established Mission San Antonio de Valero, the first of five missions built along the San Antonio River to proselytize Indians. That chapel and its grounds would later become known as the Alamo. Between 1718 and 1735, four more missions were constructed (including two in East Texas that were dismantled and moved), and in 1738 San Fernando Cathedral became the center of faith for the exclusively Catholic residents of the area.

By 1731 Spain had established Presidio de Bejar, an official civil settlement in San Antonio and the first step toward colonization. The city became the seat of Spanish government in Texas in 1772. The ten-room Spanish Governor's Palace on Military Plaza still stands today; it was there that Moses Austin petitioned the Spanish rulers in 1820 for permission to bring the first U.S. settlers into the Texas territory.

Mexico became an independent republic in 1821. In order to secure its claims on territories to the north, the Mexican government grudgingly accepted the help of the settlers Spain had welcomed from the United States. But tensions built between the American émigrés (led for the most part by Moses Austin's son Stephen) and their step-government over several issues, particularly slavery. Slave ownership was not allowed in Mexico, but some newcomers from the north saw slave labor as vital in maintaining their new homesteads.

Tension became hostility in 1833 when General Antonio López de Santa Anna proclaimed himself president of Mexico. The Texans refused to acknowledge his office, and in 1835 Santa Anna sent General Martin Perfecto de Cos to San Antonio to quell the rebellion. Cos was soundly defeated by these settler/soldiers, their forces bolstered by freelance frontiersmen.

Santa Anna, who styled himself "Napoleon of the West," was furious; he placed himself at the head of his troops to confront the Texans on February 23, 1836, demanding surrender. Their nomadic reinforcements gone, 188 Texans holed up in the Valero Mission—the Alamo. Colonel William Barrett Travis, who became the settlers' military leader pro tem when Jim Bowie became ill, answered Santa Anna's demand with a cannon shot, stoking the general's wrath and prompting a siege. Barricaded within the mission grounds, Travis penned a letter considered sacred by many modern Texans:

> To the People of Texas and All Americans in the World
> Fellow Citizens and Compatriots—
> I am besieged, by a thousand or more of the Mexicans under Santa Anna—I have sustained a continual Bombardment & cannonade for 24 hours & have not lost a man—The enemy has demanded a surrender at discretion, otherwise, the garrison are to be put to the sword, if the fort is taken—I have answered the demand with a cannon shot, & our flag still waves proudly from the walls—I shall never surrender or retreat. Then, I call on you in the name of Liberty, of patriotism & everything dear to the American character, to come to our aid with all dispatch. The enemy is receiving reinforcements daily & will no doubt increase to three or four thousand in four or five days. If this call is neglected, I am determined to sustain myself as long as possible & die like a soldier who never forgets what is due his honor & that of his country. VICTORY or DEATH.

Many myths have grown up around the fall of the Alamo, perpetually debated by Texas historians. Did Travis draw a line in the sand with his sword and ask those who would die with him to step across? Did the bedridden Bowie command that his cot be carried across that line? Did the Texans place a banner on a cannon that challenged, "Come and Take It!"? One written account of the battle—purportedly that of Santa Anna staffer Lieutenant Colonel José Enrique de la Peña—states that seven

Alamo defenders, including Davy Crockett, didn't die valiantly on the walls, as legend holds. Rather, they were brought before Santa Anna, bayoneted, then shot. Some historians are more than a little disenchanted with this chronicle.

The full truth will never be known, but one fact is clear: Travis's defiant plea for help went unheard, and after 13 days the Mexicans attacked. Overrunning the walls of the compound, Santa Anna ran up a red flag that ordered "No quarter." Mexican troops bayoneted or shot all but 16 of the Alamo occupants, the only survivors being noncombatants. Santa Anna lost nearly 1,600 troops, though he insisted to one of his officers afterward that the battle was "but a small affair." The general's aide, Colonel Juan Almonte, disagreed in his private journal: "One more such glorious victory, and we are finished."

Almonte's entry proved prophetic. On March 27, 1836, in the town of Goliad to the east, Santa Anna coldly ordered the execution of more than 300 prisoners taken at the Battle of Coleto Creek. That proved too much for the Texans, and on April 21, shouting "Remember the Alamo!" and "Remember Goliad!", 800 of them attacked Santa Anna's 1,300 troops at San Jacinto. The Mexicans were routed in minutes, losing 630 soldiers. Texan losses totaled eight. Santa Anna was captured, and the Republic of Texas was formed with General Sam Houston as its first president.

Texas was sovereign, but San Antonio ironically maintained much of its Mexican character until the 1840s. With the end of the Mexican-American War in 1848, European immigrants began settling in this frontier town. Despite the staggering culture shock, the city's population had increased tenfold by the mid-1860s, to nearly 9,000. European tastes commingled with Tex-Mex style, evinced by the elegant architecture of some of San Antonio's oldest neighborhoods and the folk-polka fusion known today as Tejano.

Downtown San Antonio

SACVB/Craig Stafford

Those same European immigrants created an atmosphere of ambivalence toward the Civil War in San Antonio. Though Texas joined the Confederacy in 1861, most of the newest residents of the Alamo City were pro-Union. In fact, this dichotomy was found in other South Texas towns, perhaps most obviously in the capital city of Austin. And the little town of Comfort, northwest of San Antonio and southwest of Fredericksburg, even erected a monument titled "True to the Union" in 1866.

Hollywood Remembers the Alamo

The Immortal Alamo, *aka* **Fall of the Alamo** *(1911)*—*Silent filmed in San Antonio.*

The Martyrs of the Alamo, *or* **The Birth of Texas** *(1915)*—*Another silent, supervised by epicmeister D.W. Griffith and filmed entirely in Hollywood.*

Davy Crockett at the Fall of the Alamo *(1926)*—*Wilson Silsby directed Cullen Landis as the King of the Wild Frontier.*

Heroes of the Alamo *(1937)*—*San Antonians cheered the film at its premiere at the Texas Theatre on Houston Street. The rest of the world thought it was pretty bad. (The theater's gone, too.)*

The Man from the Alamo *(1953)*—*Glenn Ford escapes the siege, but not his guilt.*

Davy Crockett, King of the Wild Frontier *(1955)*—*Alamo meets Disney, with Fess Parker as the last Alamo defender standing. Shot in several locations, none of them San Antonio.*

The Last Command *(1955)*—*Filmed on location at a re-created Alamo on a ranch in nearby Brackettville, directed by Frank Lloyd and starring Sterling Hayden and Ernest Borgnine.*

The Alamo *(1960)*—*John Wayne's directorial debut used an elaborate set constructed on yet another ranch in Brackettville (which is still a tourist attraction). With a budget of $12 million,* The Alamo

Texas's rebel status resulted in a slowing of growth during the war years as immigrants had second thoughts about relocating. But that didn't last long.

Isolated by distance from the rest of the state's population, San Antonio was a center for ranching and rowdiness. But with the arrival of the railroad in the 1870s and the construction of Fort Sam Houston (to defend against Native American attacks) at around the same time, the city lost some of its Wild West demeanor.

More challenges faced San Antonio in the following century. Devastating floods in 1921, and again eight years later, resulted in the construction of a concrete channel and flood-control gates in the river downtown. Some civic leaders fought to have the river filled in, eliminating the possibility of was the most expensive film ever made to that date. Wayne had to agree to star as Crockett to get the funding he needed. Far and away the best Alamo movie, it won an Oscar for sound, was nominated for five others, and garnered composer Dmitri Tiomkin a Golden Globe for the score.

Viva, Max! *(1969)—Based on a book by Dallas-born author-turned-PBS-newsreader Jim Lehrer, this controversial comedy hypothesized the retaking of the Alamo by patriotic Mexican General Maximilian Rodriguez de Santos (Peter Ustinov) and 100 soldiers. The book is very funny, as is the movie (directed by* The Dick Van Dyke Show'*s Jerry Paris). But the Daughters of the Republic of Texas tried to get the courts and city council to restrain Paris from filming in front of the Alamo. They failed, whiningly, prompting Ustinov to quip, "I am astonished to find out the cradle of Texas independence still has so many babies in it." Everyone in town but the DRT loved the movie.*

The Alamo: Thirteen Days to Glory *(1987)—Directed by Burt Kennedy on John Wayne's Brackettville set, this NBC telepic starred James Arness (Bowie), Brian Keith (Crockett), Raul Julia (Santa Anna), Alec Baldwin (Travis), and Lorne Green (Houston).*

Alamo: The Price of Freedom *(1987)—Filmed on the Brackettville set for use in the Rivercenter IMAX Theatre.*

future inundation. Had it not been for a few imaginative planners who successfully championed an alternative, San Antonio as it exists today . . . wouldn't. As it turns out, the tragedy of the floods, like the Alamo bloodbath, only temporarily obscured a silver lining for the city's future.

In 1941 the Works Progress Administration completed an elaborate project of footbridges, staircases, and sidewalks over the downtown stretch of river. Two decades later, visionary architects and business leaders helped this gilded storm sewer achieve its fullest potential. With the creation of a newly channeled bend in the river, and the addition of attractive facades and entrances on the river sides of downtown buildings, the River Walk was born.

"America's Venice" came to world attention soon after as the site of

SAN ANTONIO TIME LINE

1691	Spanish explorers discover a stream on the feast day of St. Anthony of Padua and name it Rio San Antonio.
1718	Mission San Antonio de Valero (the Alamo) established.
1718–35	Missions Concepción, San José, San Juan, and Espada built along the river.
1731	Spanish government establishes official settlement in San Antonio area.
1738	Foundation of San Fernando Cathedral laid.
1772	Spanish governor's palace built, making San Antonio the seat of New Spain's government in Texas territory.
1810	Mexican revolt against Spanish rule begins.
1820	Moses Austin receives permission from Spanish governor to bring U.S. settlers into Texas.
1821	Mexico gains independence from Spain.
1823	Mexico becomes a republic.
1833	General Antonio López de Santa Anna declares himself president of Mexico.
1835	General Martin Perfecto de Cos, sent to San Antonio to quell the settlers' rebellion, is defeated by the Texans. Texas declares its right to secede from Mexico.
1836	Santa Anna defeats the Texans at the Alamo. During the siege, Texas declares independence. Santa Anna later orders the execution of 300 prisoners at Goliad. On April 21, outnumbered Texans defeat Mexican troops at San Jacinto. Santa Anna is captured, and Texas becomes a sovereign republic.
1845	Texas becomes the United States's 28th state.
1845–60	Population of San Antonio grows from 800 to 8,000, mostly as a result of European immigration.
1846	U.S. Army begins using the Alamo grounds as a storage depot.
1848	Mexican-American War ends with Treaty of Guadalupe Hidalgo, which cedes Texas and nearly half of Mexico to the United States.
1849	U.S. Army repairs the Alamo and adds the trademark arched facade.
1850	U.S. Army brings camels to San Antonio as cargo haulers.

After a lengthy court battle, the Texas Supreme Court awards custody of the Alamo to the Catholic Church.	1855
Texas secedes from the Union.	1861
Texas readmitted to the Union. Construction of an army base begins on land donated by the city. The post is named Fort Sam Houston in 1890.	1870
First railroad arrives in San Antonio.	1877
The State of Texas purchases the Alamo chapel, currently in use as a warehouse.	1883
Apache Chief Geronimo held prisoner at Fort Sam Houston.	1886
Electricity becomes available.	1887
First Battle of Flowers parade held on the grounds of the Alamo in honor of visit by President Benjamin Harrison.	1891
The state places control of the Alamo in the hands of the Daughters of the Republic of Texas.	1905
First U.S. military aircraft flown at Fort Sam Houston.	1910
Downtown flooded by San Antonio River.	1921
After more flooding, work is completed on the river's concrete channel and flood-control gates.	1929
Works Progress Administration completes bridges, stairs, and sidewalks over the river downtown.	1941
The first company of Women's Army Auxiliary Corps (WAAC) created at Fort Sam Houston.	1942
Natural Bridge Caverns discovered north of San Antonio.	1960
Architects and business leaders work to create the River Walk.	1960s
San Antonio hosts HemisFair, the World's Fair, with the theme of "Confluence of Civilizations."	1968
The federal government establishes the San Antonio Missions National Historical Park, which includes four of San Antonio's five missions. (The state-controlled Alamo is excluded.)	1978
Rivercenter shopping complex opens on the River Walk.	1988
Alamodome sports complex completed, funded by local sales tax.	1993
San Antonio experiences some of the worst flooding in its history, with 20 inches of rain falling in 48 hours. A newly completed flood channel under downtown averts the tragedies of the '20s.	1998

San Antonio's Latino Heritage

During certain times of the year, San Antonio's links to Mexico are trumpeted and celebrated. Call the Convention and Visitors Bureau at 800/447-3372 for exact dates.

Cinco de Mayo Battle Ceremony and Festival *(first week in May)—A weeklong salute to Mexico's victory over France at the Battle of Puebla, centered around El Mercado.*

Tejano Conjunto Festival *(mid-May)—Six days of celebrating the music of South Texas and northern Mexico, featuring the finest musicians in the genre.*

Dia de los Muertos Prayer Celebration and Vigil *(November 1)— The "Day of the Dead" is a day for venerating ancestors, celebrating, and buying candy skulls.*

Feria de Santa Cecilia, Fiestas Navideñas *(Thanksgiving through Christmas)—Nearly a month of Christmas celebrations, including the blessing of the animals (pets) at San Fernando Cathedral.*

Las Posadas and Gran Posada de San Antonio *(mid-December)— Joseph and Mary's journey to Bethlehem are dramatically reenacted downtown.*

the World's Fair. The theme of HemisFair 1968—"Confluence of Civilizations"—could not have been more appropriate to San Antonio.

The People of San Antonio

Census data are cold and unromantic. A look at San Antonio's 1990 demographics—roughly 56 percent Latino, 36 percent Anglo, 7 percent African American, 2 percent "other"—may work for sociologists, but it won't begin to describe the cultural mélange that defines the city's character.

The first residents of the area that would become San Antonio were, of course, Native Americans. As settlers from New Spain began exploring lands to the north, they saw peaceful Indian encampments as fertile mission fields. Thus, Spaniards were the second settlers of south-central Texas. With the influx of European settlers and nomadic frontiersmen, yet another hue was added to the mix, and that's the way things remained

Fiesta San Antonio

throughout most of the 1800s, when San Antonio was a rowdy, notorious cow town populated by relocated Mexicans and profit-seeking Anglos. Meanwhile, the thriving Native American culture that had first attracted the Spanish settlers began to fade.

In mid-century, San Antonio became a destination for German immigrants. But rather than blending in, they chose for the most part to keep to themselves, re-creating their accustomed culture near the river in an enclave called the Little Rhine (the area now known as King William). Some of that Teutonic flavor survives in the area's architecture. Mid-century also saw the arrival of Texas's first settlers from Poland, who founded nearby Panna Maria, the oldest Polish settlement in the United States. Groups of these Polish émigrés found their way to San Antonio in the early 1900s, where they joined the recently settled Irish, whose Irish Flats neighborhood was renowned for its lively parties. Italians clustered here at about the same time, and each of these ethnic groups founded distinct neighborhoods based on memories and traditions.

Now at the end of its third century, San Antonio has lost some of its "neighborhood" feel. The city no longer has a Germantown, Polishtown, Italiantown, or Irishtown. The south and west sides of town are predominantly Latino, and while billboards and occasional mainstream radio and TV ads might lead you to believe differently, the majority of the Hispanic community is either English-speaking or bilingual. Historically, much of the city's relatively small African American population made its home on the east side, but those old neighborhoods are also becoming increasingly Latino. Native American culture has all but vanished, with fewer than 5,000 people in Bexar County claiming indigenous descent in the 1990 U.S. census.

T I P

Conventions held in San Antonio can make downtown even more crowded than usual, some of them bringing in 10,000–20,000 conventioneers. Check with the Convention and Visitors Bureau, 800/447-3372, if you want to avoid the biggest of these.

As downtown neighborhoods continue to lose their individuality, San Antonio grows away from its old heart, oozing northward. New subdivisions—many of them fenced and gated, all of them bearing trendy names—are popping up like fire-ant mounds after a rain shower, surrounded by strip malls, fast-food outlets, and self-serve gas-o-ramas. And though the city limits continue to expand as the city council annexes profitable enclaves of affluent, predominantly Anglo residents, many citizens are San Antonians by zip code only. Downtown has become a destination primarily for out-of-towners who want to see the River Walk.

But on certain days or weeks of the year—during Fiesta and other anniversaries—the proud descendants of San Antonio's builders reveal themselves, recall their roots, and draw latecomers downtown to celebrate the intricate mosaic that is San Antonio.

To understand the reverence many San Antonians feel for the Alamo is to understand Texans. And that, to most non-Texans, is a difficult proposition. The official slogan of the Texas Department of Tourism is "Texas—It's Like A Whole Other Country." It is. And Texans like it that way. The characterization of Texans that's common in the rest of the United States—fiercely independent, loyal to state first and nation after, ready to secede at the drop of a hat—is very nearly correct. In fact, some natives who are, admittedly, on the fringe, believe that Texas was made a state

San Antonio Weather

	Average High Temps (°F/°C)	Average Low Temps (°F/°C)	Average Monthly Precipitation (inches)
January	70/21	50/10	2.21
February	71/21	50/10	2.79
March	76/25	56/13	0.03
April	82/28	61/16	2.00
May	87/31	67/20	3.04
June	90/32	72/22	6.82
July	90/32	74/23	7.69
August	90/32	74/23	7.95
September	89/32	73/23	0.54
October	84/29	65/18	2.62
November	77/25	56/14	1.65
December	72/22	51/10	2.04

Source: National Weather Service

San Antonio's Weather
by meteorologist John Willing

Most visitors to San Antonio are going to find our weather "reasonable," in that it doesn't have extremely hot or cold temperatures. But if you're looking for four distinct seasons, you won't find them here.

We really have two seasons: hot and dry, and cool and "sort of" cloudy. It's pretty sunny in the summer, with 70 percent sunshine. Winter sunshine drops to 50 percent. We get about 31 inches of rain a year, much of that in spring or late summer–early fall. People who come from the Midwest or the East will find our summers less humid, since we average around 45 percent relative humidity on a typical summer afternoon.

The most comfortable days are from mid-September through early December and from mid-February through May. Summers are consistently hot, with peak temperatures around 96–97 degrees in the day and 75 at night. Our coldest average temps in winter are 61 degrees during the day and 38 at night.

Snow is rare here, so if you're sick and tired of shoveling, this is the place for you. Snow falls just once every three to four years, and we get a 2- to 4-inch storm about every ten years.

illegally and is today, as it was from 1836 to 1845, a sovereign nation: the Republic of Texas.

Fortunately for out-of-state visitors, however, Texans are equally deserving of their reputation for firm-handshake, loud-howdy friendliness. So rest assured that, should secession occur during your visit to the Alamo City, you'll probably be allowed to return home with your souvenirs from America's newest neighbor to the south—and some great stories to tell.

When to Visit

There is literally no "bad" season to visit the Alamo City. While it does get chilly in the winter, if you're from anywhere north of, say, Baton Rouge,

Top Ten Things to Bring to San Antonio
by Heloise

Multimillion-selling author of eight books on household hints, Heloise shares her San Antonio home with her plumbing contractor/ballooning partner husband, David, three dogs, two cockatiels, and a macaw. Her home is also command central for her syndicated column, "Hints from Heloise," published daily in more than 500 newspapers worldwide and on her Web site, www.heloise.com.

1. A Fiesta mood and friendly attitude. Relax and have fun!

2. Extra money! Save money by not having to use the ATMs.

3. Cool clothes. Wear light Fiesta colors to keep cool in the hot Texas sun. Temperatures can range from 90 to 100 degrees, even in the shade.

4. Antacid—so you can enjoy San Antonio's famous, spicy Tex-Mex food and tangy margaritas without grief.

5. Comfortable shoes. Take a walk around downtown to La Villita as well as the other great sites. Your feet will thank you.

6. A camera—to capture San Antonio life.

7. Extra film/batteries. Don't pay outrageous tourist prices. Buy your supplies on sale at home.

8. Sun hat. Provide your own shade.

9. Sunglasses. Need I explain?

10. Sun block. Protect your skin from the bright Texas sun.

you've seen worse. And the "off season" also carries the advantage of smaller crowds at the popular downtown tourist sites, particularly along the River Walk. Here, narrow sidewalks and imposing cypress trees (and no guardrail along the river) make negotiating the route during spring, summer, and autumn a shoulder-turning, stop-and-go, "s'cuse me" proposition with soggy consequences for the careless.

Some of the bigger attractions—Sea World and Fiesta Texas—are primarily seasonal (though the latter hosts an annual Christmas celebration). But the city's historic sites are open year-round, and the delightful climate nurtures the populace's "everything's worth a party" mindset; San Antonio has more than 100 special events and observances each year—some historical, others just for fun. The Calendar of Events, below, lists many of these events. For exact dates, call the Convention and Visitors Bureau at 800/447-3372.

Calendar of Events

January
Cowboy Breakfast, Central Park Mall; Great Country River Festival, River Walk; Martin Luther King Jr. March, throughout Downtown; River Walk Bottom Festival and Mud Parade, River Walk

February
Asian Festival, San Antonio Museum of Art; Carnaval de San Anto Mardi Gras Fiesta Masquerade, Villita Assembly Hall; River Walk Mardi Gras, River Walk; San Antonio Stock Show and Rodeo, Freeman Coliseum

March
Alamo Irish Festival, La Villita; Alamo Memorial Day Senior Olympics, to be announced; Baile de Carnaval (Cuban festival), Omni Hotel; Festival of India, La Villita; *San Antonio Express-News* Festival 10,000 Race and Masters Swim Meet, to be announced; San Antonio Watercolor Month, throughout Downtown; Tejano Music Awards, Alamodome; theme park openings, Six Flags Fiesta Texas and Sea World; St. Patrick's Day Alamo Ceremony, Parade, River Dyeing, and 10K Run, 300 Alamo Plaza; San Fernando Cathedral Passion Play, San Fernando Cathedral; Southwestern Bell Dominion Senior PGA Tournament, The Dominion

April
Fiesta San Antonio, throughout Downtown; "Incognito" Fiesta Masquerade Ball, Villita Assembly Hall; Lowrider Custom Car and Truck Festival, to be announced; River Arts Fair and Starving Artist Show, River Walk; Texas Children's Festival, Institute of Texan Cultures; Viva Botanica, San Antonio Botanical Center

May
Cinco de Mayo Battle Ceremony and Festival, El Mercado; Cloggers' Showcase, Arneson River Theatre; Helotes Cornyval, Helotes, Texas; Kerrville Folk Festival, Kerrville, Texas; Maifest, Beethoven Halle und Garten; Mama's Margarita Pour-off, Sunken Garden Amphitheatre in Brackenridge Park; Return of the Chili Queens, El Mercado; San Antonio Dance Festival, various venues; Tejano Conjunto Festival, to be announced

June
Fiesta Flamenca (through August), Arneson River Theatre; Fiesta Noche del Rio (through August), Arneson River Theatre; Fiesta Texas Summer Night Magic, Fiesta Texas; Juneteenth Festival, Sunken Garden Amphitheatre in

Great Country River Festival

Brackenridge Park; Tejano Fest, El Mercado; Texas Starlight Dance Troupe, Arneson River Theatre

July

Art in the 'Hood, King William Historic District; Bastille Day Celebration, La Villita; Beethoven Haus und Garten Gartenkonzerts, Beethoven Halle und Garten; Contemporary Art Month, throughout town; Fandango Musical Revue (through August), Arneson River Theatre; Pura Vida Music Awards, Majestic Theatre; Retama Park Thoroughbred Race Season (through November), Retama Park; Rivercenter Salute to Freedom, Rivercenter; San Antonio Conjunto Shootout, El Mercado; Summer in the City Concert Series (through August), Rivercenter; Texas Folklife Festival, Institute of Texan Cultures

August

Accordion Bash, El Mercado; El Mercado Labor Day Festival, El Mercado; El Mercado Summerfest, El Mercado; George Strait Country Music Festival, Alamodome; San Antonio CineFestival, Guadalupe Cultural Arts Center; Scout Canoe Race, River Walk

TRIVIA

The annual draining and cleaning of the river's downtown channel is a weeklong party called the River Walk Bottom Festival and Mud Parade. If you're visiting in January, learn who the new Mud King and Queen will be, dance at the Mud Ball, and watch the Mud Parade!

Celebrities Who Have Lived in the San Antonio Area

Jesse Borrego
Carol Burnett (born)
Vikki Carr
Henry Cisneros (born)
Joan Crawford (born)
Al Freeman, Jr. (born)
Dr. Bernard Harris (born)
Heloise
Tommy Lee Jones
Shawn Michaels (born)

Pola Negri
Mike Nesmith
Shaquille O'Neal (born)
John Schneider
William Sessions
George Strait
Henry Thomas
Brig. Gen. Charles E.
   "Chuck" Yeager

September
Carnaval de las Americas music festival, El Mercado; Fiestas Patrias and El Grito (Cry For Freedom) Ceremony, El Mercado; Jazz'SAlive, Travis Park; La Cantera Texas Open PGA Tournament, La Cantera

October
Bravo at the Alamo Art Festival, Alamo; Day at Old Fort Sam, Fort Sam Houston; El Mercado Chili Cook-off, El Mercado; Haymarket Festival, El Mercado; Oktoberfest, Beethoven Halle und Garten; River Art Group Show, River Walk; San Antonio Inter-American Bookfair and Literary Festival, Guadalupe Cultural Arts Center; Six Flags Fiesta Texas Fright Fest, Six Flags Fiesta Texas; Wurst Fest, New Braunfels, Texas; Zoo Boo Halloween Carnival, San Antonio Zoo

November
Beaujolais Nouveau Festival, to be announced; Dia de los Muertos Prayer Celebration and Vigil, Our Lady of the Lake University; Feria de Santa Cecilia, Fiestas Navideñas, and Blessing of the Animals (through Christmas), El Mercado; Holiday Boat Caroling (through Christmas), River Walk; River Walk Holiday Festival, River Walk; River Walk Lighting Ceremony and Holiday Parade, River Walk; San Antonio Marathon, HemisFair Park

December
Alamo Bowl, Alamodome; Downtown Apartment Tour, throughout Downtown; Fiesta de las Luminarias, River Walk; Holiday in the Park, Fiesta

Texas (through early January); Holiday River Art Fair, River Walk; Las Posadas and Gran Posada de San Antonio, La Mansión Hotel, through downtown; Los Pastores, Mission San José; Rivercenter Christmas Pageant, Rivercenter

Dressing in San Antonio

This is a casual town. Bearing in mind the dictates of temperature and a modicum of modesty, pretty much anything goes. Sunglasses (and hats for those thinning of hair) are highly recommended, and you'll frequently see umbrellas raised on very sunny days.

Downtown business folk are usually seen in the requisite suits, though jackets are usually left behind on lunch breaks. San Antonio is also the home of the guayabera shirt—a Mexican-style, button-front, short-sleeve item with bands of embroidery and pleats down both sides of the front and the back. The guayabera is worn with collar open and tails untucked to many occasions that might normally call for something dressier.

Glittering events, however, call for glittering garb, and Texans in general really enjoy dressing to the nines. If you plan to attend some of Fiesta's glitzier parties, bring your best. For an idea of just how glitzy things can be, check out the queen of Fiesta and her court—they wear the elaborate ceremonial gowns with huge trains, some nearly 20 feet long and weighing as much as a small automobile.

San Antonio's unique cuisine is featured at a festival at the Guadalupe Cultural Arts Center.

Recommended Reading

The San Antonio Story, *T. R. Fehrenbach (Fort Worth: Continental Heritage, Inc., 1978).*

The Alamo Chain of Missions, *Marion A. Habig (Quincy, Ill.: Franciscan Herald Press, 1976).*

San Antonio: Portrait of the Fiesta City, *Gerald Lair and Susan Nawrocki (Stillwater, Minn.: Voyageur Press, 1992).*

A Century of Fiesta in San Antonio, *Jack Maguire (Austin: Eakin Press, 1990).*

The Battle of the Alamo, *Ben H. Proctor (Austin: Texas State Historical Association, 1986).*

San Antonio: A Cultural Tapestry, *Jan Russell (Memphis: Towery Publishing, 1998).*

San Antonio Uncovered, *Mark Rybczyk (Plano: Wordware Publishing, Inc., 1992).*

Business and Economy

Until recently, the armed forces were San Antonio's largest industry. With the closure of Kelly Air Force Base, San Antonians have placed their hopes on tourism. Thus, tourism is now the number-one revenue generator. Annual economic impact of the tourism industry, which employs 56,000 San Antonians, is $3.15 billion.

Efforts are constantly undertaken to lure more large businesses, particularly in the attractive and lucrative high-technology sector. Unemployment is currently hovering around 5 percent, with job growth averaging 3.5 percent in the 1990s. Per capita income for San Antonio workiers is low—$20,000, or about 14 percent below the national average. Manufacturing wages are likewise low at $9.35 per hour, nearly 25 percent below the rest of the country.

Cost of Living

Except for relatively high property taxes, San Antonio is an inexpensive place to live. Tourist dollars bring a welcome glut to city coffers, and the 15-percent hotel tax helps to fund the local arts scene. Be warned: Since Texas has no state income tax, sales tax is 7.75 percent, and it applies to nearly everything but food.

Here's what you'll pay for a few select items:

Five-mile taxi ride:	$6.80
Average dinner:	$10–$15
Daily newspaper (there's only one):	50 cents
Double hotel room:	$40 and up (plus 15-percent tax)
Movie admission:	$6
Potato-and-egg breakfast taco:	$1–$1.50
Tony Lama full-quill ostrich-hide cowboy boots:	$390
Davy Crockett imitation 'coonskin cap:	$10–$20
Fuzzy armadillo key chain:	$5.50

Housing

With the average income on the low side, housing is fortunately inexpensive. The median home price is $86,800, easily the lowest in the ten largest U.S. cities. Some builders offer new homes with 2,500 square feet in the low six-figure range. Rental property is comparably low, at an average of $600 per month for a two-bedroom home. Prime sites along the river and in other rebounding downtown areas carry a premium, of course. Houston Street, in particular, is enjoying both a corporate and a residential resurgence.

Schools

San Antonio's school system is unique and labyrinthine, with 15 separate school districts serving the metropolitan area and Bexar County. Some inner-city schools are in desperate straits, scraping by with crumbling old buildings and inadequate tax bases, while growing districts to the north can't build new schools fast enough. The city is also home to some highly praised private preparatory schools, four private liberal-arts universities, a state university with two campuses, four community colleges, and a health science/education center.

2

GETTING AROUND SAN ANTONIO

San Antonio is large. The city limits encompass 377 square miles, but the entire metropolitan area, which includes parts of Guadalupe and Comal counties as well as all of Bexar, covers more than 3,000 square miles, qualifying San Antonio as the eighth-largest city in the United States. (San Antonio overtook Dallas a couple of years ago, to the delight of locals.)

Within those boundaries are a number of "suburban cities"—small communities that, for reasons of property taxes, quality of life, and pure ol' Texas pride, maintain semi-autonomy within the city limits. Chances are you won't realize you're in one of these communities unless you happen to exceed their significantly lower speed limits, thus learning that not all local police cruisers are painted in the SAPD's white and blue.

City Layout

San Antonio doesn't have the grid system of streets and roads that many cities do. You might think of the general layout as a sunburst: Streets leave the city center and radiate outward, connected by a web of cross streets. But don't depend on this as a rule—the cross streets can be few and far between. And when you're downtown, the street you're looking for may be one-way—the wrong way. Other streets set off on interesting meanders or take sudden breaks.

Adding to the fun, there is no rhyme or reason to the numbering of streets. Downtown thoroughfares that run roughly east-west start their numbering at Main Street, while north-south numbering restarts at Commerce

Street. Since negotiating your way to local sights can be confusing, keep this book and its maps handy.

The downtown area is surrounded by a rough rectangle of interstate highways that change numbers as often as drivers change lanes. Usually overhead signs explain the system, but here's how it all works:

Interstate 37 forms the eastern side of the loop around downtown. I-37 is also called I-35 and U.S. 281. To the north, U.S. 281 runs past San Antonio International Airport. The southern boundary of the downtown loop is I-10, also called I-35 and U.S. 90.

Interstate 35 to the west of downtown, also called I-10 or U.S. 81, forms the third side of the downtown loop. This north-south route separates into I-10 and I-35 north of the downtown area; and I-35, continuing east, completes the downtown loop when it intersects 37/35/281. Some of the downtown highway loop has grown into two levels to handle the downtown traffic. Watch for the sign listing your exit, and stay on the level indicated.

After circling downtown, all of these interstates and U.S. highways turn into major commuter spokes shooting out from the city center. Lending a bit of logic to the otherwise confusing starburst configuration are two highway loops surrounding the city. Loop 410, the multilane, divided innermost loop, is approximately ten minutes from downtown during non-rush hours. (San Antonio International Airport is located at the intersection of Loop 410 and U.S. 281 North.) As it describes its huge circle around the city, Loop 410 offers access to all of the highway spokes and major streets that lead downtown.

Some of those spokes also reach to Loop 1604, which is concentric with 410 but 20 minutes outside downtown. One popular San Antonio attraction, Six Flags Fiesta Texas, lies just outside 1604. Most of this loop to the north is divided four-lane, but it narrows to two on the east, west, and south.

While both loops are useful for getting from one spoke to the next, you don't want to use the loops to get from one side of the city to the other. Think of it as navigating a pie: There are shorter routes to the other side than following the edge of the crust. You can expect rush-hour

Roads with Brains

San Antonio is one of three American cities experimenting with a high-tech traffic monitoring system called TransGuide (Transportation Guidance System). This $33-million "smart highway" network uses video monitors connected by sophisticated telemetry to a central, computerized terminal from which traffic experts issue advice on dealing with changing conditions. Above several major highways, particularly around downtown, are digital message boards that advise you of conditions ahead. The most significant gain from TransGuide, according to local highway officials, has been an 18-percent decrease in "rubber-necker" accidents—those caused by people so interested in the misfortune of another that they suffer one of their own.

congestion (heading into or out of downtown) on I-35, I-10, Loop 410 between I-35 and I-10, and U.S. 281.

Public Transportation

Buses

San Antonio's enviable bus system, appropriately named VIA, is ranked fourth out of 127 U.S. transit systems in overall efficiency, according to one national evaluation. The city is blanketed by more than 100 bus routes, serving most of Bexar County and carrying nearly 40 million riders per year. Service is frequent, timely, and inexpensive (75¢; children under 5 ride free with an adult). Express buses running to and from downtown on the interstates cost $1.50, and a $15 monthly rate covers it all. For $4 you can purchase a "Day Tripper" pass for one day of unlimited use of all bus routes and streetcars. Special routes are offered to popular sights, often on motor coaches "wrapped" with pictures appropriate to the destination. For special events—concerts, Spurs basketball games, Dragons hockey games, and Fiesta events—a $5 "park and ride" service is available from many large, well-lighted lots around town. You may get back to your hotel a bit later, but riding high above the traffic will make it time well spent.

Around downtown, VIA offers 50-cent circulator streetcar service to the most popular destinations (25¢ for students, seniors, children, and the disabled). These rubber-tired, mahogany-clad specialty coaches were

How to Talk Texan

Bexar—The name of the county San Antonio occupies, pronounced "bare."

Chili/chile—One's a stew, one's a pepper, but most locals pronounce them the same: "CHILL-ee."

Culebra—This busy road is traditionally pronounced "kyoo-LAY-brah."

Fajitas—"fah-HEE-tahs." Everyone in town gets this one right. Another one nobody messes up is . . .

Guadalupe—The name of countless things in South Texas, from churches to rivers. Though the word is imported from Mexico, where the "g" would be soft, gringos universally pronounce it "gwah-deh-LOO-pay" or "gwah-deh-LOO-pee." Never say "GWAH-deh-loop."

Jalapeño—The national pepper of Texas, this "CHILL-ee" is a "hal-uh-PAIN-yoh." Note that pain is emphasized to forewarn the delicate of palate.

La Quinta—The local hotel chain is "lah KEEN-tah."

Nacogdoches—Named for the oldest town in Texas, this road is pronounced "nack-eh-DOH-chess." Easy to find, hard to say. An easier one is . . .

Tamales—"tah-MAH-lehs." Here's your chance to show off. "Tamales" is plural. The singular is "tamal." Your waiter will be impressed, as long as you don't then try to eat the cornhusk wrapper.

Tortilla—It's "tohr-TEE-ah"; "tohr-TILL-ah" was a fifth-century Hunnish raider.

And last, unless you're writing a country-and-western song and need a rhyme for "alone," the city is never called "San Antone."

---

designed for VIA, and transit companies throughout the United States have acquired identical or similar models. The most popular seat on the streetcar isn't a seat; kids in particular enjoy standing on the "balcony" in the back, holding the polished brass rail and waving to cars behind. (Occasionally the operator will allow young and young-at-heart passengers to ring the brass bell in front.) VIA streetcar stops are identified by distinctive, arch-topped markers painted in the streetcar's shade of green.

VIAtrans, VIA's paratransit system for the disabled, is the third largest in the nation. With 24 hours notice, vans provide curbside pickup and drop-off service. One-way trips cost $1, or $5 for residents who live more than three-quarters of a mile from a regular VIA route. VIAtrans-eligible passengers who can ride standard buses can do so for free.

Four other companies—Texas Trolley, San Antonio City Tours, Lone Star Trolley, and Gray Line— offer routes to major arts and tourist destinations. Gray Line has air-conditioned motor coaches, and all four services provide narrated tours.

© Gary Perkins

VIA uses both streetcars and buses.

For complete VIA route and schedule information, visit the Downtown Information Center at 112 Soledad or the tourist information center across from the Alamo. For telephone information on VIA routes, schedules, and VIAtrans eligibility and reservation information, call 210/362-2020. Tickets for Texas Trolleys and City Tours may be purchased at the Alamo Visitor

---

TOP TEN

Ten Notable San Antonio Bumper Stickers

1. *Puro San Antonio* (also seen in English, Pure San Antonio)
2. Welcome to San Antonio. Now go home.
3. ¡Symphony Si!
4. An Aggie's mom (displayed upside down)
5. Honk if I'm an Aggie
6. If God's not a Longhorn, how come the sunset is burnt orange?
7. I wasn't born in Texas, but I got here as soon as I could.
8. Remember the . . . uh . . . umm . . .
9. I'm not a cowboy. I just found the hat.
10. Cover me! I'm going to change lanes!

Center on Alamo Plaza. Prices vary with the tour selected. Information on Texas Trolleys is available at 210/225-8587 and on City Tours at 210/212-5395. Lone Star Trolleys, the only wheelchair-accessible line, depart from the Ripley's Believe It or Not!/Plaza Theatre of Wax museum across the plaza from the Alamo; call 210/224-9299. All three of the independent trolley services offer group and charter rates. Gray Line tour tickets are available by calling 210/226-1706; pickup is on Alamo Plaza at specified times.

If you're not in a hurry and want to spend a romantic hour around the central downtown area, try one of the naturally air-conditioned, one-horsepower vehicles of the Yellow Rose Carriage Company. You'll have plenty of time to see the sights, the ambience is pure Old World, and you can't beat the headroom. Prices start at $10 per person for a 25-minute tour, with up to four children under 12 tagging along for free. A 45-minute tour is $20 each, and a ride around the beautiful King William Historic District is $30. Carriage stands are located on Houston and Crockett Streets, on either side of the Alamo, and at the historic Fairmount Hotel. Tours leave continually between 9 a.m. and 11:30 p.m. Call 210/225-6490 for information.

Taxis

With more than 25 cab companies, most of which offer 24-hour service, taxis are easily obtained in San Antonio. Airport terminals have the requisite taxi stands, which will have long lines during the holidays. If you're downtown, you can occasionally flag one down, but usually a cab on the street already has a fare or is on its way to one. A more dependable alternative is to visit a taxi stand outside any of the major hotels or call a company's dispatcher. Some of the larger taxi stables are maintained by

VIA Streetcar

Al Rendon

Eight Rules for Driving in the Alamo City

1. *Wearing your seat belt is more than just a good idea. It's the law.*
2. *You may turn right on a red light, after a stop and a yield, though few drivers stop first.*
3. *Some San Antonio drivers think an amber light means, "Hurry up! You can make it!" Watch for them.*
4. *School zones, marked by signs and (sometimes) flashing lights, have a 20-mph speed limit on school days. Speeding fines double in these zones.*
5. *Area highways are undergoing constant construction. Speeding fines in work zones also double.*
6. *Crosswalk signals are observed only casually by downtown pedestrians, so look before turning or jumping through a freshly green light.*
7. *You are certainly not the type of person to use obscene gestures behind the wheel, which is a good thing. Texans can have tempers, and concealed handguns are legal with a permit. There are a few incidents combining these items and poor judgment each year.*
8. *If any portion of your stay will include more than a couple of margaritas, be aware that Texas's DWI (Driving While Intoxicated) laws are strict, unforgiving, and expensive. During holidays, Department of Public Safety officers are more prevalent on the highways than armadillos in the Hill Country.*

Checker, 210/222-2151; Yellow, 210/226-4242; and Fiesta Taxi, 210/666-6666. Fiesta accepts major credit cards.

Another option is Star Shuttle and Charter, the official airport shuttle service whose vans double as cabs all around town. While major hotels also offer shuttle service from San Antonio International, Star has a 24-hour reservation and information line (800/341-6000). Reservations shouldn't be necessary for a ride from the airport terminals unless you're arriving at an ungodly hour and want to double-check. You can also use that number to arrange a charter for a Star Shuttle vehicle or a ride back to the airport from your hotel. Star Shuttle accepts credit cards.

Driving in San Antonio

What the city lacks in navigational ease it makes up for in accessible highways, probably because of the unwritten Texas law known as "one Bubba, one pickup." Everyone drives everywhere, and many times the driver is the only passenger.

To accommodate the traffic, nearly every expressway in the San Antonio area is bracketed by one-way access roads that greatly simplify highway travel. If you find yourself headed north on I-35 when you're trying to go south, simply take the next exit to the right. (Note: Drivers on the access road are supposed to yield to traffic exiting the highway, but sometimes they forget.) Before traveling far on the access road that parallels the highway, you'll see a sign in the left lane that says "Turnaround." Take that lane, pass under the interstate, and head back the other way.

Many San Antonians think their city has serious traffic congestion. It doesn't. The average commuter trip to work or school is 22 minutes, just below the national average. But the highways are also continually under construction, significantly impeding your progress.

Rain makes traffic in San Antonio even worse. South Texas rains, when they come, aren't forceful or lengthy (usually), so road oils aren't washed away. The oil makes dampened streets and highways more treacherous than you might expect. If you've driven on ice successfully, you won't have any problem. If not, do what your mom said: Allow extra time, don't follow too closely, and watch out for people who ignore the first two rules. Also watch for standing water—storm sewers (except for the River Walk) are rare, and some streets accumulate bodies of water large enough to handle small boats, particularly near the right curb.

A warning must be issued here regarding "low-water crossings." In case of heavy or prolonged rains, a few downtown and outlying streets will be covered with standing or even flowing water. If a street is impassable, city crews are very prompt in putting out signs telling you the road is closed. These signs are gospel! Driving around them is as smart as driving around a railroad crossing barrier, and every year a number of motorists who ought to know better find themselves passengers on unscheduled float trips. Most survive.

Parking downtown is available, though you may have to walk a bit from a surface lot to your destination. Many of those lots bear signs saying "Park It and Lock It." Payment works on an honor system. There are boxes with numbered slots that correspond to the number on the parking space you choose. Don't leave the lot without anteing up, because management checks to see if you fed the parking kitty. If you didn't, your car will win a free trip to a downtown wrecker yard without you. Expired parking meters are also enforced with remarkable swiftness.

Parking rates on weekdays are anywhere from $2.50 to $5.00. Weekends are slightly higher, with "events parking" for concerts and sports higher still. An alternative to uncovered surface lots downtown is the

Nine Fascinating San Antonio Buildings Other Than the Alamo

Bexar County Court House *(Flores St. at Military Plaza)—Arguably one of the most attractive county seats in the country, this 1891 edifice is constructed of striking, deep red stone.*

Hertzberg Circus Museum *(210 W. Market St.)—This popular attraction occupies the former home of San Antonio's first public library, bankrolled by Andrew Carnegie in 1902.*

Hilton Palacio del Rio *(200 S. Alamo, on the River Walk)—This building, constructed for HemisFair in 1968, was the first in the world to benefit from all-modular construction: rooms were assembled and furnished on the ground and hoisted into place by crane.*

Mill Race Studio *(Brackenridge Park, off Broadway)—Renowned sculptor Gutzon Borglum designed Mount Rushmore from his studio in this former waterworks.*

San Antonio Museum of Art *(200 W. Jones Ave.)—Opened in 1903 as the Lone Star Brewery, the museum's digs have received national awards for a masterful renovation.*

San Fernando Cathedral *(115 Main Plaza)—The oldest cathedral in the United States (1738) was the ecclesiastical home of the Spanish Canary Island settlers who founded the city.*

Sunset Depot *(1174 E. Commerce St.)—This Spanish colonial–style entertainment complex (née 1877 Southern Pacific Depot) was the terminus for many San Antonio immigrants.*

Tower Life Building *(310 S. St. Mary's St.)—An Atlee Ayres creation dating to 1929, San Antonio's first skyscraper was once used as a blimp dock.*

Tower of the Americas *(HemisFair Park)—O'Neil Ford's 750-foot contribution to the 1968 World's Fair is one of the tallest freestanding structures in the Western Hemisphere.*

generous multilevel parking at Rivercenter. From there, a quick trolley hop or stroll will take you wherever you need to go. Buy something in the mall (even just a cup of coffee), get your ticket stamped before you return to your car, and two hours of your parking will be free.

San Antonio drivers are, by and large, friendly—though often in a hurry. Much of the time, highway speed limits of 55, 65, and sometimes 70 mph are viewed as cheerful suggestions. You may see highway signs that read "Keep Texas Moving: Slow Traffic Keep Right." Because some enhanced-velocity drivers like to give you close-ups of their grills in your rearview mirror, that's a good rule to follow. If you're unsure of your next exit, or if the pace of the left lane is a little too spirited for your blood, stay as far to the right as is comfortable. Most highway exits, with a few exceptions, are on the right anyway. And of course, signaling to change lanes is always advisable and will usually earn you a smile, a wave, and some space.

Biking in San Antonio

To date, San Antonio is not being considered for any awards as a bicycle-friendly community. Though a few new roads, according to federal law, have been built with wider shoulders or parallel bike paths, these roads are not common enough to make cycling a viable transportation option. While downtown cyclists don't have to contend with saber-toothed storm drains gnashing their rims as in other cities, many streets make up for it with potholes larger than some homes.

Biking is better in San Antonio's numerous parks. Though park streets are not particularly wide, operators of fume-spewing vehicles generally cooperate with bikers. And many of the parks feature on- and off-road bike trails. One of the more attractive of these will be the Mission Trail—a roadway and cycle trail slated for completion by the year 2000 (though much of it is already completed). Beginning downtown at the Alamo, this trail will wind its way between San Antonio's five Spanish colonial missions.

Most of San Antonio's die-hard sprocketheads rooftop their bikes outside Loops 410 and 1604 before mounting up for pleasant rides, including some challenging, winding routes through the Hill Country. There, be prepared for two-lane highways with narrow shoulders.

San Antonio International Airport (SAI)

The airport is international only in that, as you might expect, it features daily flights to and from Mexico. SAI is served by 12 commercial airlines flying 7 million passengers to or from the city each year. The airport is about 15 minutes north of downtown, just east of the intersection of Loop 410 and Highway 281 North. As the airport is not directly on 281 or any

San Antonio International Airport

other major north-south route, allow extra time before your departure; Airport Boulevard can be congested, particularly during peak flying times and rush hours. This will be alleviated somewhat with the completion of an extensive new parking system, slated for ribbon-cutting in mid-1999. Once you make it onto the airport grounds, follow the signs to one of the two close-set terminals. Airlines are clearly marked. U.S. airlines serving SAI are as follows:

America West, 800/235-9292
American, 800/433-7300
Conquest, 800/722-0860
Continental, 800/523-3273
Delta, 800/221-1212
Northwest, 800/225-2525
Southwest, 210/617-1221
TWA, 800/221-2000
United, 800/241-6522

In addition, Mexicana, 800/531-7921, and Aeroliteral, 800/237-6639, offer jumping-off service to major destinations in Mexico.

SAI isn't a hub for any major U.S. airline, which helps keep check-in and baggage-claim lines relatively short. Although SAI isn't considered a high-risk airport, allow the standard one hour before your flight in case security is tightened due to a recent crisis somewhere else.

All airport area hotels offer free shuttles, as do most of the major downtown hotels. Star Shuttle operates every 15 minutes, 24 hours a day, between SAI and downtown. The ride costs $6, and children under 5 are free. For the return trip, call 90 minutes in advance to arrange a pickup (see Taxis). The major car-rental chains have counters at or near the airport, with shuttle service to those not located in the terminals.

San Antonio Transportation Firsts

First camels *(1856)—Herd of experimental army camels rested at San Pedro Park en route to Camp Verde near Kerrville.*

First train *(1877)—Galveston, Harrisburg & San Antonio Railroad (now Southern Pacific) arrived.*

First streetcars *(1878)—Mule-pulled cars provided service between downtown and San Pedro Park.*

First electric streetcars *(1890)—"Hooray!" shouted the mules.*

First military flight *(1910)—Lt. Benjamin Foulois flew one of the Wright brothers' castoffs at Fort Sam Houston.*

First flying school owned by an American woman *(1915)—Marjorie Stinson, the fourth woman pilot in America, opened Stinson Flying School at San Antonio's first airport, now named Stinson Field, the third-oldest airport in America.*

First lucky parachute jump *(1925)—Charles Lindbergh, a cadet at Brooks Air Force Base, had to bail out of his trainer. Lindbergh's class was the first to be trained in parachute use, hence the nickname "Lucky."*

First airmail service in Texas *(1928)—When she wasn't training pilots, Marjorie Stinson flew a 30-mile mail route between San Antonio and Seguin.*

First simian astronaut *(1959)—Eleven years after his 12 minutes of fame, Sam the Space Monkey retired to the San Antonio Zoo. (Sam, a rhesus, was born at the University of Texas in Austin.)*

First Alamo City streetcars *(1983)—These rubber-tired reproductions of historic San Antonio trolleys, designed for VIA by Chance Amusement Rides of Wichita, Kansas (which also created the Brackenridge Park mini-train), are now found throughout the country.*

First "smart highway" *(1994)—The TransGuide highway monitoring system is currently being tested in San Antonio.*

Train Service

Ironically (and some say tragically) for a city that owes its settling-down to the railroads, San Antonio has no actual train station. Downtown's historic Sunset Depot, a beautiful Spanish mission–style structure built in 1903, has been turned into an entertainment complex and nightspot along the lines of Orlando's Church Street Station (see Chapter 12, Nightlife). Amtrak trains now arrive and depart from an unattractive temporary structure behind the renamed Sunset Station.

Regular train service is via the transcontinental Sunset Limited, which runs between Los Angeles and Miami, through Phoenix and New Orleans, six days a week. Contact Amtrak at 800/USA-RAIL for schedule and rate information.

The station was wheelchair accessible for some time, but current renovation efforts may change this status periodically (see Chapter 5, Sights and Attractions). The station has no baggage assistance, food service, or car-rental outlets. Because the "station" is in the shadows of both Sunset Station and the Alamodome, events traffic and nighttime merrymakers can make traffic a problem. A genuine, rail-riding trolley to connect the train station with the central downtown area is in the planning stages but will not be available for several years.

Regional Bus Service

San Antonio's small Greyhound terminal is better than the crackerbox train station, but it still needs a facelift. It has the advantage of being nearer the heart of the downtown tourist district at 500 North St. Mary's Street. It's also busy, with frequent arrivals and connections throughout the day. Schedules change, so call Greyhound at 210/270-5824 for up-to-date timetables. The Kerrville Bus Company, 210/227-5669, headquarters its local and regional services in the same building.

Bonner Garden Bed and Breakfast

3

WHERE TO STAY

Since San Antonio's number-one—some say only—industry is tourism, you would expect some choices in accommodations. You won't be disappointed. San Antonio offers a staggering variety of hostelries: no-frills chain motels for the budget-conscious; quaint, river-view bed-and-breakfasts; historic nineteenth-century "high-rises" downtown; and a rambling, first-class resort sprawling over 200 acres of the Hill Country.

Most San Antonio hotels are located for convenience—downtown, near the airport, along Loop 410, and near Sea World and Fiesta Texas. You'll pay a little more for ambience, atmosphere, and accessibility. For instance, downtown hotels close to the tourist action run higher than those on Loop 410. If you prefer a particular, popular hotel chain, most of these have locations close to downtown. The cost for any accommodations rises with proximity to the Alamo district, but the franchises inside downtown offer a nice alternative to the typical inn on the highway and will be cheaper than the more historical or ritzy establishments. But don't forget that in addition to being close to the most popular sightseeing areas, the older public houses take you back to a day when the River Walk was just a river, and San Antonio was a wilder, woollier place.

For something a bit more intimate than a multitiered hotel, try one of downtown's several bed-and-breakfasts. B&Bs located in the King William District, a historic neighborhood on the river settled by well-to-do Germans in the mid- to late 1800s, are tourist favorites. The Monte Vista neighborhood also has some outstanding B&Bs, though they're a bit farther from the center of things.

Price rating symbols:
$	**$50 and under**
$$	**$51 to $75**
$$$	**$76 to $125**
$$$$	**$126 and up**

DOWNTOWN

Hotels

ADAM'S MARK HOTEL
425 Soledad St.
San Antonio
210/354-2800
$$$$
One of downtown's newest hotels is also one of its poshest. Located in a 1958 bank building, the Adam's Mark opened its doors in 1997 following a $45-million restoration to reveal a vast lobby with giant chandeliers and tons of brass, iron, and crystal. The result is an impressive hotel that won the ASAE Inner Circle Award and a Four Diamond rating from AAA. Catch an elevator to one of 410 luxury rooms or four suites, a pool and sundeck, business facilities, and large, fully equipped workout facility with sauna and whirlpool. For dining and drinks, there is Restaurant Marbella with one of San Antonio's most lauded chefs, Michael Bomberg; Players Sports Bar; and the Tiffany Rose piano bar. Most downtown tourist and arts sites are within walking distance, and a river taxi stops just outside the back door. See www.adamsmark.com for more information. ♿ (Downtown)

CAMBERLEY GUNTER HOTEL
205 E. Houston St.
San Antonio
210/227-3241
$$$$
The Gunter has undergone several ownership changes in recent years, but none have affected the ambience of this 1800s-era hotel. In completing a recent $5-million renovation, the Camberley organization took great pains to preserve the original look of the vaulted lobby, 312 rooms, and 10 suites. The Gunter is one block away from stairs to the River Walk, four blocks from the Alamo, and across the street from the Majestic Theatre, the delightfully atmospheric home of the San Antonio Symphony and the Majestic Broadway series. The Café Suisse restaurant offers gourmet fare (though you shouldn't go if you're in a hurry), and the Gunter Bakery serves up coffee and tempting pastries. The Camberley Club offers a private lounge with complimentary breakfast, afternoon tea, and evening cordials, and there's Muldoons for cocktails. A gym, pool, and spa are available. ♿ (Downtown)

COURTYARD BY
MARRIOTT/DOWNTOWN
600 S. Santa Rosa St.
San Antonio
210/229-9449
$$$
Like most of the Marriott Courtyard

TRIVIA

The Gunter Hotel, now part of the Camberley chain, has grown significantly since it was built as San Antonio's largest building in 1909. Yet a succession of owners have taken great pains—and spent nearly $100 million—to keep the inside true to its history. Prominent on one wall is a black-and-white photo of one of the Gunter's most famous guests, Tom Mix, who is checking in at the desk while mounted on his horse, Tony.

DOWNTOWN SAN ANTONIO

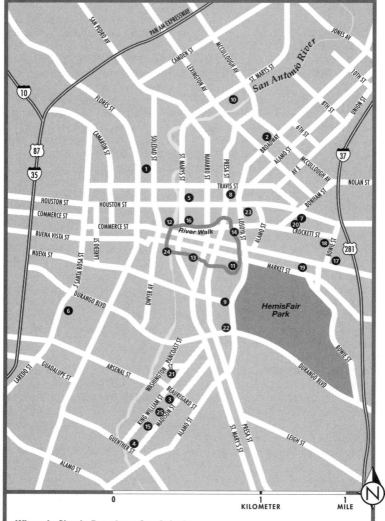

Where to Stay in Downtown San Antonio

1 Adam's Mark Hotel
2 Alamo Travelodge
3 Beauregard House
4 Beckmann Inn & Carriage House
5 Camberley Gunter Hotel
6 Courtyard by Marriott/Downtown
7 Crockett Hotel
8 Crowne Plaza St. Anthony Hotel
9 The Fairmount Hotel
10 Four Points Sheraton/River Walk North
11 Hilton Palacio del Rio
12 Holiday Inn River Walk
13 Homewood Suites Hotel
14 Hyatt Regency San Antonio
15 The Jackson House
16 La Mansión del Rio
17 La Quinta Inn/Convention Center
18 Marriott Rivercenter
19 Marriott River Walk
20 The Menger Hotel
21 Pancoast Carriage House
22 Plaza San Antonio
23 Ramada Emily Morgan Hotel
24 River Walk Plaza Hotel
25 The Royal Swan

Crowne Plaza St. Anthony Hotel

The Crowne Plaza St. Anthony, a state and national landmark, has the most beautiful lobby of any San Antonio hostelry. Dripping with gold leaf and crystal chandeliers, the lofty space is filled with antiques and art—much of which has been part of the hotel's collection since it was built in 1909. But what may have made the city's patron saint's namesake an even more attractive place to spend the night was its climate—the St. Anthony was the world's first air-conditioned hotel.

Whatever the motivation, the hotel has been the choice of many visiting luminaries, including Ronald Reagan, Bob Hope, Franklin Roosevelt, and Princess Grace of Monaco. John Wayne was such a fan that a suite in the hotel bears his name. The most ill-fated guest was labor leader Samuel Gompers, whose one night in the St. Anthony was his last on earth. But if you gotta go, go in style.

chain, the downtown Courtyard is business traveler–oriented while offering fine accommodations and amenities for visiting families. Suites and traditional rooms are available, and breakfast and dinner are served in the restaurant. A lounge provides an evening stopping-in place, and a pool, whirlpool, and gym are on-site for recreation. The seven-year-old building is located just off the downtown highway loop, near El Mercado, less than a mile from the River Walk. Pets are not allowed. ♿ (Downtown)

CROCKETT HOTEL
320 Bonham St.
San Antonio
210/225-6500
$$$
One of San Antonio's most historic

hotels, the Crockett promises you a stay "So close to the Alamo that you can almost smell the gunpowder." If you fear visits from spectral Alamo defenders, rest assured that the Crockett wasn't built until 1909, long after the dispute was settled. But the hotel is adjacent to the Cradle of Texas Liberty, as well as the Incubator of San Antonio Commerce, the River Walk. Just behind the Crockett is Rivercenter, the very popular shopping/recreation mall, and most other downtown tourist destinations are an easy walk away. The folks at the Crockett are proud not only of a top-to-bottom, historically accurate restoration, but also of some modern touches, such as a landscaped pool with waterfall, spa, and a lush, tropical courtyard. ♿ (Downtown)

CROWNE PLAZA
ST. ANTHONY HOTEL
300 E. Travis St.
San Antonio
210/227-4392
$$$$

Built in 1909, the St. Anthony offers a taste of bygone days at a price slightly lower than comparable downtown hotels. Its elaborate lobby, with gilt sculpture, posh furnishings, and tinkling chandeliers, is part of the reason it was named both a Texas and national landmark. While not right on the River Walk, it's only a block away, and across the street is lovely little Travis Park. The St. Anthony's restaurant is open for all meals, and a made-to-order pasta buffet has been a favorite of downtown business-lunchers for years. Outstanding personal service has earned the hotel AAA's Four Diamond rating for 14 consecutive years. A pool and gym are available.

E-mail stanthonyhotel@compuserve .com & (Downtown)

THE FAIRMOUNT HOTEL
401 S. Alamo St.
San Antonio
210/224-8800
$$$$

The Fairmount is one of San Antonio's finest hotels. It's also one of the most expensive. But bear in mind that it made a sacrifice a hotel should never be asked to make—it moved (see sidebar below). Now located across Alamo Street from HemisFair Park, the Fairmount was named one of *Condé Nast's Traveler* Top 50 American Hotels and is a four-star, four-diamond hotel. The hotel's Polo's Restaurant and Lounge are also perennial award-winners that host many glittering get-togethers for the local aristocracy. A gym is available, and you can bring your pets if you dress them well. & (Downtown)

Hotel on Wheels

Where Rivercenter now stands, the Fairmount Hotel previously stood for 80 years. The Fairmount had been vacant for some time when city leaders generously decided to save the historic hotel. In March 1985, the 1,600-ton structure was loaded onto 30 massive, rubber-tired dollies and lugged down Market Street to its current location on Alamo Street, across from HemisFair Park.

The Fairmount movers didn't set any speed records. The journey of four blocks or so took six days, and many San Antonians feared the hotel would fall apart before coming to rest. But supported by a web of cables and a blessing from a Catholic bishop, the Fairmount was buoyed safely to its new location, where it is now one of San Antonio's finest hotels.

Adam's Mark Hotel, p. 37

FOUR POINTS SHERATON RIVER WALK NORTH
110 Lexington Ave.
San Antonio
800/288-3927
$$$$

Located on the less-fashionable north end of the River Walk, the Four Points has the advantage of being away from the madding crowds. Nonetheless, access to the major sites is a relaxing and beautiful 15-minute stroll away on the River Walk. (You'll know which direction to go, because the river sidewalks end right outside.) A swimming pool and health club are on-site, as are a restaurant and lounge. The Four Points costs the same as some other hotels closer to where the action is, but it might be worth it to you if you need a bit more personal space. You'll have to pay for parking, however, and there's no airport shuttle. &. (Downtown)

HILTON PALACIO DEL RIO
200 S. Alamo St.
San Antonio
210/222-1400

$$$$

Though the Palace on the River is not one of central downtown's oldest hotels, what it gives up in history it makes up for in location (next to La Villita and above the River Walk), view (each room has a private balcony), and features (pool, spa, gym). Pets are welcome if they don't fear elevators. A restaurant serves breakfast, lunch, and dinner, and Durty Nellie's Irish Pub serves rowdy good times. &. (Downtown)

HOLIDAY INN RIVER WALK
217 N. St. Mary's St.
San Antonio
210/224-2500
$$$$

Few hotels can boast a back door that opens onto the River Walk. This relatively pricey sibling in the Holiday Inn family goes that one better, with quality restaurants that offer outside dining just above the Paseo del Rio level. The inn is close to all of the downtown destinations, welcomes your pets, and offers a gym, pool, and spa for loosening muscles tightened up from your sightseeing strolls. &. (Downtown)

HOMEWOOD SUITES HOTEL
432 W. Market St.
San Antonio
210/222-1515
$$$$

Outside, the Homewood is an old warehouse building above the River Walk, the former headquarters of the San Antonio Drug Co. Inside, the Homewood is a spanking new, luxurious suite hotel with topflight accommodations. It's the ideal place to stay if you want to be close to the family but everyone needs a little space to spread out. An on-site Executive Center, equipped with computer, printer,

La Mansión del Rio

A large section of this very lovely, very pricey River Walk hotel was once St. Mary's College, an all-male school founded in 1853. In 1934 it became St. Mary's Law School, which went coed in 1963. A young lieutenant named Dwight D. Eisenhower once coached football here.

The school relocated in 1966—just in time for the River Hotel Company to snatch up the original building and ready it for the 1968 World's Fair. Though additions have been made over the years, the original school building has been preserved. All together, La Mansión's complex is one of the prettiest spots on the river.

and copier, is available 24 hours. Rooms include kitchenettes and wet bars, and a free continental breakfast buffet is provided daily. An airy lounge in the lobby has overstuffed chairs that overlook the river. For the kids, Nintendo and videotaped movies are supplied. E-mail hws-riverwalk@com puserve.com ໔ (Downtown)

HYATT REGENCY SAN ANTONIO
123 Losoya St.
San Antonio
210/222-1234
$$$$

The Hyatt's prime location—on the River Walk, across the street from the Alamo—partially explains its significant room rates, as does its AAA Four Diamond rating. The style is thoroughly contemporary, particularly in its 16-story atrium lobby (where a riverlike fountain pours out into the real river) and its restaurants. The Hyatt offers a "rooftop skypool," gym, and spa, and there are several trendy shops on the river level of the lobby.

That's where you'll also find one amenity that no other San Antonio hotel can touch: The Landing jazz club, where the rightly lauded Jim Cullum Jazz Band plays in the traditional Dixieland style on weekends. Even if you decide to stay elsewhere, don't miss Cullum's band! ໔ (Downtown)

LA MANSIÓN DEL RIO
112 College St.
San Antonio
210/225-2581
$$$$

This lovely, first-class hotel was never, as its name suggests, a mansion on the river. While it is on the river, much of the present building was once the St. Mary's College. The front of La Mansión is unremarkable (boring, even), looking out on College Street and a parking garage, but the other side is a delight from inside and out, boasting Spanish colonial décor and balconies on the rooms. These overlook beautiful landscaping and one of the most popular stretches of the river, near Paesano's restaurant, the County Line Barbecue, and the Hard Rock Café. La Mansión's Las Canarias restaurant (named for the Canary Islanders who settled in San Antonio) is airy and sunny, with cuisine favored by concert- and showgoers headed across College Street to the Majestic Theatre. ♿ (Downtown)

MARRIOTT RIVERCENTER
101 Bowie St.
San Antonio
210/223-1000
$$$$

Check the address of your reservation confirmation carefully. Visitors to San Antonio (and even locals) are frequently confused between the Marriott Rivercenter and the older Marriott River Walk. These two high-rise sisters are inexplicably located directly across the street from one another. Both frequently host conventions in their glittering ballrooms and meeting rooms, and are located near the Convention Center, Rivercenter, HemisFair Park, and the Alamo.

Holiday Inn River Walk, p. 41

Holiday Inn River Walk

Amenities include a pool, gym, spa, and sauna. ♿ (Downtown)

MARRIOTT RIVER WALK
711 E. River Walk
San Antonio
210/224-4555
$$$$

Across the street from its taller, newer sibling, the Marriott River Walk is the closest hotel to the Gonzalez Convention Center (at least until the new Sheraton being built on the CC's grounds is completed) and is thus a hot spot during the convention seasons. Be prepared for a crowded lobby if your stay coincides with one of these. A Gold Key award winner from *Convention Traveler* magazine, the Marriott River Walk offers suites or rooms, a bar and restaurant, pool, spa, and gym. And even conventioneers can bring their pets. ♿ (Downtown)

THE MENGER HOTEL
204 Alamo Plaza
San Antonio
210/223-4361
$$$$

The Menger was one of San Antonio's first hotels, and many rooms still offer an ambience circa 1859, when the Menger was quite probably the finest hotel west of the Mississippi. A newer addition contains more modern accommodations, but ask for one of the historic rooms overlooking the courtyard and garden. Some rooms include kitchenettes. The south lobby's Rotunda is packed with period artworks and antiques that truly make you feel as if there's a stagecoach waiting outside at the taxi stand. Also just outside are the Alamo and Rivercenter. At a relatively reasonable price, the Menger is a great place to get the feel of Old San Antonio from right in the

The Menger Hotel

William Menger's hotel started out as a brewery in the 1850s. But entrepreneurial prescience told Menger that his lot next to the Alamo would be far more profitable as a hotel for passers-through. He was right. In 1859 he opened the first high-quality hotel west of the Mississippi.

That wasn't the Menger's only first. Inside, the hotel's Roosevelt Bar is an exact reconstruction of the one found in London's House of Lords. It was named for Teddy R., who recruited some of his Rough Riders here. Other features unique to the Menger are the King Suite, named for legendary Texas rancher Richard King, who went to the last roundup while staying here; the leather-wrapped Roy Rogers Suite, a favorite of the King of the Cowboys; and alligators. Though the scaly reptiles are no longer around, Mr. Menger used to delight in keeping an assortment of them on the patio. Only in Texas. . . .

Don't be surprised if you end up sharing your room. The Menger is reportedly haunted by at least a half-dozen former San Antonio residents, including Sally White, a housekeeper murdered by her husband; "Buckskin," who frequents the fourth floor wearing frontier regalia; and "The Maitre d'," who waits on spectral customers after the dining room closes.

center of history. E-mail menger@txdirect.net. & (Downtown)

PLAZA SAN ANTONIO
555 S. Alamo St.
San Antonio
210/229-1000
$$$$
Sitting in the courtyard of the Marriott-owned Plaza, watching peafowl and other exotic birds wander through the lush grass, you'll find it difficult to remember that the busy city center is just beyond the gate. This setting has earned the hotel a reputation as more of a resort than an overnight destination—enhanced by the on-site tennis courts, fountains, pool and spa, and workout room. The highly rated and innovative Anaqua Grill is just off the lobby. Multiple large meeting rooms make the Plaza ideal for conferences, and the small, historic buildings on the grounds lend atmosphere and even more space. That may be the Plaza's only downside—it's so nice just to stay there, you might not get out and

see the city. E-mail psasales@netex press.com. ♿ (Downtown)

RAMADA EMILY MORGAN HOTEL
705 E. Houston St.
San Antonio
210/225-8486
$$$$

The Emily Morgan isn't as old as it looks. Even though it was built in 1924, this delightfully restored building on the border of Alamo Plaza offers nineteenth-century ambience at a price lower than some other period hotels downtown. Even better, it's across the street from the Alamo and two blocks from the River Walk. Choose from traditional rooms or suites, some of which include whirlpools and refrigerators. A self-operated business center is open 24 hours, and you'll find an outdoor heated pool outside the fitness center. Inside the lobby the Yellow Rose Café serves breakfast and lunch seven days. (The original Ms. Morgan, by the way, inspired the song "Yellow Rose of Texas.") ♿ (Downtown)

RIVER WALK PLAZA HOTEL
100 Villita St.
San Antonio
210/226-2271
$$$–$$$$

As you would assume from its name, the River Walk Plaza is on the shore of San Antonio's liquid gold, albeit just above a dam at the somewhat less-popular southern tip of the downtown bend. Still, it is within a manageable walk to the downtown sights, and very near the King William Historic District. Accommodations include both suites and traditional rooms, along with amenities such as hair dryers, clock/radios, full-length and makeup mirrors, and "outstanding personal service." A full-service restaurant is open for all meals, and a gym is available to patrons. The hotel was a Howard Johnson Gold Medal Award–winner in 1996. See www.riverwalkplaza.com ♿ (Downtown)

Motels

ALAMO TRAVELODGE
405 Broadway
San Antonio
210/222-1000
$$–$$$

This partner in the ubiquitous Travelodge chain offers one of the best bargains of the downtown hotels. Located just five blocks from the Alamo and the most popular stretch of the River Walk, it's also two blocks from the downtown YMCA and one mile from golfing and horseback-riding in Brackenridge Park. A river taxi stop is 1.5 blocks away, and the VIA Trolley stops on the Travelodge's corner. Accordingly, the desk offers river-taxi and -tour tickets. The lodge has a pool, an attached restaurant for breakfast and lunch, and Sleepy Bear Dens—suites for families that feature festive décor and free kids' movies. The Travelodge isn't as historic as, say, the Menger. But the Menger doesn't give away "huggable Sleepy Bear plush toys." ♿ (Downtown)

LA QUINTA INN/
CONVENTION CENTER
1001 E. Commerce St.
San Antonio
210/222-9181
$$$

Driving around San Antonio, you might be led to believe "La Quinta" (lah KEEN-tah) is Spanish for "next door to Denny's." Several of the representatives of this San Antonio–based chain are indeed near the family-style restaurants. That is only one of the advantages of the La Quinta Inns. Their reputation for providing very good accommodations at an affordable price could be envied by other, more far-flung national chains, and makes them an ideal choice for traveling families. Each La Quinta offers similar features—Southwestern-style architecture and décor, pools, continental breakfast, data ports, free stays for children under 18 (in parent's room), and laundry and dry cleaning services. Newer to the chain is the La Quinta Suite, with landscaped courtyards, additional business features, and fitness centers. The Convention Center La Quinta offers both rooms and suites (at an adjacent facility), along with easy access to the River Walk, the Alamo, the Alamodome, Rivercenter, and all of the other downtown magnets. Special rooms are offered for physically challenged guests, and discounts are available for AARP members. If La Quinta sounds attractive but you don't want to be quite so close to the center of things, try one of the ten other locations around town. Some will be slightly lower in price than others, due

to location, but all bear AAA Three Diamond ratings and are held to the same high standards. Call 800/687-6667 for reservation information, or log on to www.laquinta.com. ♿ (Downtown)

Bed-and-Breakfasts

BEAUREGARD HOUSE
215 Beauregard St.
San Antonio
800/841-9377
$$$
Owner Ann Trabal invites you to "Come as a stranger, leave as a friend." Three room styles are offered in this 1910 two-story Victorian. One room is wheelchair accessible, and another features a sleeping porch. Breakfast is served in the dining room, on the tree-shaded backyard deck, or on the front porch. Downtown activities are within a short walk, and the trolley stop is a block away. Laundry facilities are available, as is transportation to Sea World and Fiesta Texas, and parking is free. No pets. ♿ (Downtown)

Ramada Emily Morgan Hotel, p. 45

Ramada Emily Morgan Hotel

TIP If you plan to spend most of your time at historical sites, stay in or near downtown. Trying to get downtown in the morning for a day of sightseeing puts you in the middle of rush hour. Likewise, going back at the end of the day.

BECKMANN INN & CARRIAGE HOUSE
222 E. Guenther St.
San Antonio
210/229-1449
$$$

Choose from suites or rooms at this 1886 property, which is listed in the National Register of Historic Places and as a City of San Antonio Historic Landmark. The Beckmann's signature is a wraparound sunporch on the main house and matching architecture on the carriage house. Interior architecture includes 14-foot ceilings, beveled windows, and arched pocket doors. Bedrooms feature private baths; ornately carved, high-back queen-size beds; and ceiling fans, with only the phone, air-conditioning, refrigerator, and TV to detract from the Old World ambience. Breakfast is served in a formal dining room with china, crystal, and silver. The Beckmann has received "excellent" ratings from IIA, Mobil, and AAA. It is not wheelchair accessible, and pets are not allowed. www.beckmanninn.com. (Downtown)

THE JACKSON HOUSE
107 Madison St.
San Antonio
210/225-4045
$$$

Don and Liesl Noble, sixth-generation residents of the King William District, have restored two neighborhood homes as bed-and-breakfasts. The 1894 Jackson House, in its AAA-rated

modern incarnation, offers traditional rooms and suites, a luxurious landscaped garden, and a lofty, glass-enclosed conservatory with a pool and spa. First-floor rooms have 12-foot ceilings and two-person spa bathtubs. Upstairs are sloping ceilings, claw-foot tubs, and roof windows looking out on the Victorian surroundings. For an extra touch of elegance, a 1960 Rolls Royce Silver Cloud is available as an airport shuttle or to other destinations by appointment. No pets. ♿ (Downtown)

PANCOAST CARRIAGE HOUSE
202 Washington St.
San Antonio
210/225-4045
$$$

Built in 1896 for Don Noble's great-grandfather, this tidy Victorian carriage house contains three suites, all with queen-size beds, full kitchens, and separate living/dining areas. Through the French doors downstairs are an enclosed brick patio and a garden with swimming pool, spa, tables, chairs, and chaises. Call for the Rolls instead of a cab (see above). No pets. ♿ (Downtown)

THE ROYAL SWAN
236 Madison St.
San Antonio
210/223-3776
$$$

With stained-glass windows looking out on the King William Historic

GREATER SAN ANTONIO

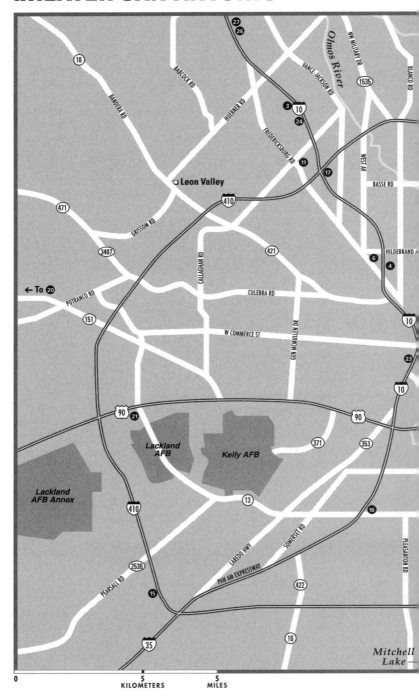

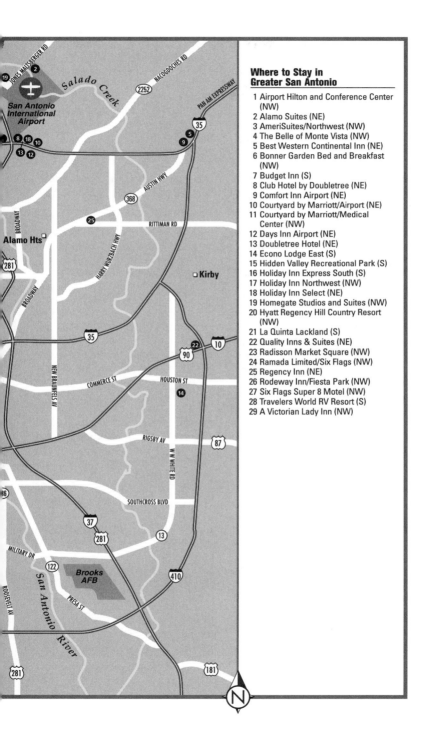

Where to Stay in Greater San Antonio

1 Airport Hilton and Conference Center (NW)
2 Alamo Suites (NE)
3 AmeriSuites/Northwest (NW)
4 The Belle of Monte Vista (NW)
5 Best Western Continental Inn (NE)
6 Bonner Garden Bed and Breakfast (NW)
7 Budget Inn (S)
8 Club Hotel by Doubletree (NE)
9 Comfort Inn Airport (NE)
10 Courtyard by Marriott/Airport (NE)
11 Courtyard by Marriott/Medical Center (NW)
12 Days Inn Airport (NE)
13 Doubletree Hotel (NE)
14 Econo Lodge East (S)
15 Hidden Valley Recreational Park (S)
16 Holiday Inn Express South (S)
17 Holiday Inn Northwest (NW)
18 Holiday Inn Select (NE)
19 Homegate Studios and Suites (NW)
20 Hyatt Regency Hill Country Resort (NW)
21 La Quinta Lackland (S)
22 Quality Inns & Suites (NE)
23 Radisson Market Square (NW)
24 Ramada Limited/Six Flags (NW)
25 Regency Inn (NE)
26 Rodeway Inn/Fiesta Park (NW)
27 Six Flags Super 8 Motel (NW)
28 Travelers World RV Resort (S)
29 A Victorian Lady Inn (NW)

District, the Swan is a tidy 1892 Victorian home with gabled roof, verandas, front and back porches, fireplaces, exotic woods, and luxurious claw-foot tubs. The parlor boasts a floor-to-ceiling library, couches, wingback chairs, a chess set, and fireplace. Another fireplace is found on the wicker-furnished veranda. Several suite options with contrasting characters are offered, though each offers a private bath, queen-size bed, cable TV, and phone with data port. Full hot-and-cold breakfast is served daily, with different selections each morning. Snacks and non-alcoholic drinks are available at all times, and a liqueur nightcap is provided in your room. The Swan received three diamonds from AAA and "excellent" from the American B&B Association, Mobil/Frommers, and Historic Accommodations of Texas. The River Walk and downtown are only blocks away, and you can use your complimentary passes at the trolley stop one block away. Pets are not allowed, and the Swan is not wheelchair accessible. Children over 12 welcome. www.royalswan.com. (Downtown)

NORTHEAST

Hotels

ALAMO SUITES
12079 Starcrest Dr.
San Antonio
210/494-1008
$$$
If you suspect you might like to extend your stay in San Antonio, the Alamo Suites offer a lush option to a standard hotel, with daily, weekly, and monthly rates. Suites include fine furnishings and housewares, microwave ovens in the kitchenettes, and wash-

ers and dryers. A large, inviting pool is secluded behind the building. The location on Loop 410 isn't particularly close to the historical sites or theme parks. E-mail mangum@connecti.com ♿ (Northeast)

CLUB HOTEL BY DOUBLETREE
1111 NE Loop 410
San Antonio
210/828-9031
$$$
Like many of the airport-area hotels, the Club caters to the business traveler. Suites are available, as are traditional rooms. A 3,000-square-foot business center includes a large-screen TV, conference rooms, work stations, data ports, fax machines, copiers, computers, and—when you're tired of working—a lounge. If you're coming to get away from work, enjoy the pool, spa, gym, and full-service restaurant. North Star Mall, the very popular shopping mecca, is an easy walk away, across a bridge spanning Loop 410. The airport is a short shuttle hop in the other direction. ♿ (Northeast)

Crowne Plaza St. Anthony Hotel, p. 40

Crowne Plaza St. Anthony Hotel

COURTYARD BY MARRIOTT/ AIRPORT
8615 Broadway
San Antonio
210/828-7200
$$$

Obviously, this Courtyard is very near the airport. Guests in suites and traditional rooms are served by an outdoor pool and indoor whirlpool, a weight room, laundry room, breakfast and dinner restaurant, and lounge. Getting there from the airport is easy on the complimentary shuttle, which serves a two-mile radius 24 hours a day. (Note: Jets are loud on takeoff, so you may want to opt for another Courtyard location that's farther from the airport but nearer North Star Mall. But you'll have to give up the restaurant and fitness center. 210/530-9881.) ♿ (Northeast)

DOUBLETREE HOTEL
37 NE Loop 410
San Antonio
210/366-2424
$$$

This AAA Four Diamond–winner offers Cascabel, one of the city's most interesting restaurants, whose intriguing, Southwestern-inspired cuisine is a perennial award-winner. The DoubleTree also provides you with an expertly outfitted gym, pool, spa, and sauna to work off your meal (and those signature Double-Tree chocolate-chip cookies) before heading back to your room or suite. A shuttle is available to and from the very nearby San Antonio International Airport. The Loop 410 site is only 15 minutes from downtown via U.S. 281, and slightly farther from Sea World/Fiesta Texas. It is also very near the population center of San Antonio, so there are many eateries and activities to take advantage of,

including the lauded Quarry Golf Club and Quarry Market shopping extravaganza. Nearer yet, a safe walk over the highway, is the very popular North Star Mall. No pets. E-mail hotel@sanantonio.doubletree-hotels.com ♿ (Northeast)

HOLIDAY INN SELECT
77 NE Loop 410
San Antonio
210/349-9900
$$$

Across the highway from North Star Mall, this upscale inn is located near the airport—a prime location for business travelers. Features include two restaurants, a lobby bar, health club, and pool. A welcome bonus is the Executive Edition floor, tailor-made for those needing to mix business and pleasure during their stays. Downtown is 15 minutes away, Sea World and Fiesta Texas are within 20 minutes, and a number of good-to-outstanding restaurants are nearby. Take the shuttle to and from the airport. ♿ (Northeast)

Motels

BEST WESTERN CONTINENTAL INN
9735 I-35 N.
San Antonio
210/655-3510
$$$

This northeastern version of the popular, nationwide chain offers the advantages of being just 10 minutes from the airport (via Loop 410) and 15 non–rush hour minutes from downtown (via I-35), which means it's comfortably east of the very busy U.S. 281/Loop 410 intersection. It's also between downtown and Randolph Air Force Base, so if your stay includes Independence Day, you'll be right down the highway from the city's best fireworks display, an annual Randolph event. If you're partial to Best Westerns but don't want to stay in San Antonio's northeast corner on the SA/Austin corridor, you can try one of the other five local members of the chain. This one features a restaurant (with room service) and a pool. There's no airport shuttle, but the taxi ride will be very short. ⚬ (Northeast)

COMFORT INN AIRPORT
2635 NE Loop 410
San Antonio
210/653-9110
$$

Another chain location that's not too close to the busiest corridors, this one has an airport shuttle. The 203 rooms are served by a restaurant, pool, and fitness center. The Comfort Inn is also near one of San Antonio's largest and most incomprehensible (to Yankees) nightspots, Far West Rodeo (see Chapter 12, Nightlife). North Star Mall isn't far, and access to downtown is straight south on nearby I-35. Six other Comfort Inns are scattered throughout the city, and some offer suites in addition to traditional rooms. ⚬ (Northeast)

DAYS INN AIRPORT
542 NE Loop 410
San Antonio
210/930-3300
$$$

Days Inns are found in nine locations throughout the city. This one offers the advantage of easy access to the airport and North Star Mall, and is 15 minutes from Fiesta Texas and 20 from Sea World. All feature pools with few other amenities, and some are cheaper than others. All have restaurants nearby. A location at Loop 410 and I-35, also northeast, of-

fers kitchenettes (210/650-9779), and a far northwest sibling near Fiesta Texas offers suites (210/696-7922). Most of the locations are wheelchair accessible. ⚬ (Northeast)

QUALITY INNS & SUITES
3817 I-35 N.
San Antonio
210/224-3030
$$

In addition to its traditional rooms, Quality offers two-room suites with sitting areas, recliners, pullout love seats, desks, minibars with refrigerators, two TVs and phones, and king-size beds. Extended-stay rates are available for four or more nights. A pool is on-site, and Quality has a reciprocity agreement with the nearby World Gym to help you work off the complimentary breakfast doughnuts and cereals. Restaurants are nearby when continental isn't enough, and pets can come with you. ⚬ (Northeast)

REGENCY INN
1131 Austin Hwy.
San Antonio
210/824-1441
$

The Regency is a budget inn 20 minutes from both downtown and Sea World/Fiesta Texas. The inn offers a pool, and you may bring your pets along. ⚬ (Northeast)

NORTHWEST

Hotels

AIRPORT HILTON AND CONFERENCE CENTER
611 NW Loop 410
San Antonio
210/340-6060
$$$

Though this Hilton's primary lodgers are business types, the hotel also has a family plan that allows children 18 and under to stay for free—but only in your room. Pets can, too. The Hilton features rooms and suites; a pool, gym, and spa; and a nine-hole putting green for warming up before you hit the links. Free transportation is available to the airport (two miles away), and two major shopping malls are across the highway. There is a full-service restaurant, and a sports bar for after you put the kids to bed. & (Northwest)

AMERISUITES/NORTHWEST
4325 AmeriSuites Dr.
San Antonio
210/561-0099
$$$

This collection of suites targeting the corporate traveler offers refrigerators, microwaves, wet bars, and coffeemakers in rooms, as well as data ports. Laundry facilities, free continental breakfast, and complimentary local transportation are available. Outdoors are a heated pool and fitness center. & (Northwest)

COURTYARD BY MARRIOTT/
MEDICAL CENTER
8585 Marriott Dr.
San Antonio
210/614-7100
$$

If you plan to become ill during your visit, this is the place to stay. The Courtyard is located on the edge of the vast Medical Center area in the northwest and is thus a step closer to Fiesta Texas. Suites are available, as are a pool, whirlpool, and weight room. The restaurant serves breakfast only, and a lounge is available. No pets, please. & (Northwest)

HOMEGATE STUDIOS
AND SUITES
11221 San Pedro Ave.
San Antonio
210/342-4800
$

Newly renovated, Homegate is an extended-stay hotel near the airport. Suites include living rooms, kitchens, and work areas with data ports and voice-mail service. On site are a pool, spa, gym, and laundry. Access to all

Bonner Garden Bed and Breakfast, p. 55

Bonner Garden Bed and Breakfast

tourist sites is easy. Prices are based on three- or seven-night packages. No pets. ♿ (Northwest)

HYATT REGENCY HILL COUNTRY RESORT
9800 Resort Dr.
San Antonio
210/647-1234
$$$$

Not so much a hotel as a universe, located on 200 oak-shaded acres adjacent to Sea World, this relative newcomer has become one of the most desirable vacation destinations in the area. On the vast grounds are an 18-hole golf course designed by Arthur Hills (which earned a "Best American Resort" title from *Golf* magazine), two swimming pools separated by waterfalls, a 950-foot river for on-site tubing, tennis courts, a health club with beauty and massage services, and a special Camp Hyatt area for kids. The massive main building holds four restaurants, from outstanding Texas barbecue to the luxurious Antlers Lodge. ♿ (Northwest)

RADISSON MARKET SQUARE
502 W. Durango St.
San Antonio
210/224-9130
$$$

A quality hotel close to El Mercado, the Radisson brims with amenities, including laundry facilities, meeting and banquet rooms, a pool, whirlpool, and gym. The restaurant serves breakfast, lunch, and dinner, and the lounge serves libations. Another perk is complimentary van service between the hotel and downtown from 7 p.m. to midnight. ♿ (Northwest)

The Sporting District

San Antonio has long had a reputation for friendliness—particularly after the Civil War, when the Alamo City's most legendary hospitality was found in a downtown neighborhood bordered by Market, Durango, Santa Rosa, and Frio Streets. This was the "Sporting District," a collection of brothels that even provided a Blue Book guide to the area complete with a quality rating system. Brothels were assigned a grade of A, B, or C. "A" houses were large, usually mansion/hotels for extended stays, offering gambling tables for patrons who tired of other amenities. "C" houses were basically shacks suitable only for very short stays. (Note: The triple-A rating system for contemporary hotels is unrelated.)

The Sporting District is long gone. Much of the formerly libertine neighborhood is now occupied by a Kmart, prompting the local joke that the city traded its red lights for a flashing blue one.

Motels

HOLIDAY INN NORTHWEST
3233 NW Loop 410
San Antonio
210/377-3900
$$

The HI offers some features not commensurate with its reasonable price: a gym, spa, and indoor/outdoor pool. It's closer to Sea World and Fiesta Texas than it is to downtown, but all sights are easily accessible by highway. A full-service restaurant is provided. Pets have to stay home. & (Northwest)

RAMADA LIMITED/SIX FLAGS
9447 I-10 W.
San Antonio
210/558-9070
$$

There are three members of the Ramada Limited family in town. All have similar amenities, which are basically pools and bargain prices, though there are plenty of restaurants nearby. This one offers the additional advantage of being near its namesake (though not next door, as its name might lead you to believe), and thus also closer to Sea World than the downtown and northeast Limiteds. & (Northwest)

RODEWAY INN/FIESTA PARK
19793 I-10 W.
San Antonio
210/698-1438
$$

This Rodeway is a good choice if you'll be spending significant amounts of time at Fiesta Texas (half a mile away) or Sea World (15 minutes), if you can afford the Dominion or La Cantera golf courses (less than a mile away), or if you'd like to get outdoors at Friedrich Wilderness Park (three miles) or Eisenhower Park (one mile). Rodeway has both traditional rooms and "mini-suites" and a pool, and will accommodate your pets. & (Northwest)

SIX FLAGS SUPER 8 MOTEL
5319 Casa Bella St.
San Antonio
210/696-6916
$$

As the name says, this Super 8 is near Six Flags Fiesta Texas. It's one of the few motels that offers a mini-playground for kids, including a hoop for the budding Michael Jordans in your brood. A pool is also on-site. Free continental breakfast is included in the room price, and pets are allowed. The motel is a AAA award–winner and was named to the "Pride of Super 8." There are five other Super 8 locations around town. & (Northwest)

Bed-and-Breakfasts

THE BELLE OF MONTE VISTA
505 Belknap Pl.
San Antonio
210/732-4006
$$

The gabled and turreted 1890 Belle is slightly farther from downtown than other B&Bs, but it makes up for that distance with a bargain price and easier access to the zoo and Brackenridge Park. There are five bedrooms done up to the Victorian hilt, and breakfast is full Southern-style. Host Jim Davis (a retired teacher) also offers a shuttle from the airport and bus or train stations at a small fee. No pets and no wheelchair accessibility. (Northwest)

BONNER GARDEN BED AND BREAKFAST
145 E. Agarita Ave.
San Antonio
210/733-4222 or 800/396-4222
$$$

Ramada Emily Morgan Hotel, p. 45

The 1910 Bonner house is unique among San Antonio B&Bs in that it is not a Victorian but instead a replica of a two-story Italian villa created for artist and printmaker Mary Bonner. Also unlike some of its peers, the Bonner offers a 50-foot pool, in-room spas, and an exercise room. A rooftop patio overlooks the downtown skyline. All five rooms—Bridal Suite, Garden Suite, Studio, Portico, and Ivy—have private baths, and three have fireplaces for fireside enjoyment of books or movies from the Bonner's library. The lush gardens invite strolling, and protected parking is provided. Pets are not allowed, and the Bonner is not wheelchair accessible. (Northwest)

A VICTORIAN LADY INN
421 Howard St.
San Antonio
800/879-7116
$$$
This AAA Three Diamond–rated, elegant, century-old mansion offers private baths for each of eight spacious rooms. Sumptuous breakfast fare (with classical music) is served in the

formal dining room, which, like the rest of the Lady, is furnished with era-appropriate antiques. Bicycles are available for your short trek to downtown, or you can use complimentary passes for a trolley ride from a stop two blocks away. Upon your return, unwind in the outdoor hot tub surrounded by tropical palms and banana trees. Room rates include beverages, off-street parking, and local calls. Honeymoon and corporate packages and meeting space are available. Smoking and pets are not allowed, and the Lady is not wheelchair accessible. www.viclady.com. (Northwest)

SOUTH

Motels

BUDGET INN
2717 Roosevelt Ave.
San Antonio
210/534-6066
$$
The Budget Inn offers few amenities—no pool, no fitness center, no food. But it has one thing no other hostelry in town can boast: it's right on the Mission Trail. In fact, the Spanish missionaries who settled San Antonio might have stayed here between setting up Missions Concepción and San José. If you're intent on biking for part of your stay in San Antonio, the Budget will put you right next to the midstretch of the Mission Trail biking path. Not completely wheelchair accessible. (South)

ECONO LODGE EAST
218 S. W.W. White Rd.
San Antonio
210/333-3346
$$
If your entire vacation budget will be

blown just getting here, this Econo Lodge offers an attractive alternative to eating all of your meals (aside from the free continental breakfast) at McDonald's. A pool is on-site, as are a coin-operated laundry, meeting room, and fax and copy services. Rooms include massaging showers and hair dryers, and for a small fee, will include a microwave and refrigerator. A grocery store is nearby. All of the downtown destinations are only five miles away from this Ruby Award and AAA Three Diamond–winner, which offers discounts to AAA and AARP members, senior citizens, government, commercial, and corporate travelers. & (South)

HOLIDAY INN EXPRESS SOUTH
606 Division St.
San Antonio
210/927-4800
$$
Besides offering Holiday Inn dependability and a pool, the Express South is on the same side of town as Sea World, though it's still a 15-minute drive. Air Force history aficionados will also appreciate the Express, as it offers easy access to Lackland AFB and the Air Force museum there (see Chapter 6, Museums and Galleries). Downtown is 10 minutes or so the other way. & (South)

LA QUINTA LACKLAND
6511 Military Dr.
San Antonio
210/674-3200
$$
This southwest edition of the very good La Quinta chain is, as the name implies, just outside the fence of Lackland Air Force Base. Sea World is 15 minutes away. The motel has a pool, and the lack of a restaurant is compensated for by several nearby spots, fast-food and otherwise. & (South)

Campgrounds

HIDDEN VALLEY RECREATIONAL PARK
12515 Fischer Rd.
San Antonio
210/623-6737
$
Hidden Valley is well named. It offers over 100 rustic acres just inside Loop 1604 in the city's southwest corner. Full hookups are available on shady lots at $19 per night for a four-person RV. Tent camping is $17 for four. If a visit to Sea World puts you in the mood, come back to the Valley and fish in one of two four-acre lakes, or swim in the creek. A store with bait shop is on-site, and a pavilion is provided for large groups. Should you want to caravan to San Antonio, Hidden Valley will help you plan a party for your party. Access to downtown is easy via I-35 North. (South)

TRAVELERS WORLD RV RESORT
2617 Roosevelt Ave.
San Antonio
210/532-8310
$
The closest RV resort to the River Walk and the Alamo, Travelers World RV Resort is ideal for campers who like to spend more time at historical sites than campsites. Just south of the downtown loop, this "urban oasis" is one mile north of Mission San José. Cyclists, take note: Travelers World is nearly on the Mission Trail and would be a good starting point for a bike tour of the missions. Full showers, rest rooms, a store, and a service center are on-site, as well as a pool and hot tub. Rates start at $26 (full 30-amp hookup) for a party of four. Tent campsites are $18.50 per night. (South)

Texas Department of Transportation

4

WHERE TO EAT

OK, San Antonio has great Mexican food. You'd expect that. And within the category of Mexican eateries alone, you'll find a wide variety of offerings, from Tex-Mex (blend of north and south of the border) to mostly Tex to strictly traditional Mexican food. If you love Mexican food, San Antonio is nirvana.

But don't let your interest in Mexican comestibles blind you to the many other delicious bills of fare in the Alamo City. For instance, some argue that South Texas boasts America's very finest barbecue (though Kansas City and St. Louis might disagree). Contemporary continental cuisine is also respectably represented in some unique and nationally renowned dining houses. And the immigrants of the 1800s and later, as well as today's international settlers associated with the medical center, brought with them some decidedly non–Tex-Mex menus.

While San Antonio's dining establishments are many and varied, their locations are not. You'll note in the following listings that few restaurants appear in the South sector. That doesn't mean the South zone has none, but they're small—mostly mom-and-pop operations—and vary widely in quality. Listed below are San Antonio's most popular or otherwise notable restaurants. To get the most out of your dining experiences, pick a restaurant or two from each category and taste the many flavors of San Antonio. Or just stick with Mexican—you can't go wrong there.

This chapter begins with a list of restaurants organized by the type of food offered. Each name is followed by a geographic zone abbreviation (see page vii) and the page where you will find a description of the restaurant. The price coding reflects the cost of a typical appetizer and entrée.

Price rating symbols:
$ $10 and under
$$ $11 to $20
$$$ $21 and up

RESTAURANTS BY FOOD TYPE

American/Contemporary

Boudro's (DT), p. 60
Cappy's (NE), p. 67
Carranza (NE), p. 67
Earl Abel's (NE), p. 70
EZ's (NE, NW), p. 70, 79
Hard Rock Café (DT), p. 63
Los Patios Brazier and Gazebo
    Restaurants (NE), p. 71
Magic Time Machine (NE),
    p. 71
Planet Hollywood (DT), p. 65
Tower of the Americas Restaurant
    (DT), p. 66

Bar and Grill

Fat Tuesday (DT), p. 62
Liberty Bar (NW), p. 80
Willie's Grill and Icehouse (NW),
    p. 84

Barbecue

Bob's Smokehouse (S), p. 84
The County Line (DT, NW),
    p. 60, 78
Rudy's Country Store and Barbecue
    (NW), p. 82
Tom's Ribs (NE, NW), p. 75, 83
Tony Roma's (DT, NW), p. 66, 83

Cajun

Acadiana Café (S), p. 84
Pappadeaux Seafood Kitchen (NW),
    p. 82

Chinese

Ding How (NW), p. 78
Hu-Nan River Garden (DT), p. 63
Mencius Gourmet Hunan (NW),
    p. 81

Coffee/Tea

Espuma Coffee and Tea Emporium
    (DT), p. 62
Madhatters Tea (NW), p. 81

Continental

Biga (NW), p. 76
Ernesto's (NW), p. 78
Mesón European Dining (NW),
    p. 81
Powerhouse Cafe (NE), p. 75

Delis/Sandwiches

Boston Subworks (NW), p. 76
Pecan Street Delicatessen (DT),
    p. 64
Schilo's Delicatessen (DT), p. 65

Diners

DeWese's Tip Top Café (NW), p. 78
G/M Steakhouse (DT), p. 62
Pig Stand (DT, NE, S), p. 64, 75, 85

Fine Dining

Old San Francisco Steak House (NE),
    p. 71
Ruth's Chris Steak House (NW), p. 82
Victoria's Black Swan Inn (NE),
    p. 76

French

L'Etoile (NE), p. 71

Greek

Mina & Dimi's Greek House (S),
    p. 85

Hamburgers

Chris Madrid's Nachos & Burgers
    (NW), p. 78

Fuddrucker's (NE), p. 70
Little Hipp's (NW), p. 80

Indian

India Oven (NW), p. 79
Simi's (NW), p. 82

Italian

Fratelli's Caffè Italiano (NW), p. 79
Paesano's (DT), p. 64
Piatti (NE), p. 74
Spaghetti Warehouse (NE), p. 75

Japanese

Tokyo Steak House (NW), p. 83

Mexican

Alamo Café (NE, NW), p. 66, 76
Canyon Café (NE), p. 66
Chuy's Comida Deluxe (NE), p. 67
Don Pedro (S), p. 84
La Calesa (NE), p. 70
La Fiesta Patio Café (NE), p. 71
La Fogata (NW), p. 80
Los Barrios (NW), p. 81
Maverick Café (NW), p. 81
Mi Tierra Café and Bakery (DT),
    p. 64
On The Border Mexican Café (NE,
    NW), p. 74, 82
Rio Rio Cantina (DT), p. 65
Tomatillo's Café y Cantina (NE, NW),
    p. 75, 83

Steaks/Seafood

Barn Door Restaurant (NE), p. 66
Dick's Last Resort (DT), p. 62
Joe's Crab Shack (DT, NE, NW), p. 63,
    70, 79
U.R. Cooks Steakhouse (NW), p. 83
Water Street Oyster Bar (NE), p. 76
Water Street Seafood Co. (NW),
    p. 83

Thai

Thai Kitchen (NW), p. 83

DOWNTOWN

BOUDRO'S
421 E. Commerce St.
San Antonio
210/224-8484
$$
When Broadway star Tommy Tune visited the Alamo City some years ago, one of the first things he asked was, "How do I get to Boudro's? Joel Grey told me I have to eat there!" Boudro's (BOO-drohz) is one of the best-known dining facades on the River Walk—famous for its lighthearted blending of Southwest, Cajun, and continental cuisines. Specialties of the house include herb-cured salmon tacos, blackened prime rib, and Colorado lamb chops with basil/lemon/mint sauce. The décor is pure "Texas bistro," and dining on the sidewalk at the river level is romantic when tourist flow isn't too heavy. If you don't have a reservation, you'll wait a long time. Open for lunch and dinner seven days, till midnight Fri and Sat. ♿ (Downtown)

THE COUNTY LINE (RIVER WALK)
111 Crockett St.
San Antonio
210/229-1941
$$
Founder Randy Goss proudly states the raison d'être of his barbecue house is to "get it all over you." Within the Texas roadhouse you'll find fine pork and beef ribs, with a thick, hearty sauce that you won't mind wearing home. All meats are slow-smoked and accompanied by generously portioned, home-style side orders. Best of all, well-thought-out combos let you

DOWNTOWN SAN ANTONIO

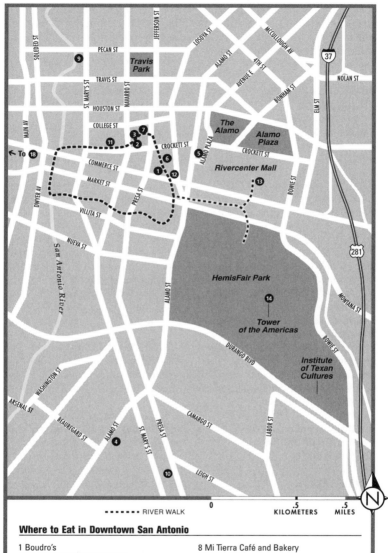

RIVER WALK

0	.5	.5
	KILOMETERS	MILES

N

Where to Eat in Downtown San Antonio

1 Boudro's
2 The County Line (River Walk)
3 Dick's Last Resort
4 Espuma Coffee and Tea Emporium
2 Fat Tuesday
5 G/M Steakhouse
2 Hard Rock Café
6 Hu-Nan River Garden
7 Joe's Crab Shack

8 Mi Tierra Café and Bakery
2 Paesano's
9 Pecan Street Delicatessen
10 Pig Stand
11 Planet Hollywood
1 Rio Rio Cantina
12 Schilo's Delicatessen
13 Tony Roma's
14 Tower of the Americas Restaurant

try a bit of everything. The County Line on the far north side of the city is so popular, in spite of the distance, that Goss decided to open this riverside version. Open for lunch and dinner seven days. Reservations unnecessary. ♿ (Downtown)

DICK'S LAST RESORT
406 Navarro St.
(on the River Walk)
San Antonio
210/224-0026
$–$$

If you like your meal served up with a side order of abuse, try Dick's. This madcap eatery prides itself on its testy waitpersons and generally antisocial attitude—but it's all in fun. Several of Dick's specialties, such as ribs, chicken, and painfully hot crawfish, are served in buckets. Burgers and the like arrive on butcher paper. Plates do not exist. A fully stocked bar (with the best Bloody Marys in town), live jazz, and rowdy banter add to the funhouse feeling. Warning: Don't ask for directions to the rest room. Just look around until you find it. Lunch and dinner seven days. Call in a reservation, and Dick will throw you in the river when you arrive. ♿ (Downtown)

ESPUMA COFFEE
AND TEA EMPORIUM
928 S. Alamo St.
San Antonio
210/226-1912
$

San Antonio doesn't have a hip, happenin' coffee bar on every corner like Seattle does, but the King William–area Espuma is a step in the right direction. In addition to an endless list of specialty coffee drinks and smooth, rich granitas, Espuma boasts several marvelous desserts. Treats are also on hand for your eyes and

ears: a new artist is featured in the gallery every month, and Friday and Saturday offer Spanish folk music. Open daily. Credit cards not accepted. Not wheelchair accessible. (Downtown)

FAT TUESDAY
111 W. Crockett St.
San Antonio
210/212-7886
$

Fat Tuesday's menu is as short as its list of specialty drinks is long. Short list first: burgers, chicken, salads, appetizers. Specialty drinks: too many daiquiris to list. The décor of this River Walk saloon can be described as "simply Mardi Gras." A local poll named FT the coolest hot spot after 9 p.m., and its margaritas were named the People's Choice in the local annual margarita pour-off. FT's cheerful barkeeps will be happy to call you a cab. Open 11 a.m.–2 a.m. daily. ♿ (Downtown)

G/M STEAKHOUSE
211 Alamo Plaza
San Antonio
210/223-1523
$

If the prices at Ruth's Chris Steakhouse send a shiver through your wallet, G/M is for you. The most popular item in this antiquey storefront is the lunch special: chopped sirloin steak, baked potato, salad, Texas toast, and tea or coffee, for $3.95. Equally reasonably priced are the top sirloin and chicken-fried steak. Or arrive early and try the *huevos rancheros* for breakfast. No, it's not haute cuisine. The location is so perfect—across the street from the Alamo—that it's rumored Santa Anna and his troops stopped in for T-bones during the siege. Breakfast, lunch,

Top Ten Places to Eat on the River Walk

1. Rio Rio Cantina (Tex-Mex)
2. Boudro's (contemporary)
3. Paesano's (Italian)
4. The County Line (barbecue)
5. Dick's Last Resort (rowdy)
6. Rivercenter food court (eclectic)
7. Fat Tuesday (bar and grill)
8. Hu-Nan River Garden (Chinese)
9. Tony Roma's (barbecue)
10. Joe's Crab Shack (seafood)

and dinner daily. Reservations are unheard of. க (Downtown)

HARD ROCK CAFÉ
111 W. Crockett St.
(on the River Walk)
San Antonio
210/224-ROCK
$$
The food is unremarkable but the hype is overwhelming. The San Antonio version of this worldwide pop phenomenon boasts a large collection of rock 'n' roll memorabilia, some of it specific to regional stars such as Stevie Ray Vaughan. Open daily, 11 a.m.–2 a.m. க (Downtown)

HU-NAN RIVER GARDEN
506 River Walk
San Antonio
210/222-0808
$$
With appropriate Chinese décor inside and the River Walk outside, the Hu-Nan is a unique blend of East and Southwest. Lunch specials are popular with the downtown business

crowd, and large-scale family dinners are attractive to tourist groups. The standard Chinese menu includes specialties such as Hunan crispy whole trout and Hunan chicken in spicy brown sauce, and a full bar offers exotic Polynesian libations. Reservations are accepted for lunch and dinner, seven days. க (Downtown)

JOE'S CRAB SHACK
212 College St.
San Antonio
210/271-9981
$$
"Peace, love, and crabs" is the theme of this casual seafood place that might be located on a dock . . . somewhere . . . in an era . . . oh, sometime ago. And crabs are what you'll find, in more versions than you might have known existed. The barbecued crabs are a spicy, greasy treat, and for all of the signature dishes, the tabletop instructions on how to eat them are appreciated by novices. Other seafoods are available, and everything goes better with a beer or drink from the

bar. Reservations are not necessary, but the Quarry Market location can get very busy. While you wait at that one, there's a playground for the kids. Here at downtown Joe's, tables are available in the semi-open overlooking the river. & (Downtown)

MI TIERRA CAFÉ AND BAKERY
218 Produce Row
(in Market Square)
San Antonio
210/225-1262
$

This Market Square institution is the place for late-night dining after downtown events (read: long lines). The menu offers good Tex-Mex, and Mi Tierra is an ideal source for your first *cabrito*. For afters, an in-house bakery fries up highly regarded *empanadas* and Mexican cookies. Live mariachi bands perform at your table, but not for free. Reservations accepted for ten or more. Open 24 hours every day. & (Downtown)

PAESANO'S
111 W. Crockett St.
(on the River Walk)
San Antonio
210/227-2782
$$

Two words—shrimp Paesano. This garlicky signature dish is highly recommended by locals to everyone except honeymooners. All of the pasta dishes are good, as are the veal and seafoods, and the Caesar salad is exceptional. The riverside patio offers a relaxing place in which to sample Paesano's wine list under a canvas umbrella. Reservations are accepted for lunch and dinner daily. & (Downtown)

PECAN STREET DELICATESSEN
152 E. Pecan St.

San Antonio
210/227-3226
$

The oil bust of the eighties may have ended Doug Weatherston's career as a petroleum engineer, but it was a great thing for the downtown San Antonio lunch crowd—Weatherston really knows how to run a deli. At his storefront location just off the River Walk, he lets you select your own sandwich fixin's from an expansive list of 24 items, eight of which meet healthy-heart guidelines. Mediterranean and Middle Eastern specialties include homemade dolmas and outstanding *muffulettas* (veggie and not), hummus, and tabbouleh. All salads are made from scratch, and baguettes, focaccia, cookies, and brownies are baked on-site each day. Olive fans, take note: The olive sampler will take you around the world for only a buck. Lunch only, Mon–Sat until 3 p.m. & (Downtown)

PIG STAND
801 S. Presa St.
San Antonio
210/225-1321
$

The McDonald's of the pork-loving set, this old-style, local fast-food mini-chain is most famous for one thing: the Pig Sandwich—a sort of porcine hamburger. All dishes are basic but good, and stepping into a Pig Stand is stepping into the past. The Pig Stand folks make several claims for "firsts," including the first drive-in restaurant ever. Whether or not it was, it celebrates each weekend with classic-car nights. (Fords and Chevys separately, please.) And some nights, you'll be treated to a live performance by one of the best country-and-western bands in town—which just happens to be fronted by

EZ's, p. 70

Pig Stand's owner—Richard Hailey and Neon Stars. Open for lunch and dinner. ⟨⟩ (Downtown)

PLANET HOLLYWOOD
245 E. Commerce St.
San Antonio
210/212-STAR
$$

The only place in town where you are guaranteed to see Schwarzenegger, Willis, and Stallone—or cardboard cutouts of them, anyway. This glitzy chain eatery is very popular on weekends, perhaps less for its California cuisine than for the fact that everyone wants to say, "I've been there" and get a T-shirt. The rare movie memorabilia is a big draw, too. Valet parking is available in the evening. Open for lunch and dinner seven days, until 2 a.m. ⟨⟩ (Downtown)

RIO RIO CANTINA
421 E. Commerce St.
San Antonio
210/226-8462
$$

Be hungry. Rio Rio's plates are the size of Roman battle shields, and just after you've finished eating far too many chips with salsa, they arrive full. The menu is standard Tex-Mex but very well done—particularly the chicken enchiladas verdes. The signature libation, Rio 'Rita, is also delightful but potent. Best of all, however, is the location: Rio Rio offers patio dining overlooking the madding crowd on the River Walk. Lunch and dinner seven days. Reservations accepted for large groups. ⟨⟩ (Downtown)

SCHILO'S DELICATESSEN
424 E. Commerce St.
San Antonio
210/223-6692
$

With the exception of the Beethoven Halle und Garten, nowhere is San Antonio's Germanic heritage more obvious than at this busy downtown spot. Try the split-pea soup, even if you don't usually like pea soup, and the made-in-house root beer. The sandwich meats are top-flight, the dessert pastries and cheesecake are not to be missed, and the traditional dinner dishes and sauerkraut may have you longing for the Schwartzwald (as will the live oompah music on Friday and Saturday nights). Be warned—the hot mustard will slam your sinuses open. Breakfast, lunch, and dinner Mon–Sat, with take-out food, meats, cheeses, and desserts available. & (Downtown)

TONY ROMA'S
Rivercenter
San Antonio
210/225-7662
$$

Tony's slogan says it all: "A Place for Ribs." Baby backs are the most popular entrée at this casual chain eatery, though there are many other tempting, smoky comestibles. Reservations are accepted for lunch and dinner every day. & (Downtown)

TOWER OF THE AMERICAS RESTAURANT
222 HemisFair Plaza
San Antonio
210/223-3101
$$

The menu in the sky has often been inconsistent, but the view is not to be missed. San Antonio revolves once every 90 minutes around this restaurant in the World's Fair tower. Inside is a Hill Country/Southwest/Mexican atmosphere in which aged beef and fresh seafood entrées are served. On Friday and Saturday evenings a jazz pianist adds to the ambience. Open for lunch and dinner seven days, with reservations recommended. & (Downtown)

NORTHEAST

ALAMO CAFÉ
14250 U.S. 281 N.
San Antonio
210/495-2233
$–$$

This newest version of a familiar San Antonio eatery is very popular. The parking lot is always full, so while you wait, stroll around the fountain and pool outside and enjoy an excellent margarita. When your name is called, you'll find a standard Tex-Mex menu, but everything on it is good. The fajitas are particular standouts, and the pre-meal chips and salsa are dangerously habit-forming. Lunch and dinner seven days. & (Northeast)

BARN DOOR RESTAURANT
8400 N. New Braunfels Ave.
San Antonio
210/824-0116
$$

The Barn Door is down-home simple: it looks like a barn, and its menu features standard country cuisine— steaks, chicken, and lamb—with the addition of softshell crab and other seafood fresh from the Texas Gulf Coast. Pasta dishes are starting to creep onto the menu, too, but the Door will never get trendy. Chef Sonny, who's been at the grill for 40 years, does mouthwatering steaks that have become favorites of business lunchers and noontime birthday celebrants. Reservations recommended. If you go for lunch, be prepared for a full parking lot. Lunch and dinner Sun–Fri, dinner only Sat. & (Northeast)

CANYON CAFÉ
255 E. Basse Rd.
San Antonio
210/821-3738
$$

In the hip new Quarry Market, Canyon Café's nouveau industrial architecture is almost as intriguing as

TIP

With 19 locations in San Antonio, Taco Cabana is the McDonald's of Mexican food. The Tex-Mex menu is not gourmet, but it is fast, with drive-ups available. Patio dining and music add to the fun. The kids will have fun watching the tortilla machine at work, and parents can enjoy the product of the margarita machine.

its nouveau Southwestern menu. Almost. Grilled chicken and tuna are the hot items, usually dusted or rubbed pre-grilling with just the right spices. There are lots of sauces for lots of uses on the menu. One of the best of these is the *chipotle* mayonnaise, made with those hot little peppers—the perfect condiment for what is proudly (and maybe accurately) listed as "The Greatest Chicken Sandwich in the World," and a vegetarian sandwich containing a whole portobello mushroom cap. The Canyon gets busy and doesn't take reservations, so get there early. Or wait in the excellent and attractive bar for your table. ♿ (Northeast)

CAPPY'S
5011 Broadway
San Antonio
210/828-9669
$$

Cappy Lawton is San Antonio's restaurant genius—he also created the lively EZ's burger joints. Cappy's is a popular, if not exotic, lunch and dinner locale featuring a mostly Southwestern menu. Chef Mark Dortman recommends the oak-grilled tenderloin, "Snapper Cappy," or mustang chicken. Seating is available outdoors, or enjoy the rough-hewn, airy interior. Lunch and dinner seven days. Reservations accepted. ♿ (Northeast)

CARRANZA
701 Austin St.

San Antonio
210/223-0903
$$

There's a taste of everything on Carranza's menu, but the seafood offerings are standouts. Italian and Texas mesquite barbecue dishes also come highly recommended. Close to downtown, Carranza is in a two-story historic limestone near the beautiful Sunset Depot. Open for lunch and dinner Mon–Fri, and dinner only on Sat. Reservations accepted. ♿ (Northeast)

CHUY'S COMIDA DELUXE
7959 Broadway
San Antonio
210/930-6775
$

The mid-1998 debut of Chuy's was welcomed by many San Antonians. Yes, it's another casual Mexican restaurant. But locals who frequent Austin were endeared to the original's outlandish décor and better-than-most cuisine. Both have made the transition to San Antonio just fine. For the former, there is a ceiling covered entirely in hubcaps and hundreds of hand-painted fish. The latter includes Tex-Mex standards such as cheese enchiladas (with Tex-yellow rather than Mex-white cheese) in chili gravy, and chiles rellenos (stuffed peppers). Other dishes such as shrimp cakes are more imaginative. And, of course, margaritas. The food is good, and the mood is pure

GREATER SAN ANTONIO

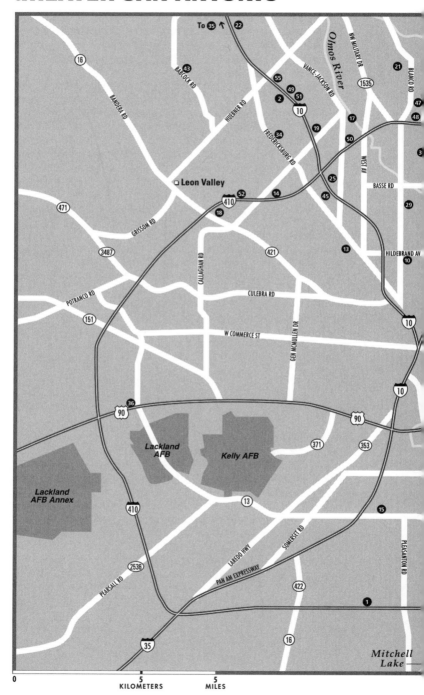

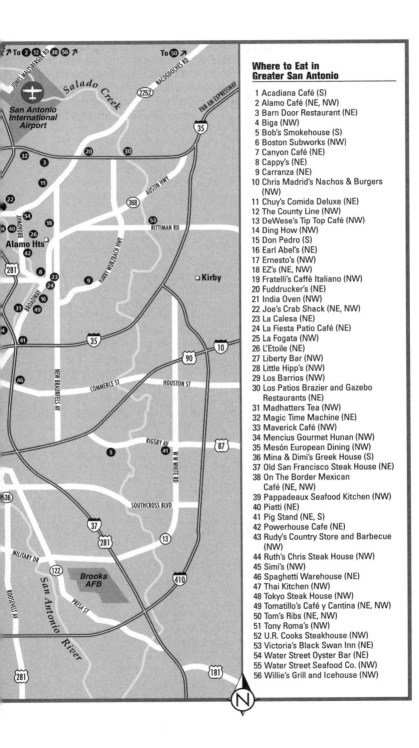

Where to Eat in Greater San Antonio

1 Acadiana Café (S)
2 Alamo Café (NE, NW)
3 Barn Door Restaurant (NE)
4 Biga (NW)
5 Bob's Smokehouse (S)
6 Boston Subworks (NW)
7 Canyon Café (NE)
8 Cappy's (NE)
9 Carranza (NE)
10 Chris Madrid's Nachos & Burgers (NW)
11 Chuy's Comida Deluxe (NE)
12 The County Line (NW)
13 DeWese's Tip Top Café (NW)
14 Ding How (NW)
15 Don Pedro (S)
16 Earl Abel's (NE)
17 Ernesto's (NW)
18 EZ's (NE, NW)
19 Fratelli's Caffè Italiano (NW)
20 Fuddrucker's (NE)
21 India Oven (NW)
22 Joe's Crab Shack (NE, NW)
23 La Calesa (NE)
24 La Fiesta Patio Café (NE)
25 La Fogata (NW)
26 L'Etoile (NE)
27 Liberty Bar (NW)
28 Little Hipp's (NW)
29 Los Barrios (NW)
30 Los Patios Brazier and Gazebo Restaurants (NE)
31 Madhatters Tea (NW)
32 Magic Time Machine (NE)
33 Maverick Café (NW)
34 Mencius Gourmet Hunan (NW)
35 Mesón European Dining (NW)
36 Mina & Dimi's Greek House (S)
37 Old San Francisco Steak House (NE)
38 On The Border Mexican Café (NE, NW)
39 Pappadeaux Seafood Kitchen (NW)
40 Piatti (NE)
41 Pig Stand (NE, S)
42 Powerhouse Cafe (NE)
43 Rudy's Country Store and Barbecue (NW)
44 Ruth's Chris Steak House (NW)
45 Simi's (NW)
46 Spaghetti Warehouse (NE)
47 Thai Kitchen (NW)
48 Tokyo Steak House (NW)
49 Tomatillo's Café y Cantina (NE, NW)
50 Tom's Ribs (NE, NW)
51 Tony Roma's (NW)
52 U.R. Cooks Steakhouse (NW)
53 Victoria's Black Swan Inn (NE)
54 Water Street Oyster Bar (NE)
55 Water Street Seafood Co. (NW)
56 Willie's Grill and Icehouse (NW)

fun. Lunch and dinner, seven days. &
(Northeast)

EARL ABEL'S
4200 Broadway
San Antonio
210/822-3358
$
Established in 1933, Earl Abel's is a
third-generation, family-owned San
Antonio institution. Don't expect
haute cuisine but do expect good
food. Portions are large, the server
could be your aunt (some employees
have been there 40 years), and the atmosphere is "howdy!" friendly.
Breakfast at Earl's is a local favorite,
particularly for business types, and
lunch and dinner offer home-style
specials such as roast turkey and excellent chicken-fried steak. The fried
chicken is legendary. The only nega-
tive thing about Earl Abel's is having
to make your choice among the
fresh-baked pies sadistically displayed on the counter. Breakfast,
lunch, and dinner daily. & (Northeast)

EZ'S
6498 N. New Braunfels Ave.
San Antonio
210/828-1111
$
Imagine that Al's Diner from "Happy
Days" fell through a wormhole in
space and ended up in the 1990s.
That idea hints at the atmosphere of
EZ's, the trendy burger joints founded
by local restaurant whiz Cappy Law-
ton. This one's the original, but there
are four other locations. One of them
is sure to be handy for you. Tongue-
in-cheek décor featuring long
stretches of neon and sculpted fish
wearing scuba gear gives kids plenty
to look at while waiting for their oak-
grilled burgers and low-fat gourmet
shakes and malts. EZ's has also

updated pizza to include Santa Fe
chicken and chicken pesto, and the
roast rosemary chicken is worth
every trip to get more napkins. The
Caesar salad is excellent and generous, and the only menu item that isn't
cooked over or in an oak fire. Open
for lunch and dinner seven days. &
(Northeast)

FUDDRUCKER'S
8602 Botts Ln.
San Antonio
210/824-6703
$
Now a national chain, Fuddrucker's
was once only San Antonio's. And this
Botts Lane location, hidden in an of-
fice/industrial complex north of Loop
410 off Broadway, was the very first.
(There are three other San Antonio locations, including one on Alamo
Plaza.) Pick a sizzling one-third– or
one-half–pound burger, dress it with
everything from lettuce to jalapeños,
and try to get through it before the bun
falls apart. Chicken and fish sandwiches are also available, but that's
not why you're at the Fudd. Fries are
hefty, beer and wine are available,
shakes are thick and great, and a rack
of fresh-made pies stands mocking
you as you exit. & (Northeast)

JOE'S CRAB SHACK
255 E. Basse Rd.
(in the Quarry Market)
San Antonio
210/930-1736
$$
See description in Downtown sec-
tion, page 63. (Northeast)

LA CALESA
2103 E. Hildebrand Ave.
San Antonio
210/822-4475
$

La Calesa not only offers one of the most traditional Mexican menus in town (the cheese is white, as it should be), but also does so at a bargain price. The salsa, chiles rellenos, and refried black beans are signatures, and dishes such as shrimp have a taste of southern Mexico and the Yucatan. Open for lunch and dinner daily and for breakfast on weekends, this unassuming house-cum-restaurant deserves a visit. Try the sangría. ᕕ (Northeast)

LA FIESTA PATIO CAFÉ
1421 Pat Booker Rd.
San Antonio
210/658-5110
$

It's not downtown, but La Fiesta is worth the drive for at least two things: its bargain prices and its salsa—a first-place winner in a recent Austin contest. (The competition included restaurants from San Antonio, Austin, and all points in between.) The menu of Tex-Mex fare is distinguished by all-natural Mexican foods such as whole-grain brown rice. Bright colors and lots of plants and fish contribute to the casual atmosphere. Open for breakfast, lunch, and dinner every day but Mon. ᕕ (Northeast)

L'ETOILE
6106 Broadway
San Antonio
210/826-4551
$$–$$$

In the tony Alamo Heights area, L'Etoile truly is a star. The service is formal but the atmosphere is more bistroesque. Seafood is the focus and thus is seasonal—but if you're here when the L'Etoile crab cakes are, get 'em. Also recommended are the red snapper pauprette, salmon

Xeres, and choose-it-yourself lobster. Beef tenderloin and veal are popular year-round. The only downside is no wheelchair accessibility. The masterminds behind L'Etoile recently opened a new dining and entertainment experience, Powerhouse Cafe in the Quarry Market. Open Mon–Sat. lunch and dinner. (Northeast)

LOS PATIOS BRAZIER AND GAZEBO RESTAURANTS
2015 NE Loop 410
San Antonio
210/655-6171
$$

Secluded in a surprisingly quiet wood off Loop 410, the two restaurants of Los Patios have also become popular as wedding reception sites. The Brazier is essentially a high-class grill and the more expensive of the two. The Gazebo offers Tex-Mex and American, including soups, salads, and sandwiches. One or the other will suit your palate. The Gazebo is open seven days for lunch and dinner, and an outstanding Sunday brunch. The Brazier is open Tue–Sun for lunch, and dinner on Fri and Sat. Reservations are recommended for both. (Northeast)

MAGIC TIME MACHINE
902 NE Loop 410
San Antonio
210/828-1470
$$

See Chapter 7, Kids' Stuff, page 125. ᕕ (Northeast)

OLD SAN FRANCISCO STEAK HOUSE
10223 Sahara Dr.
(at San Pedro Ave.)
San Antonio
210/342-2321
$$$

Ordering Mexican Food

Some of the names will be familiar to you from the drive-up window at Taco Bell. But when you come to a city where you can find real Mexican food, the menu might seem . . . well . . . foreign. Here's a quick and easy guide. (Hint: Roll your rs.)

Al carbon *(ahl car-BOHN)—generic term for grilled meat*

Barbacoa *(bar-bah-KOH-ah)—this is not Mexican barbecue. Traditionally, the head of a calf was buried in hot coals overnight and the meats peeled off the next morning. An acquired taste.*

Burrito *(buh-REE-toh)—flour tortilla wrapped around meat or beans and cheese*

Cabrito *(kah-BREE-toh)—grilled young goat*

Cerveza *(sehr-VEH-zah)—beer*

Ceviche *(seh-VEE-cheh)—not beer; a stew of raw fish, lime or lemon juice, and spices. Better than it sounds.*

Chalupa *(chah-LOO-pah)—corn tortilla fried flat, topped with just about anything*

Chile or Chili *(CHEE-lee)—a pepper, in any of several varieties and degrees of discomfort*

Chile relleno *(CHEE-leh reh-YEH-noh)—pepper stuffed with meat and spices, cheese, or raisins*

Chili *(CHEE-leh)—ground beef stew. Real chili does not contain beans.*

Chipotle *(chih-POH-tleh)—a really hot pepper, not to be eaten by itself by humans*

Chorizo *(choh-REE-zoh)—spicy, greasy Mexican sausage. Good with eggs in breakfast tacos.*

Enchilada *(ehn-chih-LAH-dah)—tortilla, usually corn, stuffed with meat or cheese and topped with green or red salsa*

Fajitas *(fah-HEE-tahs)—one of San Antonio's most popular dishes: flour (or corn) tortillas filled with sizzling grilled beef or chicken and slathered with onions, green peppers, cheese, tomatoes, sour cream, guacamole, and salsa*

Flan *(flahn)—a custard dessert, usually served in a caramel sauce*

Flautas *(FLOW-tahs)—corn tortillas filled with chicken or beef, fried hard*

Guisada *(whee- [or gwee-] SAH-dah)—usually* carne guisada, *beef tips in gravy*

Habañero *(hah-bah-NYEHR-oh)—a red pepper significantly hotter than the jalapeño, and not often eaten by itself*

Lengua *(LEHN-gwah)—beef tongue in broth*

Margarita *(mahr-gah-REE-tah)—the quintessential San Antonio beverage: tequila, lime juice, and orange liqueur. Served frozen (slushy) or on the rocks. Some are dangerously good.*

Menudo *(meh-NOO-doh)—thin stew with corn and tripe, often served for breakfast*

Mole *(MOH-leh)—a hearty, thick, brown sauce that contains chocolate; usually served over chicken*

Pico de gallo *(PEE-koh deh GAH-yoh)—a condiment of chopped onions, tomatoes, and cilantro*

Pollo *(POH-yoh)—chicken*

Puerco *(PWEHR-koh)—pork*

Quesadilla *(keh-sah-DEE-ah)—sometimes called Mexican pizza; stiff tortilla "sandwich" filled with cheese or other fillings*

Queso *(KEH-soh)—cheese; authentic Mexican cooking usually uses a mild white variety*

Taco *(TAH-koh)—tortillas, crisp or soft, filled with meats, cheese, beans, lettuce, guacamole, and just about anything you'd like*

Tamales *(tah-MAH-lehs)—beef, chicken, or pork wrapped in a thick layer of cornmeal. The singular is "tamal." Do not eat the cornhusk wrapper.*

Tortilla *(tohr-TEE-ah)—flat bread of cornmeal (masa) or flour.*

Tostada *(toh-STAH-dah)—in some parts of the country, this term refers to chalupas. It is more appropriate to crispy fried chips of corn—or sometimes flour—tortillas.*

Verde *(VEHR-deh)—green, as in "salsa verde;" a mild sauce often served over chicken enchiladas*

Los Patios Brazier and Gazebo Restaurants, p. 71

Many San Antonio restaurants have historical ambience, but only one takes you back to the Barbary Coast of the 1890s. As you enjoy pre-meal Swiss cheese and fresh-baked bread, take in the nineteenth-century memorabilia. Watch the renowned "Girl on the Red Velvet Swing" as she performs suspended from the 30-foot ceiling, accompanied by Gay '90s music played on twin grand pianos. OSFSH's steaks and prime rib earned the restaurant fourth place on revered and feared Texas steakhouse critic Tom Horan's list of Top Ten Texas Steakhouses in 1997, and the wine list and the seafood and lamb dishes are equally admirable. Dinner only, seven days. Reservations accepted. & (Northeast)

ON THE BORDER MEXICAN CAFÉ
255 E. Basse Rd.
San Antonio
210/828-8833
$$
This relatively new addition to San Antonio's Tex-Mex scene puts some

interesting twists on the standards. The chips come hot, fresh out of the fryer and ready for OTB's hearty salsa. Fajitas—a staple so common in San Antonio that you can get it at fast-food counters—can be ordered with the standard beef or chicken, or topped with buffalo for the more adventuresome. Seafood entrées a la Veracruz are also highly recommended, as are the enchiladas and chiles rellenos. Be warned, however: Go easy on the chips. Portions are generous to a fault. There's another location at 18008 U.S. 281, 210/495-4224. & (Northeast)

PIATTI
255 E. Basse Rd.
San Antonio
210/832-0300
$$
Like all of its neighbors in the Quarry Market, Piatti features great architecture you probably can't find in any of the Italian chain's 15 counterparts in other cities. The menu has been localized as well, beginning as Italian, then heading southwest. A standout

is the *gnocchi di patate*—familiar potato flour dumplings with portobello mushrooms and hot chiles added. Pasta is prevalent, but seafood, beef, and veal are also well represented. Salads and appetizers are too unique and interesting to resist. Lunch and dinner daily. Piatti is still new and very popular, so reservations are highly recommended. & (Northeast)

PIG STAND
1508 Broadway
San Antonio
210/222-2794
$
See description in Downtown section, page 64. (Northeast)

POWERHOUSE CAFE
255 E. Basse Rd.
(in the Quarry Market)
210/930-5155
$$–$$$
One of the most highly anticipated San Antonio restaurant openings in recent years brought much more than a restaurant: the Powerhouse Cafe in the Quarry Market. The same culinary masters who succeeded with cuisine Francaise at L'Etoile in Alamo Heights spent more than two years planning this massive, industrial-chic eating experience that combines French flair with Texas tradition. Powerhouse has 28,000 square feet spread across three floors with three bars. The largest of these, seating 150, has a stage behind the bar that features live music (primarily jazz and swing) and live entertainment, including the original "Alamotion" show. A patio restaurant can only be described as Tex-Mex-French, with onion soup, shrimp quesadillas, cactus salad, and the like. A dinner-and-show package ($39.95) lets you choose from four entrées, including crab cakes with remoulade sauce,

pasta, rotisserie chicken, and blackened fish with papaya salsa, all while enjoying trendy entertainment. Call for show days and times. Lunch and dinner, seven days (dinner served till midnight). & (Northeast)

SPAGHETTI WAREHOUSE
1226 E. Houston St.
San Antonio
210/299-1114
$
The name is accurate—this is a warehouse in the heart of one of San Antonio's downtown warehouse/industrial districts just north of the Alamodome. Inside you'll find antiques and memorabilia, and the best seats in the house are in a re-created trolley. Dishes favored by locals include the 15-layer lasagna and, well, just about any of the pastas and parmigianas. The Warehouse has won several local awards, including Restaurateur of the Year for chef Chez Logan. Open for lunch and dinner seven days. & (Northeast)

TOMATILLO'S CAFÉ Y CANTINA
3210 Broadway
San Antonio
210/824-3005
$–$$
Tomatillo's prides itself on providing a fiesta atmosphere night and day, year-round. Specialties are standard Tex-Mex, with the fajitas highly recommended. Even less authentic (but who cares?) are several iterations of nachos, which won the Best Nachos prize in the *San Antonio Current*'s Best of San Antonio awards. Lunch and dinner seven days, though lunches are busy with the business crowd. & (Northeast)

TOM'S RIBS
13323 Nacogdoches Rd.

San Antonio
210/654-7427
$$

The big smiling pig on the sign tells it all. Tom's is a San Antonio–owned and –operated place for big portions of slow-smoked barbecue. All kinds of barbecue, of course, but Tom's namesake is the highlight. Choose from several varieties and cuts, including the new St. Louis style. The sauce is thick, tangy, and hearty, and the accompanying sides (potato salad, beans, corn on the cob) are better than the best church picnic. Tom's caters to families with generous family meals at a very reasonable price. Beer and wine are available, but Texas barbecue always seems to go better with iced tea. Open seven days for lunch and dinner. & (Northeast)

VICTORIA'S BLACK SWAN INN
1006 Holbrook Rd.
San Antonio
210/590-2507
$–$$$

If you can get to Victoria's, you'll have struck nineteenth-century gold. This out-of-the-way plantation in the Salado Valley is frequently described as "the most romantic place in San Antonio." The menu offers shrimp Wellington, Cajun stuffed filets, and fresh pastries, and—in true Victorian style—high tea. But if the Old World doesn't suit you, the same lovely locale offers the more affordable and familiar Ugly Duckling Barn & Grill. The Swan is closed Sat–Mon, but open for lunch and dinner Tue–Fri. Tea is at 2:30. The country setting is not wheelchair accessible. (Northeast)

WATER STREET OYSTER BAR
7500 Broadway
San Antonio
210/829-4853

$$

See description in Northwest section (Water Street Seafood Company), page 83. (Northeast)

NORTHWEST

ALAMO CAFÉ
10060 I-10 W.
San Antonio
210/691-8827
$–$$

See description in Northeast section, page 66. (Northwest)

BIGA
206 E. Locust St.
San Antonio
210/225-0722
$$–$$$

Biga may be located in a 100-year-old mansion, but the menu at this upscale, casual bistro is up-to-date; the list of Southwestern, Mediterranean, and nouvelle dishes changes daily. Depending on the season of your visit, expect fresh seafood and pasta and a variety of beef and game, including antelope, pheasant, and venison. Pastries and breads are exceptional. For an appetizer, try the onion rings, fried in a batter of Shiner (Texas) Bock beer and served with a lively habañero ketchup. Reservations are recommended for groups of five and more. Open for dinner Mon–Thur 5:30–10:30 and Fri and Sat until 11 p.m. Wheelchair accessible inside but there are four steps in front. & (Northwest)

BOSTON SUBWORKS
441 W. Nakoma Rd.
San Antonio
210/341-6624
$

The winner of San Antonio's Best

Texas Barbecue

Only in the movies is Texas's ranching heritage better represented than in its barbecue. Dating back to days when cooking a big chunk of meat over an open fire was the only option, the tradition is carried over, celebrated, and treasured today.

Most 'cue joints ("joint" is an honorable title in Texas) offer pretty much the same menu. Brisket is by far the most prevalent, along with sausage, chicken, turkey, and lamb in some places, and of course, ribs. Side dishes are nearly always pinto beans (in thin broth), potato salad, coleslaw, jalapeños, and white bread for sopping (wheat and tortillas are sometimes available). These commonalities understood, the variations are found within the cooking method and the sauce.

Cooking styles always involve smoke. Favored woods are native mesquite and pecan, and hickory and oak. Some 'cue chefs build the fire directly under the meat, while others prefer the indirect method—a firebox mounted to the side of the smoke chamber. Whichever method is employed, time is the taskmaster. Many barbecuists feel that the longer you can smoke the meat without losing vital juices or adding unnecessary charring, the better. This can make preparing a meal a full day's work. But a good brisket with a dark crust and juicy center is the reward.

In San Antonio's fine barbecue establishments, always try the meat sans sauce first. You may find the smoky flavor best unaccompanied. If you opt for slathering, you'll find a spectrum of sauces ranging from thin, vinegary concoctions to doctored ketchups to sweet, tomatoey blends. Some houses also offer fiery-hot varieties.

If you doubt the popularity of barbecue in South Texas, keep an eye open as you travel the roads. Chances are you'll pass—or be passed by—a truck hauling a cylinder-shaped trailer with a smokestack. For outdoor parties and ranch shindigs, some Texans bring the barbecue joint to them.

Cheese Steak Sub award, the Sub-works freely admits its atmosphere is "East Coast Hustle and Bustle." The Eastern seaboard is also reflected in the décor of Boston memorabilia. Breakfast, lunch, and dinner seven days. 点 (Northwest)

CHRIS MADRID'S NACHOS & BURGERS
1900 Blanco Rd.
San Antonio
210/735-3552
$

These are serious burgers. Choose from quarter- or half-pound (also called "Macho") hefts. The meat is thin and wide, but juicy. Variations include the Old Fashion, the Cheeseburger (with American cheese), and the Cheddar Cheezy. All familiar varieties. Then you get to the "Only In San Antonio" end of the menu: the Tostada Burger, with tortilla-chip fragments and a smear of refried beans; and the Flaming Jalapeño Burger, which is just what you think. Accompanied by an order of Macho Nachos, Madrid's fare promises you at least one night of pleasure and regret in the Alamo City. Outdoor seating available. 点 (Northwest)

THE COUNTY LINE
Loop 1604 west of U.S. 281
San Antonio
210/496-0011
$$

See description in Downtown section, page 60. (Northwest) This location is scheduled to move to U.S. 281 N. and Bitters Road in September 1999.

DEWESE'S TIP TOP CAFÉ
2814 Fredericksburg Rd.
San Antonio
210/732-0191
$

Nostalgia is DeWese's theme. Family-owned since 1938, the café offers simple country fare such as award-winning chicken-fried steak and onion rings, and other menu items that have won enviable reviews in *Texas Monthly* and local newspapers. In true forties and fifties style, DeWese's doesn't accept credit cards or reservations. Open for lunch and dinner every day except Mon. 点 (Northwest)

DING HOW
4531 NW Loop 410
San Antonio
210/340-7944
$

Ding How, translated by Manager Maurice Huey, means "The Best." Many San Antonians agree, making this "restaurant on stilts" popular for lunch and dinner, and garnering it the local Silver Spoon Award for several years. The décor is very Chinese inside and out, and the menu leans toward the familiar and away from the adventurous. If you're with a group, the family and deluxe dinners offer healthy portions of everything at a reasonable price. Reservations are accepted. Open for lunch and dinner seven days. 点 (Northwest)

ERNESTO'S
2559 Jackson-Keller Rd.
San Antonio
210/344-1248
$$

Ernesto Torres describes his menu as "seafood gourmet, beef and veal, Mexican style," but seafood takes the lead. Several varieties of fish fillet, as well as shrimp or crab meat, can be prepared in any one of nine regional Mexican sauces. Some French influence is evident as well in the crab and shrimp crêpes. The eclecticism works: Torres has been honored with a trophy case full of honors: an American Express My Favorite Restaurant award, a San Antonio's People's Choice award, a Best Table Green Sauce in Texas award, and Best Fried Oysters in Texas. Ernesto promises to prepare anything the way you want it "to make you feel at home." Unlike home, reservations are recommended. Open for lunch and dinner Mon–Fri, and dinner only on Sat. &. (Northwest)

EZ'S
5720 Bandera Rd.
San Antonio
210/681-2222
$
There's an additional Northwest location at 734 W. Bitters Rd., 210/490-6666. (Northwest) See description in Northeast section, page 70.

FRATELLI'S CAFFÈ ITALIANO
8085 Callaghan Rd.
San Antonio
210/349-7997
$$
"Italian food, St. Louis style" is a strange slogan anywhere outside St. Louis. But that midwestern city is home of "the Hill," an Italian community with some of the finest traditional pastas you'll find anywhere, and the San Antonio contingent of the Fratelli clan grew up there. All pastas are made fresh in-house, and the best is the toasted ravioli. More complex dishes such as shrimp fano and chicken maritata are highly recommended. The atmosphere is casual and relaxed, and cozy booths are available. Fratelli's is a past winner of San Antonio's Silver Spoon Award for the best Italian restaurant. Reservations are accepted for lunch and dinner seven days. You can visit the restaurant online at www.fratellis.com. &. (Northwest)

INDIA OVEN
1031 Patricia Dr., No. 106
San Antonio
210/366-1030
$$
This elegant eatery's comprehensive North Indian bill of fare has garnered awards from the *San Antonio Express-News*, *Texas Monthly* magazine, and AAA. Chef Charanjit Bassi came to San Antonio after stints in New York, Houston, and San Jose. He recommends the mixed grill tandoori or the chicken *tikka masala*, but it's difficult to read farther down the menu than the jumbo prawns. And the ten varieties of Indian bread may have you asking for a sample of each. Bassi reminds you that your meal can be prepared to any preference of mild or spicy. Reservations are accepted. Open for lunch and dinner all week. &. (Northwest)

JOE'S CRAB SHACK
12485 I-10 W.

Outside the Liberty Bar, p. 80

Liberty Bar

San Antonio
210/699-9779
$$
See description in Downtown section, page 63. (Northwest)

LA FOGATA
2724 Vance-Jackson Rd.
San Antonio
210/340-1348
$$

La Fogata's patio, replete with hand-painted tile, fountains, and plants that would feel right at home south of the border, is one of the most relaxing places in town to enjoy Mexican food. It's also one of the most popular, so make a reservation. A huge menu with well-chosen combo platters allows you to sample a bit of all the standards such as enchiladas, fajitas, chiles rellenos, and the like. Seafood is also very good, and the margaritas are outstanding. But best of all are the chips with the dark, smoky salsa, made by first broiling the peppers. Lunch and dinner seven days, breakfast on weekends. ♿ (Northwest)

LIBERTY BAR
328 E. Josephine St.
San Antonio
210/227-1187
$$

If you can talk yourself into going through the door of an antique house

that's San Antonio's version of the tower at Pisa, you'll be rewarded. An eclectic menu of grilled meats such as quail and redfish and a tasty vegetarian menu—accompanied by more than a few imported beers—make this perpendicularly challenged bar and grill a favorite after-concert gathering place for members of the San Antonio Symphony and other artsy types. Lunch and dinner seven days, with occasional live entertainment. ♿ (Northwest)

LITTLE HIPP'S
1423 McCullough Ave.
San Antonio
210/222-8114
$

Rarely is a restaurant's name such a poor descriptor of the effect of its food—but don't let that stop you. Hipp's ain't fancy, though the dining room is called the Grand Ball Room. It's festooned with rubber, plastic, and leather balls of all types, in tribute to its predecessor, Hipp's Bubble Room. The burgers are very large and very juicy, and you can get all of the standard dressings. Try the jalapeño cheese Hippburger with a basket of Hippuppies (tater tots anywhere but Hipp's) and a frosty Shiner Bock. Don't try the Jumbo Bacon Cheeseburger (one pound of beef, 10 slices of bacon, eight slices of cheese) without help or

---

T I P

On a budget and in a hurry? Try Bill Miller's, a San Antonio institution for Texas barbecue. Each Bill Miller's includes a dining room and a drive-through. The familiar barbecue fare is very popular, as are the baked potatoes with all the trimmings. Pies are baked fresh daily. Open for lunch and dinner seven days. Locations all around town.

a ride home. For something found only at Hipp's try the Shypoke Eggs. They look exactly like fried eggs, but they're actually tortilla chips with white and yellow cheese on top. Why? Who cares? Open for lunch and dinner Mon–Fri. ♿ (Northwest)

LOS BARRIOS
4223 Blanco Rd.
San Antonio
210/732-6017
$–$$

Los Barrios ("the neighborhood") is so popular that General Manager Louis Barrios takes calls for business folk who list the restaurant's number on their cards. Louis's mom, Viola, handles the Mexican/continental cooking duties, and her favorite concoction is *cortadillo*: Zuazua-style beef tenderloin with fresh vegetables and herbs. Los Barrios was named one of the 100 Best New Restaurants in America by *Esquire*, and Louis B. was the San Antonio Restaurant Association's 1996 Restaurateur of the Year. Eat here, and he'll probably drop by to ask you how you like the food. Reservations are accepted for lunch and dinner every day, with live Latin jazz on weekends. ♿ (Northwest)

MADHATTERS TEA
3606 Avenue B
San Antonio
210/821-6555
$

A coffee bar that doesn't flaunt coffee. Owner/Chef Rene Guerrero's passion is tea—70 varieties—and she invites you to the tea parties she hosts anytime between 11 a.m. and 11 p.m. every day (9 a.m. on Sun). Madhatters' location is as relaxing as its herbal espressos: a 60-year-old house looking out on Brackenridge Park. Comestibles—all with an Alice

in Wonderland nonsensibility—include a variety of gourmet sandwiches and salads and the award-winning pork tenderloin salad. Reservations are accepted for groups of six or more. Open until midnight Fri and Sat. ♿ (Northwest)

MAVERICK CAFÉ
6868 San Pedro Ave.
San Antonio
210/822-9611
$–$$

East meets Southwest. The Maverick is San Antonio's—perhaps the world's—only combination Mexican/Chinese restaurant. The menus from both hemispheres are standard but good, and there are some fascinating culture-blending combo plates. Open for lunch and dinner seven days. ♿ (Northwest)

MENCIUS GOURMET HUNAN
7959 Fredericksburg Rd.
San Antonio
210/615-1288
$$

Much of the ethnically eclectic medical-center crowd gathers at Mencius for lunch. Simple yet elegant, softly colored décor is the backdrop for outstanding Chinese food, including shrimp and scallops (Hunan style), Mencius beef, and sautéed string beans in garlic sauce. Saturday evenings are accompanied by live classical guitar. Lunch and dinner seven days, with reservations recommended for dinner. (Northwest)

MESÓN EUROPEAN DINING
5999 DeZavala Rd., Suite 150
San Antonio
210/690-5811
$$

This relative newcomer quickly became a local standout. Despite its unimpressive strip-mall location, Mesón offers a very good, nearly elegant dining experience at an excellent price. Lunch fare, basically lighter, includes some inventive chicken dishes (the breast stuffed with broccoli and cheese in a cream sauce is delicious), pastas, and salads. The dinner menu moves upscale a bit to include grilled salmon in béarnaise sauce, two varieties of lamb chops, and horseradish-crusted filets. Reservations usually aren't necessary. Lunch and dinner every day. ⑤ (Northwest)

ON THE BORDER MEXICAN CAFÉ
11745 I-10 W.
San Antonio
210/690-3700
$$
See description in Northeast section, page 74. (Northwest)

PAPPADEAUX SEAFOOD KITCHEN
76 NE Loop 410
San Antonio
210/340-7143
$$
Authentic Louisiana cuisine makes it worth fighting the airport-area traffic to get to Pappadeaux ("papa-doze"). Bayou-fresh classics include the crawfish platter with étouffée and dirty rice and shrimp étouffée. Less-Cajunized seafood is available, as are beef and chicken dishes. But it's the Louisiana coastal dishes that really shine, with their rich, roux-thickened sauces and spicy aromas. Pappadeaux is very popular, so it starts to get busy around 7 on weekends. And they don't take reservations, so you might want to get there a bit earlier. Lunch and dinner every day. ⑤ (Northwest)

RUDY'S COUNTRY STORE AND BARBECUE

24152 I-10 W.
(at Boerne Stage Rd.)
Leon Springs
210/698-2141
$
A perfect day in San Antonio? Fiesta Texas all day, then out I-10 a little farther for supper at Rudy's. Don't expect to be made a fuss over. You'll wait in line for your South Texas–style smoked meat, which will be handed to you wrapped in white butcher paper—Rudy's china. Pull a beer or soft drink out of a galvanized tub of ice. Siddown at an outside table and enjoy. Then go back for homemade peach cobbler with a big ol' scoop of Promised Land Dairy Vanilla. It really doesn't get any better than this. Lunch and supper (not dinner) every day. (Northwest)

RUTH'S CHRIS STEAK HOUSE
7720 Jones Maltsberger Rd.
San Antonio
210/821-5051
$$$
It's not a San Antonio original, and its location doesn't have a lot of River City ambience. But if you're a serious steak fan, this is the place. The limelight shines on U.S. prime beef and live Maine lobsters. The décor is a blend of Southwestern and early English accents. The steaks are impeccable, and the wine list is a multi-award winner from *Wine Spectator*. Open for dinner seven days, with reservations recommended. ⑤ (Northwest)

SIMI'S
4535 Fredericksburg Rd.
San Antonio
210/737-3166
$–$$
Sukhwinder Bal's Indian menu includes a couple of mainstays for

couples: the Empire Dinner for two (chicken, shrimp, lamb, et al.) and seafood for two. Simi's also offers highly regarded dishes for the weight-conscious and non-carnivorous. Bal's craft has earned recognition from *Texas Monthly* and the *San Antonio Current*. Reservations are accepted for lunch and dinner daily. & (Northwest)

THAI KITCHEN
445 McCarty Rd.
San Antonio
210/344-8366
$
Sam Suwanasung's Thai Kitchen—actually Thai and Chinese—is a candlelit, romantic taste of the East that has been named San Antonio's Best Thai Restaurant for several years running. You might want to place a reservation for lunch or dinner. Open daily. & (Northwest)

TOKYO STEAK HOUSE
9405 San Pedro Ave.
San Antonio
210/341-4461
$$
The menu at this mostly Japanese eatery is eclectic, with an emphasis on gourmet steaks and seafood. For raw-fish fanatics, a sushi bar is also provided. Open seven evenings for dinner only; reservations are recommended. & (Northwest)

TOMATILLO'S CAFÉ Y CANTINA
9911 I-10 W.
San Antonio
210/641-6417
$$
See description in Northeast section, page 75. (Northwest)

TOM'S RIBS NO. 2
2535 NW Loop 410
San Antonio

210/344-7427
$$
See description in Northeast section, page 75. (Northwest)

TONY ROMA'S
9502 I-10 W. (in The Colonnade)
San Antonio
210/432-7427
$$
See description in Downtown section, page 66. (Northwest)

U.R. COOKS STEAKHOUSE
4907 NW Loop 410
San Antonio
210/647-4846
$$
If you look forward to vacation as a welcome relief from the kitchen, U.R. Cooks may change your mind. Select your own giant cut o' beef and grill it yourself. The ambience is much like that of a backyard cookout: open, casual, and fun. That may be why the local hotel Concierge Association voted U.R. one of the city's top ten restaurants. (If you don't want to turn your own beef, Chef Jesse Campos—whose mother loves him, according to Manager Mark Gray—can do it for you.) Reservations are unnecessary. Open for dinner seven days and for lunch on Sat and Sun. & (Northwest)

WATER STREET SEAFOOD CO.
10855 I-10 W.
San Antonio
210/696-3474
$$
Water Street is like a school classroom: The first thing to do upon entering is look at the blackboard. In lieu of a math assignment, you'll find the day's specials, which can be prepared blackened, mesquite-grilled, sautéed, broiled, or fried. The high ceiling and net-and-line décor will

make you feel like you're dining on the Gulf. Open for lunch and dinner every day, until midnight Fri and Sat. ♿ (Northwest)

WILLIE'S GRILL AND ICEHOUSE
15801 San Pedro Ave.
San Antonio
210/490-9220
$

In Texan parlance, an ice house is a convenience store—a place to get a cold, inebriating drink nearly any time of day. Willie goes that one better by offering grilled catfish, chicken tenders, and chicken-fried steak in an open-air café filled with antiques and collectibles. Open for lunch and dinner seven days. Requests for reservations will be laughed at. ♿ (Northwest)

SOUTH

ACADIANA CAFÉ
1289 SW Loop 410
San Antonio
210/674-0009
$

Acadiana is one of a few San Antonio reflections of the recent Cajun-food craze. Chef Frenchy Guidry, who describes his menu as "country Cajun," recommends the various catfish dishes, although his gumbo and étouffée are local award-winners. Also try alligator nuggets, Cajun popcorn, *boudin*, and (believe it or not) fried dill pickles. The café occasionally offers live Cajun music during dinner. With 20-foot vaulted ceilings and two fireplaces, Acadiana is a delightful place to stop after a day at nearby Sea World. Reservations recommended for lunch and dinner daily. ♿ (South)

BOB'S SMOKEHOUSE
3306 Roland Ave.

Dining on the River Walk

San Antonio
210/333-9338
$

"Cafeteria style" and "casual dining" may not sound promising. So how about Best Beef Ribs in America, according to *People* magazine? Or the only San Antonio barbecue house on *Texas Monthly*'s 50 Best Barbecue Joints in Texas list? Bob Wells offers the other Texas staples: brisket, pork, sausage, chicken, and even lamb ribs. Home-style sides such as potato salad, beans, and coleslaw are perfect accompaniments, and a $20 family special gives you a whole bunch of everything. Lunch and dinner seven days. Cash only. ♿ (South)

DON PEDRO
1526 SW Military Dr.
San Antonio
210/922-3511
$–$$

The Sepulveda brothers set their table with standard Tex-Mex fare, but it's good and reasonably priced. One unique offering is *parrillada Norteña*, a feast for four with *agujas, pollo al carbon*, *costillas al horno*, *chorizo al carbon*, and *queso flameado*. (It's worth the southwest trek just to hear them explain what this embarrassment of riches includes.) Casa Sepulveda is located near the Mission Trail, which makes it an oasis the Spanish missionaries would gladly have patronized. ☺ (South)

MINA & DIMI'S GREEK HOUSE
7159 Hwy. 90 W.
San Antonio
210/674-3464
$–$$
Owner Mina (Sidler) and her son, Chef Dimi(tri Tsandoula) invite you to trade the Texas climate for a taste of the Mediterranean at what Dimi calls "the only real Greek restaurant in town." Murals of Greece and Turkish artifacts overlook entrées such as moussaka, *pasticcio*, lamb chops, and *taramosalata*. Less traditional is the finest calamari in town. For afters, enjoy stout Greek coffee along with an indescribably tasty baklava cheesecake. The first Thursday of the month brings a wine-tasting, and every Friday and Saturday night features live belly dancing. Open for lunch and dinner every day but Sun, with reservations recommended on Fri. ☺ (South)

PIG STAND
3054 Rigsby Ave.
San Antonio
210/333-8231
$
See description in Downtown section, page 64. (South)

Texas Department of Transportation

5

SIGHTS AND ATTRACTIONS

A general formula to keep in mind when dividing up your sightseeing time is the following: downtown = history, north = theme parks. The historical sights are within a time radius of 15 to 25 minutes of each other. Getting out to the mega-attractions such as Sea World and Fiesta Texas takes 20 to 30 non–rush hour minutes from downtown. But all of the trips are worthwhile.

If you want to take in as much history as you can but you don't have a lot of time, opt for one of the excellent trolley or bus tours of the most famous sights. You'll see them all, have the advantage of a knowledgeable guide, and have time left over for less weighty pursuits. If getting home in a hurry is not a concern, you can walk to many of the downtown attractions and enjoy the city at a leisurely pace.

Whatever your downtown destination, an excellent place to start is the Alamo. Not only is this where San Antonio's history looms largest, it is also tourist central. The friendly folks at the tourist center on Alamo Plaza can answer your questions and provide discount coupons to some of the more popular attractions.

DOWNTOWN

ALAMEDA THEATRE
318 W. Houston St.
San Antonio
210/299-4300

Many San Antonians breathed a sigh of relief when the Alameda reopened in 1998. This crumbling structure, once a great movie palace erected in the 1940s, had been promised a rebirth for several years. But funding and planning never seemed to come together. It's appropriate that the now-reconstituted Alameda, once the largest theater to be dedicated to Spanish-language entertainment, will serve as a multi-venue performance

DOWNTOWN SAN ANTONIO

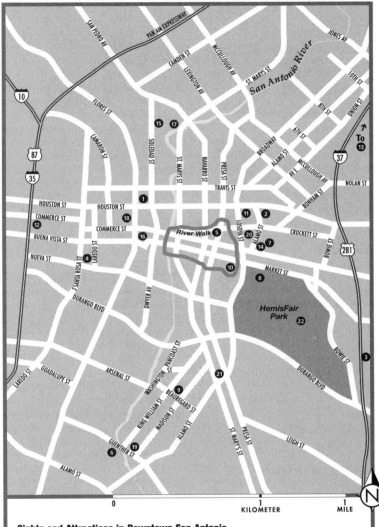

Sights and Attractions in Downtown San Antonio

1 Alameda Theatre
2 The Alamo
3 Alamodome
4 Casa Navarro State Historical Park
5 The Edge
2 Gray Line Tours
6 Guenther House
7 IMAX Theatre
8 Instituto Cultural Mexicano

9 King William Historic District
10 La Villita Historic District
11 Lone Star Trolley Tours
12 Market Square (El Mercado)
13 Pearl Brewery
12 Ripley's Believe It or Not!/Plaza Theatre of Wax
14 The Rivercenter
15 San Antonio Central Library

16 San Fernando Cathedral
17 Southwest School of Art and Craft
18 Spanish Governor's Palace
19 Steves Homestead
20 The Texas Adventure
21 Texas Highway Patrol Museum
8 Texas Trolley
22 Tower of the Americas
2,14 Yanaguana Cruises

hall and teaching facility for Latino arts and culture. In fact, the importance of the Alameda to Hispanic San Antonians has been compared to that of Harlem's Apollo Theatre to African Americans. Call for tour information and special events and exhibits. ♿ (Downtown)

THE ALAMO
300 Alamo Plaza
San Antonio
210/225-1391

The most common remark overheard from tourists outside the Alamo is, "It's much smaller than I thought." It is. It's also much smaller than it used to be. The chapel (what most people think of as "The Alamo") and grounds look much different than they did before the 1836 battle that transformed San Antonio's first mission into the Cradle of Texas Liberty. For instance, there was no Burger King across the street. But the Daughters of the Republic of Texas, executors of the Alamo legacy, go to great lengths to maintain Texas's number-two tourist attraction with dignity and reverence. In front of the chapel, serving as centerpiece to Alamo Plaza, is the Cenotaph—a pink granite and gray marble monument designed by Pompeo Coppini and inscribed with the likenesses and names of the battle's heroes. Legend may sometimes take precedence over fact, but the Alamo is still a stirring place. (Note: No photography allowed inside the chapel.) Mon–Sat 9–5:30, Sun 10–5:30. Free. ♿ (Downtown)

ALAMODOME
Durango St. and I-37
San Antonio
210/223-DOME

San Antonio's 72,000-seat domed stadium is a monument to ingenious financing and unfulfilled promises. Seeking the 1990s El Dorado of a National Football League franchise, San Antonians voted to fund the stadium through a sales tax levied by the local bus company (which explains the lack of parking around the dome and the large bus lanes). While locals have used the dome for concerts, rallies, and exhibition games—including the 1996 NBA All-Star Game and the 1993 Olympic Festival—the NFL has yet to bite. But the dome is still worth a look for its very San Antonio colors, latticework towers anchoring the cable-suspended roof, and the world's largest retractable seating system. Call for tour information and event schedules. ♿ (Downtown)

CASA NAVARRO
STATE HISTORICAL PARK
228 S. Laredo St.
San Antonio
210/226-4801

This unassuming little building, somewhat buried downtown, is the former home of José Antonio Navarro (1795–1871). Navarro was an eminent statesman and rancher, and one of two Native Texans (of Mexican nationality) who signed the state's declaration of independence from Mexico. Thus, his homestead is an ideal place to get "the rest of the story"—San Antonio's history from the point of view of one of its early settlers. Conversational, interactive tours are offered through the restored and accurately furnished interior, and the operators will enjoy talking with you and answering your questions from documentary sources, with a guarantee of "no tall tales." Special hands-on activities are available for kids. Wed–Sun 10–4. $2 adults, $1 children 6–12. ♿ (Downtown)

THE EDGE
245 E. Commerce St.
San Antonio
210/225-EDGE

A relative newcomer to downtown, The Edge is billed as "the ultimate thrill ride." Realistic video is combined with high-tech sound and motion-controlled seats for experiences including a runaway mine train, an outer-space demolition derby, a haunted house, and an "intergalactic pinball machine." It has nothing to do with San Antonio except that it's here. Take the kids, but only before eating at the next door Planet Hollywood. Mon–Thu 11 a.m.–11 p.m., Fri 11 a.m.–1 a.m., Sat 10 a.m.–1 a.m., Sun noon–11 p.m. Admission: $5 (no credit cards). Note: Patrons must be at least 42 inches tall and able to brace their upper and lower bodies. Wheelchairs will not fit in the ride. (Downtown)

GRAY LINE TOURS
Alamo Plaza
San Antonio
210/226-1706

Gray Line offers three tours of the most popular tourist destinations. Tour 1 follows the Mission Trail, beginning at the Alamo and including San Fernando Cathedral. Tour 2 visits Brackenridge Park, the zoo and botanical gardens, Fort Sam Houston, the Institute of Texan Cultures, and the King William District. Tour 3 combines 1 and 2 and adds a river barge trip. Tour 1: departs daily 9 a.m., returns 12:30 p.m. Tickets: $20 adults, $10 children 5–12. Tour 2: Departs daily 1:30 p.m., returns 5:15 p.m. Tickets: $20 adults, $10 children. Tour 3: Departs daily 9 a.m., returns 5:15 p.m. Tickets: $35 adults, $17.50 children. No tours on Easter, Thanksgiving, Christmas, or New Year's Day. (Downtown)

GUENTHER HOUSE
205 E. Guenther St.
San Antonio
210/227-1061

Carl Hilmar Guenther, founder of the Pioneer Flour Company, created this beautiful home and its sculpted grounds in 1860. Stepping inside is like stepping into Germany of more than a century ago, with crystal chan-

The River Walk, p. 94

SACVB/Craig Stafford

RIVER WALK

Sights and Attractions on the River Walk

1 Arneson River Theatre
2 Barge Ticket Terminal
3 Barge Ticket Terminal (Holiday Inn)
4 Esquire Tavern
5 Henry B. Gonzalez Convention Center
6 Jim Cullum's Landing Jazz Club (Hyatt Regency Hotel)
7 La Mansión del Rio
8 La Villita Historic District
9 North Loop Gate
10 Old Mill Crossing
11 Padre Damian Massanet's Table
12 Rivercenter and Barge Ticket Center
13 Sniper Cypress
14 South Loop Gate
15 Waterfall Fountain

Map labels:

BOWIE ST
Alamo Plaza
Alamo
HemisFair Park
CROCKETT ST
BONHAM ST
Rivercenter Mall
Convention Center
ALAMO PLAZA
ALAMO ST
LASOYA ST
ALAMO ST
PRESA ST
PASEO DE LA VILLITA
KING PHILIP V ST
NACIONAL
NAVARRO ST
HOUSTON ST
COLLEGE ST
CROCKETT ST
COMMERCE ST
MARKET ST
PRESA ST
ST. MARY'S ST
ST. MARY'S ST
VILLITA ST
NUEVA ST
JACK WHITE AV
San Antonio River
SOLEDAD ST
DWYER AV
MAIN AV

------- RIVER WALK

.5 MILES
.5 KILOMETERS
0

deliers, abundant gold leaf, and period furniture. The King William District home is maintained today as a museum and gift shop and features a cozy restaurant serving breakfast, lunch, and an outstanding Sunday brunch. Mon–Sat 9–5, Sun 10–2:30. Free. (Downtown)

IMAX THEATRE
Rivercenter
849 E. Commerce St.
San Antonio
210/225-IMAX
There are always two or three spectacular films to choose from at the IMAX; each one will overwhelm you visually (from a 60-foot-high screen) and aurally (from a six-channel, gigawatt sound system). But if you have another IMAX near your hometown, you can probably catch the same flicks there. The one you can't miss during your visit is a San Antonio exclusive—the 45-minute docudrama *Alamo: The Price of Freedom*. See it before or after visiting the real thing, and the battle—and San Antonio's roots—takes on new meaning. Daily 9 a.m.–10:20 p.m. (last show). $6.95 adults, $6.75 seniors, $4.75 children 3–11. (Discount offered for two-show packages.) ⅃ (Downtown)

INSTITUTO CULTURAL MEXICANO
600 HemisFair Plaza
San Antonio
210/227-0123
The calendar of events at the Instituto includes music and dance performances, art exhibits, lectures, and films—all presented in the interest of preserving and strengthening San Antonio's cultural and social bonds with Mexico. Call for information and schedules. Mon–Fri 9–5:30, Sat and Sun noon–6. Free or nominally priced for most events. Much of the insti-

tute is not wheelchair accessible. (Downtown)

KING WILLIAM
HISTORIC DISTRICT
Bounded by S. St. Mary's,
Washington, Beauregard, and
Madison Sts.
San Antonio
210/224-6163
In the mid-1800s, shortly before Mexico ceded Texas to the United States, European immigrants began settling in San Antonio, at that time still very much a frontier town. Perhaps out of homesickness, the newcomers built the elegant, pillared, gabled, and porched Victorian-era mansions of the King William neighborhood. The largest of these were built for entrepreneurs who found new wealth in the new state, and many of the homes retain their dignified splendor. Visit the San Antonio Conservation Society office at 107 King William and pick up a map of the neighborhood, then take yourself on one of the city's most enjoyable walking or driving tours. The best time to visit is during Fiesta's King William Fair (in April), when live music and food booths point the way to some of the most beautiful houses opened for visits. Daily until dusk. Free. (Downtown)

LA VILLITA HISTORIC DISTRICT
Bounded by Villita, S. Presa,
Nueva, and Alamo Sts.
San Antonio
210/207-8610
The "little village" is the site of the original Spanish settlement on the San Antonio River, and General Santa Anna set up his cannon line here for the Alamo siege. Much of this National Historic District has been restored to the look of a century ago, though the tidy buildings now contain

Fun Facts about the Alamo

- It was established as Mission San Antonio de Valero in 1718, the first of six Spanish missions built along the San Antonio River to proselytize the natives. (One mission didn't last long.)
- What is commonly called "The Alamo" is actually just the mission chapel. The original mission grounds covered more than twice the space of what is now Alamo Plaza.
- The Catholic Church had abandoned the Alamo years before the battle.
- The trademark arched facade of the chapel was added 14 years after the battle by the U.S. Army, which was using the building for storage.
- In 1855 the Texas Supreme Court granted ownership of the Alamo to the Catholic Church, over the protestations of the city and the army. The church sold the chapel to the state in 1883 for $20,000.
- Not a national historic site, the Alamo is managed by the Daughters of the Republic of Texas (DRT), whose members trace their lineage to the original citizens of the republic.
- Street repairs in front of the Alamo uncovered a Native American burial ground.
- On a 1985 concert visit to San Antonio, rock star Ozzy Osbourne was nabbed urinating on the Alamo Cenotaph. He paid $10,000 in reparations to the DRT.

craft studios, galleries, restaurants, and boutiques. One of these is the Cos House, where General Martin Perfecto de Cos surrendered after unsuccessfully attempting to quell a rebellion by the Texan settler/soldiers. Another is the Little Church of La Villita, which still holds services on Sunday mornings. Visit the second floor exhibit in Bolivar Hall and take in the "Old Villita" exhibit. This will give you a much stronger sense of the history of the settlement itself, and the city's origins. A few steps toward the river from La Villita are the grassy terraces of the Arneson River Theatre, one of the earliest River Walk projects, home to many summer performances by local dance and music troupes. During Fiesta, La Villita hosts one of the festival's most popular weeklong events, A Night in

Old San Antonio. Daily 10–6. Free. &
(Downtown)

LONE STAR TROLLEY TOURS
301 Alamo Plaza
San Antonio
210/224-9299
Board Lone Star's red and green,
turn-of-the-century-style trolleys at
Ripley's Believe It or Not!/Plaza Theatre of Wax. This is the only fully
wheelchair-accessible trolley service
in town. One-hour narrated tours of
the downtown sights include the
Alamo, San Fernando Cathedral, El
Mercado, the King William District,
HemisFair Park, the Southwest Center of Art and Craft, and the River
Walk. Tours leave every 30 minutes
and last 90 minutes, with opportuni-
ties to step off and reboard later. Daily
10–6. $7.50 adults, $4 children 5–11. &
(Downtown)

MARKET SQUARE (EL MERCADO)
514 W. Commerce St.
San Antonio
210/207-8600
If you had only one afternoon in San
Antonio to experience the spirit of the
city, Market Square would be the
place to spend it. A century ago, this
two-block commercial reserve was
filled with farmers's stalls and food
stands—notably, those of the Chili
Queens, who gathered to dispense
their spicy fare to farmers, downtown
businessfolk, and passing ranchers
and tourists. Today the square is souvenir heaven. Its many shops display
a staggering array of merchandise of
wide-ranging price (and quality), surrounded by myriad restaurants and
food stands. From spring through fall,
you would be hard-pressed to find a
weekend without some kind of celebration going on in the open spaces.
& (Downtown)

PEARL BREWERY
312 Pearl Pkwy. and Ave. E
San Antonio
210/226-0231
This delightful, fairy-tale castle–like
1886 structure contains the headquarters of one of Texas's official
beers (the other is Lone Star). Tours
are offered most days, but call ahead.
Don't miss the replica of a combination saloon and courthouse once
owned by legendary frontier enforcer
Judge Roy Bean. No barroom brawls
endanger the piano player here—this
version is a gift shop. Call for tour
hours. Free. & (Downtown)

RIPLEY'S BELIEVE IT OR NOT!/
PLAZA THEATRE OF WAX
301 Alamo Plaza
San Antonio
210/224-WAXX
Whether your tastes run to history or
the sensational, this combo-museum
across the street from the Alamo provides a bit of both. The "I didn't know

The Fort Sam Houston Quadrangle,
p. 100

Fort Sam Houston Museum

that!" spirit of the Ripley's exhibits will be familiar from the long-running Sunday morning comic feature. And while the Theatre of Wax may not quite be Madame Tussaud's, its creepily accurate displays offer glimpses into Texas history and religion and show business themes. (Some of the horror settings may be too intense for the very young, but these are in the cellar and can be avoided.) Mon–Sun 9 a.m.–10 p.m. Combination ticket $11.95 adults, $7.95 children 4–12. ♿ (Downtown)

THE RIVER WALK
(El Paseo del Rio)
Throughout Downtown
San Antonio
210/207-8480
Anthony of Padua may be the patron saint of San Antonio, but he has some competition from Robert Hugman, the visionary young architect whose 1929 idea of turning the downtown bend of the San Antonio River into an asset rather than a flood threat charted the city's future. Beginning near Municipal Auditorium off Lexington Street, and continuing through the King William District, the River Walk offers an undeniably romantic stroll past shops, restaurants, fountains, nightclubs, hotels, and towering cypress trees. The 2.5-mile route is often clogged with tourists during the busy season and calls for considerable shoulder-turning and "pardon me"-ing, but it is well worth the trouble. The River Walk is particularly difficult to navigate during special festivals and holidays, when the river serves as a parade route. (See Calendar of Events in Chapter 1.) Note: There is no guardrail, but the river isn't very deep and it's shark-free. Open 24 hours. Free. Wheelchair accessible via Rivercenter elevators, but stairs and other obstructions are frequent on the walk. (Downtown)

SAN ANTONIO CENTRAL LIBRARY
600 Soledad St.
San Antonio
210/207-2500
Internationally renowned Mexican architect Ricardo Legoretta set off quite a flurry of controversy in 1995. His progressive design for this immense downtown structure was hotly debated—particularly its predominant color, dubbed "enchilada red" in a local contest. But few San Antonians now second-guess the architect, and the library is an unmitigated success. Within the angular structure, which stands out for its combination of red, purple, and yellow hues, is contained a six-floor atrium, art gallery, and high-tech auditorium. Glass doors allow access to terrace gardens for special events. Oh, and there are lots of books, with a popular children's library (with spots for reading to young 'uns) and a genealogy collection. Mon–Thu 9–9, Fri–Sat 9–5, Sun 11–5. Free. ♿ (Downtown)

SAN FERNANDO CATHEDRAL
115 Main Plaza
San Antonio
210/227-1297
In the heart of downtown, San Fernando boasts the oldest cathedral sanctuary in the United States. It was founded in 1731 by Spanish Canary Island settlers as the religious—and geographic—center of their new home. In fact, Main Plaza where the cathedral sits was first called Plaza de las Islas—Place of the Islands. The cathedral has seen many milestones, such as the marriage of Alamo defender James Bowie in 1831, and several rebuildings following floods and fire. It is also the legendary—and probably apocryphal—burial place of Bowie, William Travis, and Davy Crockett. Daily 6–6. Free. (Downtown)

SOUTHWEST SCHOOL OF ART AND CRAFT
300 Augusta St.
San Antonio
210/224-1848
In 1965 the San Antonio Conservation Society purchased this breathtaking riverside property from the Ursuline Academy School for Girls and formed the Southwest Craft Center. Since then, the art institute has continued to reinvent itself, growing and expanding into an important source of art education and a retreat for budding painters, sculptors, and potters. The Ursuline Academy was founded in the 1850s, and the look and feel of that era has been elegantly preserved—particularly in the stained glass–clad chapel. Today the center is a place to learn contemporary and traditional arts and crafts with expert local and visiting instructors, and to view professional artists' works in the several galleries. Frequent special programs are offered for children. All of the school's programs have proven so popular, in fact, that additional classroom and exhibit space has been constructed in a remodeled auto-parts store across the street. The Copper Kitchen cafeteria serves lunch, and the center offers a picturesque site in which to enjoy it. Most areas are wheelchair accessible. Daily 10–10. Free, but there's a fee for classes—call for schedule. ♿ (Downtown)

SPANISH GOVERNOR'S PALACE
105 Plaza de Armas
San Antonio
210/224-0601
The title may be misleading. This 1700s-era home of the military governors of Spanish Colonial San Antonio isn't quite palatial by today's standards. It is, however, a fascinating bit of history and the state's only existing example of an early aristocratic Spanish home. Inside the thick adobe walls, studded with protruding timbers, are period furnishings and artifacts. (The few stairs in the building are antique, too, so watch your footing.) The back door leads to a restful, luxuriantly foliated courtyard that provides a lovely and cool place to rest

---

Do You Know the Way to San José?

Of the five missions in San Antonio, only one is an operating parish church: Mission San José. One of the most popular services here takes place each Sunday at noon—when Catholicism meets Mexican folk music in a mariachi mass. The chapel's trademark Rose Window shines down on a not-so-traditional service with music provided by local mariachi musicians, including trumpeters, accordionists, marimba players, singers (singing the liturgy in Spanish, of course), and various other instrumentalists from time to time. Arrive early, as seating is limited and services are very popular.

How to Make *Cascarones*

Just about every celebration in town is greeted with cascarones *(kah-skah-ROH-nehs; singular,* cascarón*). These confetti-filled eggs are traditionally broken above (preferably not on) the heads of loved ones and partymates, thus imparting good luck. After Fiesta, dead* cascarones *litter downtown streets. To make your own, you'll need raw eggs, colored tissue paper, markers or paint, and confetti. ("Dots" punched from colored paper work nicely.)*

1. *Carefully crack a nickel-size hole in the pointy ends of the eggs. (If you get past this stage, you're home free.)*
2. *Empty and rinse the eggshells and place them upside down to dry.*
3. *Hold a shell by placing a finger in the hole. Decorate it by gluing on tissue and confetti, painting it, or using stickers. Repeat at least a dozen times. Let the shells dry overnight.*
4. *Next morning, fill the shells with confetti (birdseed, for the environmentally aware). If you preserved the egg carton, it makes a handy rack for holding the shells until you . . .*
5. *Close the shells by gluing circles of tissue around the edges of the holes. Let dry.*
6. *Your* cascarones *are ready to use. Note: If you plan on smashing a* cascarón *over the head of a Yankee, you might explain the tradition first, just to avoid a cultural confrontation.*

If this all sounds like too much trouble, you can also buy your cascarones. *They are sold on every street corner downtown.*

during your downtown travels. Just outside the walls is Military Plaza (Plaza de Armas), once the heart of area government and still the site of San Antonio City Hall. El Palacio del Gobernador Español was restored in 1929 and designated a National Historic Landmark in 1970. Mon–Sat 9–5, Sun 10–5. $1 adults, 50¢ children 7–13.

Wheelchair accessible except for a few steps. (Downtown)

STEVES HOMESTEAD
509 King William St.
San Antonio
210/227-9160
Prominent German businessman Edward Steves built his family retreat on

the banks of the San Antonio River in 1876. Donated to the San Antonio Conservation Society in 1952, the home and grounds have been preserved as an outstanding example of some of the King William District's gorgeous architecture. Inside the limestone, French/Italian villa–style main house are many of the heirloom furniture pieces passed down in the Steves family. Outbuildings include a carriage house (complete with antique carriages), gardener's quarters, laundry house, and natatorium (enclosed swimming pool). The elegant garden includes a bronze fountain Steves purchased at the 1876 Philadelphia Centennial Exhibition. Definitely a must-see. Daily 10–4:15 (subject to change). $2. Wheelchair accessible with advance arrangements. (Downtown)

THE TEXAS ADVENTURE
307 Alamo Plaza
San Antonio
210/227-8224
This century-spanning attraction on Alamo Plaza uses startling high-tech

The Alamo, p. 88

SACVB/Al Rendon

effects to present the birth of Texas narrated by the ghosts of Davy Crockett, Jim Bowie, Juan Seguin, and Colonel William B. Travis. Dubbed "an Encountarium F/X Theatre," the adventure will draw in even those who find history a bit on the dusty side. Daily 10–10; shows begin every 30 minutes. $6.50 adults, $5.90 seniors and military, $4.50 children 3–11. ⑂ (Downtown)

TEXAS HIGHWAY PATROL MUSEUM
812 S. Alamo St.
San Antonio
210/231-6030
This fledgling museum, opened in 1998, was a five-year labor of love by current Texas State Troopers and the families and survivors of those who have fallen in the line of duty. The 13,000-square-foot exhibit space houses displays dedicated to the Highway Patrol Medal of Valor, History Hall, and "A Day in the Life of a Trooper." The museum is not only a memorial to 73 troopers who have given their lives, but also an educational resource dedicated to history and prevention. The near future will bring an expansion of the museum to 20,000 square feet which will include a driver education facility. Open Tue–Sun 10–4. Free. ⑂ (Downtown)

TEXAS TROLLEY
Alamo Visitor Center
216 Alamo Plaza
San Antonio
210/228-9776
Texas Trolley offers the most comprehensive tour service in town. There are 60-minute narrated tours and on-and-off Trolley Hop passes for the Historic Tour (Alamo, River Walk, HemisFair Park, Missions San José and Concepción, Lone Star

What Is Fiesta?

If you read the accounts of the Alamo and San Jacinto battles in Chapter 1, you might think the middle of April would be more suited to mourning than celebrating. But it's during that month that San Antonio holds its signature event: Fiesta San Antonio, aka Fiesta.

And, boy, is it a party. For ten days, Downtown is useless as a business center. There are just too many parades, festivals, feasts, and frivolities—far too many to list here. But the highlights are:

Oyster Bake—*This music-filled kickoff event on the campus of St. Mary's University sends 90,000 of the little guys to meet their maker every year.*

A Taste of New Orleans—*San Antonio's Mardi Gras salutes the original with jazz bands and all things Cajun at Sunken Garden Amphitheatre.*

Fort Sam Fiesta and Fireworks—*The military gets the Fiesta spirit with a day of picnicking, concerts, and aerial pyrotechnics.*

Texas Cavaliers River Parade—*More than 40 river barges become floats for a parade on the downtown bend. Crowds are huge, pomp is palpable, and the fun is infectious.*

NIOSA *(Night in Old San Antonio)—This is actually four days and nights of food and music in La Villita and the surrounding area.*

Battle of Flowers Parade—*The tradition started in 1891 with a few church ladies throwing posies at each other. Today this event is one of the city's largest parades, with over 7,000 participants.*

King William Street Fair—*The historic neighborhood opens its streets, and some of its houses, to 1 million neighbors. (See King William District, this chapter.)*

Fiesta Flambeau Parade—*Yes, another parade, this time in the evening. Now you know why float manufacturers in town stay busy all year.*

There are many, many more Fiesta facets—over a hundred. Call the Convention and Visitor's Bureau at 800/447-3372 for a schedule.

Ten Best Reasons to Visit the River Walk

1. **River Walk Bottom Festival and Mud Parade** (late January)
2. **River Walk Mardi Gras** (early February)—arts and crafts, music, food, and another parade
3. **Starving Artists Show** (early April)—outstanding art along the banks and in La Villita
4. **Fiesta** (mid-April)
5. **Fiesta Noche del Rio** (June–August)—nightly music and dance at the Arneson River Theatre
6. **Pachango del Rio** (early September)—sample more than 25 River Walk restaurants
7. **River Art Group Show** (early October)—hundreds of artists from across Texas offer their wares
8. **River Walk Lighting Ceremony and Holiday River Parade** (Friday after Thanksgiving)
9. **Holiday Boat Caroling** (late November–Christmas)—floating serenaders salute the season
10. **Fiesta de las Luminarias** (throughout December)—River Walk is lined with thousands of *luminarias* (candles)

Museums, El Mercado, San Fernando Cathedral, and La Villita) and Uptown Tour (Fort Sam Houston, Botanical Center, McNay Art Museum, Olmos Park, Zoo, Brackenridge Park, Witte Museum, and San Antonio Museum of Art). Also available are the Grand Tour of San Antonio (departing 9–5), which includes both of the above, and Highlights of San Antonio Tour (Alamo, San José and Concepción, Lone Star, and El Mercado). To get out of downtown, opt for the Hill Country Magic Tour (See Chapter 13, Day Trips). Prices range from $8.95 for one-hour tours to two-day Hop passes for $19.95 (children half-price). (Downtown)

TOWER OF THE AMERICAS
HemisFair Park
San Antonio
210/207-8615
This might be the ideal place to begin exploring San Antonio. The 750-foot tower—taller than both Seattle's Space Needle and the Washington Monument—was built for HemisFair and stands in the middle of the park of the same name. Its glassed-in observation deck at around the 600-foot mark offers a panoramic view of the city. For the vertigo-free, a second observation area is open to the elements. Above them both is a restaurant that rotates once each hour (See Chapter

4, Where to Eat). Sun–Thu 9 a.m.–10 p.m., Fri–Sat 9 a.m.–11 p.m. $3 adults, $2 seniors, $1 children 4–11. Ꮭ except for outside observation area. (Downtown)

VIA STREETCAR
All around Downtown
San Antonio
210/227-2020
VIA Metropolitan Transit's vintage-look streetcars—rubber-tired reproductions of the elegant trolleys that operated in San Antonio 50 years ago—continuously circulate among the most popular downtown tourist destinations. Each ride costs 25¢, and commemorative tokens are available at several locations as take-home mementos. Call for route and schedule information, or look for the distinctive green, arch-top trolley stop signs. Hint: Ask the driver if you can ring the bell. (Downtown)

YANAGUANA CRUISES
The River Walk
San Antonio
210/244-5710

The name Yanaguana (yah-nah-GWAH-nah), meaning "clear water," was given to the San Antonio River by the Payaya Indians. This cruise line offers round-trip, 35-minute rides along 2.5 miles of the river's downtown route, complete with a live-narration guide to historic and popular sites. For a more expensive, though far more romantic trip, call ahead and reserve a place on a dinner cruise catered by one of the River Walk's fine restaurants. Daily tours leave hourly 9 a.m.–10 p.m. (including holidays). $4 adults and children 6 and over, $3 seniors and military, $1 children 5 and under. Tickets are available at the Alamo Visitors Center and on the lagoon at Rivercenter. (Note: Only one barge is wheelchair accessible. It leaves from the Rivercenter station.) Ꮭ (Downtown)

NORTHEAST

FORT SAM HOUSTON
N. New Braunfels Ave.
at Grayson St.
Fort Sam Houston

Splashtown, p. 104

SACVB/Al Rendon

Fun Facts about the River Walk

- *After the floods of 1921 and 1929, city leaders wanted to drain and pave over the downtown stretch of river. Robert Hugman, a farsighted young architect, convinced them to turn lead into gold by converting the river into a park. Due to the Great Depression, groundbreaking didn't happen for ten years.*

- *The Works Progress Administration began constructing the footbridges, staircases, sidewalks, and dams in 1938 and completed them by 1941. More than 11,000 trees were planted on the banks.*

- *One of the first businesses to locate facing the river was an architect's office—Robert Hugman's—in 1946. Next to him was the river's first restaurant, Casa Rio (River House).*

- *The River Walk District and River Walk Advisory Board were formed in 1962 as riverside businesses took an interest in creating attractive facades on the "backs" of their buildings.*

- *In preparation for the 1968 World's Fair, HemisFair, the city dedicated $500,000 to river improvements.*

- *HemisFair brought world attention to the River Walk and secured for San Antonio the nickname "America's Venice," bestowed by columnist Ernie Pyle nearly 30 years earlier.*

- *The downtown bend is drained and its concrete bottom cleaned each year in January, prompting the Bottom Festival and Mud Parade.*

- *Park rangers get around in boats.*

- *Most stretches of the river are shallow enough to stand up in. (Note: This is discouraged.)*

- *River Walk fish and the occasional turtle have developed a taste for little pieces of tortilla.*

GREATER SAN ANTONIO

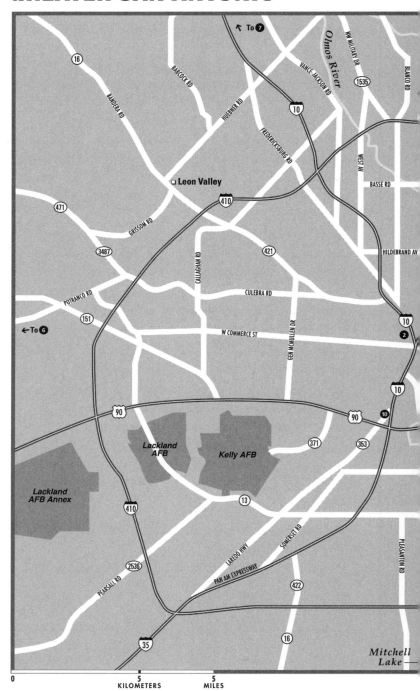

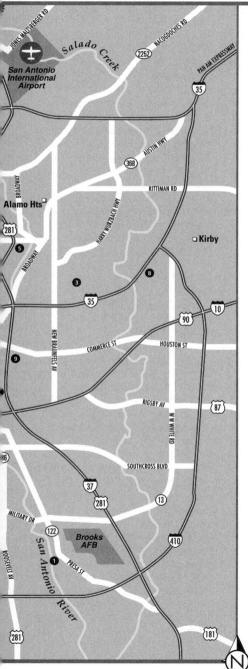

Sights and Attractions in Greater San Antonio

 1 Acequias and Aqueduct (S)
 2 Chapel of the Miracles (NW)
 3 Fort Sam Houston (NE)
 4 Mission Trail (S)
 5 San Antonio Zoological Gardens and
   Aquarium (NE)
 6 Sea World of Texas (NW)
 7 Six Flags Fiesta Texas (NW)
 8 Splashtown (NE)
 9 Sunset Depot (NE)
10 Union Stockyards (NW)

210/221-1886

Home of the U.S. Army Medical Command, Fort Sam offers a microcosmic study of San Antonio's history. The base has too many interesting facets to list here, but a visit to the museum in Building 123 will get you a self-guided tour map and a list of the many interesting sights within the fort's gates. These include the site of the first military aircraft flight, the U.S. Army Medical Museum, the home occupied by newlyweds Lt. and Mrs. Dwight D. Eisenhower, the FSH National Cemetery, as well as the first WAAC (Women's Army Auxiliary Corps) unit. The Fort Sam Quadrangle, where Apache Chief Geronimo was held prisoner in 1886, is a favorite with kids, who enjoy hand-feeding the deer herds that have lived here for over 100 years. Wed–Sun 10–4. Free. ₺ (Northeast)

SAN ANTONIO ZOOLOGICAL GARDENS AND AQUARIUM
Brackenridge Park
3903 N. St. Mary's St.
San Antonio
210/734-7183

The collection of animal life at the zoo may only be Texas' third-largest (at 3,400 examples), but the surrounding grounds must surely be some of the state's prettiest. There's plenty of shade to ensure cool strolling from one animal to the next amid native and exotic plants and some free-roaming birds. Animals are separated by habitat type, such as African veldt, Amazon rain forest, and Australian Outback. Several feeding and behavior shows run continuously throughout the day. A play area is available for the kids when they tire of nature's wonders, and a petting zoo lets them get up close and personal. Memorial Day–Labor Day daily 9–6:30, rest of

the year 9–5. Note: You can stay in the park past closing time, till 8 p.m., in summer. $6 adults, $4 children 3–11. ₺ (Northeast)

SPLASHTOWN
3600 I-35 N.
San Antonio
210/227-1400

This elaborate, 18-acre waterpark features a multitude of very wet attractions, from enclosed and open waterslides high in the air to wave pools and "river raft" rides on the ground. In summer months Splashtown presents "dive-in movies," projected on the shore of one of the many pools. Season openings and closings vary. Sun–Thur 11–9, Fri– Sat 11–11. $17.99 adults, $12.99 children shorter than 48 inches. ₺ (Northeast)

SUNSET DEPOT
St. Paul Square
1174 E. Commerce St.
San Antonio
210/227-5371

You'll also find this historic structure listed in Chapter 12, Nightlife, and some San Antonians aren't happy about it. The constant press by city leaders to offer tourist-oriented activities downtown led to a transformation of the depot into an entertainment and dining complex, along the lines of Orlando's Church Street Station. Actual train service has been relegated to an unimpressive temporary building out back. The remarkably beautiful pink "adobe" Sunset Depot was San Antonio's Ellis Island, the terminus for immigrants from around the globe. The architecture of the 1903 edifice is a salute to the Spanish missions and is itself nearly church-like. The effect is completed by the elegant stained glass of the Rose Window on the south end looking out on the Alamodome.

Oddball and Obscure

Close Encounter: *While many cities discourage illegal aliens, they're welcome at 103 Old Towne Road in Seguin, just east of San Antonio. That's the address of the Mutual Unidentified Flying Object Network, America's largest UFO research center.*

East Meets Southwest: *On Highway 87 just outside the eastern city limits is the tiny hamlet of China Grove. The town would be completely unknown if it hadn't been for the Doobie Brothers's song.*

Heads of State: *A small but elegant waterworks building in Brackenridge Park off Broadway once served as the studio for renowned sculptor Gutzon Borglum. It was here that Borglum did his miniature studies for the sculpting of Mount Rushmore in the 1920s.*

Back to Nature: *Southeast of the city on Old Corpus Christi Road is the community of Elmendorf, home of the Riverside Nudist Resort. This 17-acre campground and community on the banks of the San Antonio River welcomes those who want to get a little more Texas sun than everyone else.*

Their Honored Dead: *The Fort Sam Houston National Military Cemetery has row upon row of markers for U.S. war dead. But far in the back is a small plot dedicated to German, Japanese, and Italian soldiers who died as prisoners of war at Fort Sam during World War II.*

Bovine Bane: *San Antonio's City Hall is famous for barbs—political and otherwise. It was on the grounds now occupied by that edifice that entrepreneur John Gates demonstrated the new-fangled barbed wire to ranchers in the 1870s, ending the era of open-prairie grazing.*

A Tree Grows in Alamo Heights: *San Antonio's most historic bus stop is found outside a supermarket on Broadway in Alamo Heights. Designed by Dionico Rodriguez in the late 1920s, the shelter/sculpture shades waiting riders under lifelike concrete trees.*

Santa's Helper: *At the intersection of Dewey Street and Main Avenue is a marker reading "North Pole—4,189 miles." No one knows why, though it's rumored St. Nick has a fondness for margaritas and needs a point home once a year.*

The controversial redevelopment did bring some welcome additions, including the re-creation of a long-lost stained-glass window on the north end. If you're interested only in history, just drive by and look. If you're interested in entertainment, see Chapter 12.

Just outside the depot's front door is a historic commercial area named St. Paul Square, once a center of African American businesses and gateway to the city's once predominantly black East Side. The square is also undergoing redevelopment. ♿ (Northeast)

NORTHWEST

CHAPEL OF THE MIRACLES
Salado St. at I-10
San Antonio
Nearly hidden beneath the interstate is one of the Alamo City's oldest religious institutions—El Capilla de Milagros, or the Chapel of Miracles. Constructed in the 1870s, El Capilla has been the pilgrimage terminus for thousands of believers who seek healing from physical afflictions. The source of that healing, which many swear by, is El Señor de los Milagros. This crucifix on display in the nave of the sanctuary is thought to be more than four centuries old. The chapel and crucifix are not officially sanctioned by the church, and both are privately owned. There is a small admission charge. (Northwest)

SEA WORLD OF TEXAS
10500 Sea World Dr.
San Antonio
210/523-3611
One of San Antonio's two large-scale tourist attractions, Anheuser Busch's Sea World boasts 25 shows, exhibits, rides, and attractions on its 250 acres,

Tower of the Americas, p. 99

SACVB/Al Rendon

nearly all with an aquatic theme. While the park claims an active role in sealife research, it is nonetheless a theme park—and a very successful one. The star attraction is—are—Shamu, the killer whale(s). (There's actually no single whale named Shamu, but don't tell the kids.) Shamu's arena is a vast pool and stadium in which whales and their trainers perform mind-boggling stunts. Other shows feature sea lions, exotic birds, an exciting troupe of waterskiers, and megapop concerts throughout spring and summer. Park opens at 10 a.m.; days and closing times vary with the season, so call ahead. $29.95 adults (10 percent off for seniors), $19.95 children 3–11. ♿ (Northwest)

SIX FLAGS FIESTA TEXAS
17000 I-10 W.
San Antonio
210/697-5050
This 200-acre family entertainment complex has undergone some changes since it was purchased by the Time Warner/Six Flags chain in

1995. Though the original concept of a musical theme park has not been completely abandoned, additional rides have been added, as have kid-centered shows featuring cartoon characters and superheroes. High-quality musical entertainment for all ages can be found in the park's Mexican, Old West, American (circa 1950), and German areas. Fiesta Texas includes a water park, so go prepared to get wet, then stay late for a spectacular laser/fireworks show. Special celebrations are planned for Halloween and Thanksgiving through Christmas. Days open vary with season, so call ahead. $32 adults (48 inches and taller), $22.50 seniors, children (under 48 inches), and physically challenged. Parking $5 additional. See www.sixflags.com for more information. &. (Northwest)

UNION STOCKYARDS
1716 S. San Marcos St.
San Antonio
210/223-6331
San Antonio's ranching heritage lives on in the oldest livestock market south of Kansas City. Monday and Wednesday mornings bring livestock auctions conducted by hyperspeed auctioneers, acting much as they did when the stockyards opened in the

---

Ten Commandments for Fiesta-Goers

- *Don't drive downtown if you can help it. Take VIA Park and Rides instead.*
- *Allow extra time. Fiesta traffic moves very slowly.*
- *Fiesta royalty has the right of way day and night during Fiesta. Watch for motorcades of new cars with flags, accompanied by police motorcycles.*
- *Dress for heat and sun during the day.*
- *There are three parades: two on the streets and one on the river. Catch all of them.*
- *A Night in Old San Antonio at La Villita is a great place to start getting the Fiesta spirit.*
- *Crowds can occasionally get thick, so hold on to the kids.*
- *Don't overdo the margaritas. They sneak up on you.*
- *Take money for sampling all of food and drink (good luck!) as well as for souvenirs.*
- *Learn the Chicken Dance at Sauerkraut Bend in La Villita Assembly Hall.*

1880s. City slickers take note: The atmosphere at the stockyards is full of more than just history. Open daily. Free. Mostly wheelchair accessible. (Northwest)

SOUTH

ACEQUIAS AND AQUEDUCT
Mission Rd. north of U.S. 281
San Antonio
210/229-5701
The Spanish missionaries who settled this arid land quickly learned the value of a steady water supply. With the help of natives who were proselytized while they worked, the Franciscans oversaw the construction of an elaborate, 15-mile web of *acequias*—irrigation ditches modeled on Muslim-built canals in Spain. Water trapped by the Espada Dam was collected in the *acequia madre* (the mother of all ditches), then routed via the other *acequias* to 3,500 acres of land. Most of the canals are gone

Mission Espada at San Antonio Missions National Historic Park

© John Elk III

now, though examples can still be found within the Alamo compound and in HemisFair Park next to the playground. The most impressive segment of the network is the Espada Aqueduct, which bore river water over Piedras Creek. This double-arched stone span, over 250 years old, still carries water to area farms. (South)

MISSION TRAIL
San Antonio Missions National
Historical Park
Beginning on Mission Rd.
at S. St. Mary's St.
San Antonio
210/534-8833
Retrace the path of the Spanish missionaries along the Mission Trail. The Alamo is the oldest mission and the northern terminus, but Mission Road begins just north of U.S. 90/I-10. The road, which roughly follows the San Antonio River, can be confusing, so follow the signs. The entire trail has been designated a National Historical Park, and is currently being reshaped to include greenbelt spaces and a bike trail by the year 2000. (The trail is too far to walk, unless you're a dedicated missionary.) Along the trail you'll find the other four missions in the Alamo chain. Their names have been shortened considerably over time, but the words are still as beautiful as the old structures themselves:

Mission Concepción (1731): Concepción is one of three missions built in East Texas, then moved to San Antonio when their original mission fields proved unfruitful or unfriendly. All that remains of the Concepción compound is a beautiful, twin-towered church constructed in 1755, its interior displaying remarkable wall paintings. With its two impressive bell towers

MISSION TRAIL

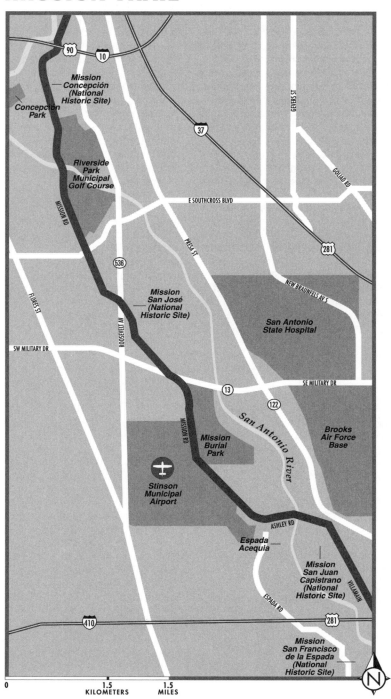

visible for quite a distance, it became headquarters for decades of regional religious festivals.

Mission San José (1720): The largest and best known (in its day) of the San Antonio River missions, San José at one time housed 300 people within its grounds. The mission also picked up an unfortunate second vocation as a fortress against attacks by Apaches and Comanches. So successful was it as a stronghold that it was favorably compared to military forts in the region. San José's trademark is the chapel's legendary Rose Window.

Mission San Juan Capistrano (1731): Another East Texas émigré, San Juan became a renowned supplier of produce to the region, including the other missions. So prolific were the San Juan farmers that their fruits and vegetables were traded as far east as Louisiana and south to Mexico. Today the mission is fertile in another way—as a parish church hosting daily Mass.

Mission San Francisco de la Espada (1731): The chapel of the third relocated mission is perhaps the most stereotypical in appearance. The three bell niches in its arched facade are familiar from countless films set in Mexican villages, though the church's most striking feature is an elaborately arched doorway nearly Moorish in appearance. Espada was beset with misfortune brought by Apaches and smallpox, but weathered them all to remain the most charming—and most remote—of the five missions.

Before taking on your mission mission, stop at the Visitor's Center in the 3200 block of Roosevelt Avenue. The center features a multilingual, interactive video introduction to the park. Hours: 9–5 daily except Thanksgiving, Christmas, and New Year's Day. Admission: Free. Wheelchair accessible but with some difficulty at San Juan and Espada. ♿ (South)

6

MUSEUMS AND GALLERIES

While some of San Antonio's arts persona is nurtured by its Southwestern location and heritage, so far the Alamo City has managed to avoid Santa Fe Syndrome: an overwhelming glut of Cowboy and Indian art. In fact, there is remarkable representation from all cultures and eras throughout the city's aesthetic sites—along with some regional kitsch, which only adds to the local personality and ambience.

Serious art lovers will find collections rivaling those in larger cities, while folk-art devotees may decide to stay. They might even choose to move in, in fact, to the spanking new Nelson A. Rockefeller Center for Latin American Art at the San Antonio Museum of Art. The sciences are well-represented in several museums, and of course San Antonio's military heritage has incubated important profiles of American warfare on some of the local bases. Similar variety is found in local galleries, which offer everything from the cheerful skeletons of Mexico's Dia de los Muertos to cutting-edge contemporary works. If you're intent on seeing it all, you'd better shop for a house while you're here.

ART MUSEUMS

MCNAY ART MUSEUM
6000 N. New Braunfels Ave.
San Antonio
210/824-5368

Art lover Marion Koogler McNay would be delighted at what has become of her Atlee and Robert Ayres–designed Mediterranean and Southwestern–style mansion. It's filled with flat and 3-D works by some of the greatest masters of the last 150 years, including Picasso, Cézanne, Gauguin, Rodin, and Matisse, on permanent display. In fact, when it opened to the public in 1954, the McNay was Texas's first museum of modern art. It also proffers frequent, highly regarded visiting exhibits, so call ahead to see what's here while you are. Outside the mansion is as beautiful as in, with 23 acres of virtuosic landscaping particularly in the courtyard and sculpture garden, and a reflecting pool buoying a striking metal sculpture. Tue–Sat 10–5, Sun noon–5. Best of all, the museum is free. & (Northeast)

SAN ANTONIO MUSEUM OF ART
200 W. Jones Ave.
San Antonio
210/978-8100
One of San Antonio's most acclaimed renovation projects, SAMA is housed in the former Lone Star Brewery, Texas' largest at the turn of the century. SAMA's lofty galleries on the

Public Art

San Antonio is not a hotbed of public art, unless you include the omnipresent, usually unwelcome (though often fascinating) works of "taggers"—graffiti artists. In fact, a 1997 vote of the people to set aside 1 percent of the cost of city-funded construction projects for public art passed by the narrowest of margins, and only after acrimonious debate in city council chambers and the media. The ordinance was rescinded soon after.

One form of art, however, is almost universally accepted by Alamo City residents. The mural, which has its roots in Mexican folk art, is a prized addition to the interior and exterior walls of many San Antonio buildings. Notable, large-scale pieces are found in the lobby of the U.S. Post Office on Alamo Plaza, in HemisFair Park, and at the Lila Cockrell Theatre in the Convention Center. Particularly impressive is The Spirit of Healing, a stunning six-story tile mural by Jesse Treviño on the outside of Santa Rosa Children's Hospital (519 W. Houston St.). But the true spirit of San Antonio is found in newer murals created by local artists, some with the volunteer assistance of neighborhood residents and children. Any street on the predominantly Hispanic west side will proffer numerous such examples on neighborhood buildings and community centers.

A related work of public art is the Mission Bridge, which carries Houston Street over the river downtown. The 1990 bridge's lampposts feature representations of the historic missions, interpreting San Antonio's religious beginnings and heritage in colorful ceramic tile.

banks of the river house substantial permanent collections of Chinese, Greek, Roman, and pre-Columbian antiquities. Its palette of paintings is more varied than the McNay's, with works dating as far back as the 1800s. Folk-art lovers will find nirvana at SAMA, with three major collections of Americana and similarly attractive groups of Mexican and Texan quilts, crafts, and furniture. The two foremost among these collections are housed in the astounding new Nelson A. Rockefeller Center for Latin American Art. The center, occupying an $11 million new wing, is America's most important statement about the art of Central and South America. Pieces in the collection span 3,000 years, from 1,000 B.C. to today. Mon–Sat 10–5 (Tue to 9 p.m.), Sun noon–5. $4 adults, $2 seniors and students (with I.D.), $1.75 children 4–11; free Tue 3–9. ♿ (Downtown)

SCIENCE AND HISTORY MUSEUMS

HERTZBERG CIRCUS MUSEUM
210 Market St.
San Antonio
210/207-7810
Not only does the Hertzberg offer circus history, it's in a historic building: San Antonio's first public library, built with $50,000 from Andrew Carnegie in 1902. Today the building houses one of the largest collections of circus memorabilia in the world, the nucleus of which was donated by local circus maven Harry Hertzberg in 1940. Over 20,000 items are on display, including posters, photographs, sheet music, and artifacts. Among the latter are a 1902 circus parade wagon, a wooden sphinx from the Ringling Brothers' wagon, and gadgets and props associated with

Hertzberg Circus Museum

legendary circus performers. Performance videos are shown hourly. See also Chapter 7, Kids' Stuff. Mon–Sat 10–5, Sun and holidays noon–5. $2.50 adults, $2 seniors, $1 children 3–12, free to active military. One-hour free parking across Market Street in River Bend Garage. (Downtown)

INSTITUTE OF TEXAN CULTURES
HemisFair Park
Bowie and Durango Sts.
San Antonio
210/458-2300
If one goal for your visit is learning about Texas history and you haven't a clue where to start, make the institute your first stop. This low-slung building in HemisFair Park served as the Texas Pavilion during the 1968 World's Fair, then was taken over by the University of Texas. It's a treasure trove of Texas's roots, with special emphasis on the 27 native and immigrant cultures that have contributed to the state. Large, fascinating exhibits are family-friendly, as are frequent programs and presentations. The best time to be here is late

July/early August for the Texas Folklife Festival, when Texan cultures really come to life with food, crafts, and entertainment on the museum grounds. You'll be so fascinated, you'll forget the heat. Tue–Sun 9–5 (except Thanksgiving and Christmas). $4 adults, $2 seniors and children 3–12. Prices do not include Folklife Festival. & (Downtown)

LONE STAR
BUCKHORN MUSEUMS
Houston St. at Presa St.
San Antonio
210/270-9467
This San Antonio landmark only recently moved to central downtown from the old Lone Star Brewery, ending an era. Not all of the collection was able to make the move and some was purchased by collectors, but much of the contents of the several museums remains. This includes the famous Halls of Horns, Feathers, and Fins, displaying taxidermied examples of native Texas and exotic fauna. The Hall of Texas History Wax Museums bring to life the people and events that birthed the state between 1532 and 1898, and the contents of the O. Henry House includes artifacts from the life of the legendary Texas writer.

Note: The Hall of Horns, which contains the world's largest collection of antlery, began as a "bring your own" decorating project at the Buckhorn Saloon in the 1880s, where cowpokes and trappers would trade their wares for drinks. Leave your own trophies at home, however. The "New Buckhorn" will include a restaurant in the transplanted Buckhorn Saloon, with Texas-size appetizers and alcoholic and soft drinks. Daily 9:30–5. $5 adults, $4 seniors and children 6–11. & (Downtown)

TEXAS TRANSPORTATION
MUSEUM
11731 Wetmore Rd.
San Antonio
210/490-3554
This labor of love by local train aficionados features preserved and restored transportation pieces from

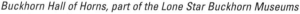

Buckhorn Hall of Horns, part of the Lone Star Buckhorn Museums

SACVB/Al Rendon

Public Sculptures Worth Spotting

Carmen Luna y Canto *(Victor Gutierrez, 1990)—Galeria Ortiz, 102 Concho St.*

Father Demian's Table *(Rolando Briseño, 1987)—River Walk south of Navarro St. bridge*

Hill 881 South, *Vietnam memorial (Austin Deuel, 1986)—105 Auditorium Circle*

Mi Casa es Su Casa, *tr. "My House Is Your House" (Diana Calvillo de Chapa, 1992)—HemisFair Park at Market St.*

Steel Sculpture *(Michael Bigger, 1981)—Universidad Nacional Autónoma de Mexico in HemisFair Plaza*

Sunset Spiral fountain *(Richard Harell Rogers, 1985)—Nations Bank Plaza, Convent and Navarro Sts.*

Three Way Piece No. 1 *(Henry Moore, 1964)—1 Alamo Center, Commerce and St. Mary's Sts.*

Triumph *(Larry Graber, 1981)—Vista Verde at I-10*

Untitled *(Sandy Stine, 1989)—Bexar County Justice Center, 300 Dolorosa St.*

Untitled fountain *(Marmon Mok Architects, 1974)—Soledad at Martin Sts.*

Texas history. Horse- and people-powered vehicles are on display, as well as noisier transport options from the steam and fossil-fuel eras and an antique depot. Miniature railroads re-create lost or forgotten rail equipment, and most weekends feature rides behind the museum's antique switch engine. The auto collection spans the '20s to the '70s. Train cars are not wheelchair accessible. Thu, Sat, Sun 9–4. Trains run Sun 12:30–3:30, leaving every 45 minutes. $4 adults, $2 children, $10 family maximum. (Northeast)

WITTE MUSEUM
Brackenridge Park
3801 Broadway
San Antonio
210/357-1900
The Witte (WIT-ee) stands out among Alamo City museums not only because it's in a dedicated museum building rather than a restored mansion or brewery but also because its mission is to make natural and local history enjoyable for families. Permanent exhibits showcase area residents, from dinosaurs through the defenders of the Alamo, in the main

La Villita Historic District

Set aside an afternoon. The "Little Village," which was the site of the original Spanish settlement (see Chapter 5, Sights and Attractions), is now a haven of craft studios, galleries, and boutiques. You'll find a broad spectrum of artistic offerings in all media, from antique to very contemporary paintings, sculpture, jewelry, fabric, stained glass, and photography. When hunger for art is overcome by physical cravings, tasty, casual dining establishments offer a ready remedy. Several art exhibitions and festivals are held throughout the year, with the liveliest during spring's Fiesta. Some buildings are not wheelchair accessible. For more information, call 210/207-8610.

building and restored houses out back. But traveling, high-tech exhibits of the microscopic and the monstrous have proven to be real family favorites. Call to see who's visiting when you are. A favorite for local and visiting youngsters is the four-story Science Treehouse. Featured in the public television series "TeleVentures," the Treehouse tempts with science-based entertainment such as musical laser beams and launchable tennis balls. See also Chapter 7, Kids' Stuff. June–Aug Mon–Sat 10–6 (Tue to 9 p.m.), Sun noon–5; rest of the year Mon–Sat 10–5, Sun noon–5. $5 adults, $3 children. & (Northeast)

MILITARY MUSEUMS

Note: When you visit any of San Antonio's bases, military security protocols apply. Weapons are not allowed, and vehicles are subject to search. As a courtesy in the evening, approach sentry stations with only parking lights on.

**AIR FORCE HISTORY
AND TRADITIONS MUSEUM**
Lackland Air Force Base
Orville Wright Dr.
San Antonio
210/671-3444
Lackland's base museum boasts a collection of historic aircraft to delight the aerophile in the family, as well as photographic, static, and dioramic displays of San Antonio and America's rich military aviation history, from balloons to rockets. Tue–Sat, call for times. Free. & (South)

MUSEUM OF FLIGHT MEDICINE
Brooks Air Force Base
Lindbergh Dr.
San Antonio
210/536-2203
Hangar Nine, which houses the museum, is the oldest such structure in the United States. And while Air

Many San Antonio art lovers lean toward the conservative. But in July, the more adventuresome venture out for Contemporary Art Month, a 14-year-old celebration of the cultural avant garde. Nearly a hundred exhibits of more than 250 artists are featured at most San Antonio art spaces, particularly Southtown's "Art in the 'Hood" and the Blue Star Art Space.

Force history is well represented, this museum-in-progress has definitely moved into the late twentieth century with exhibits of aerospace and astronaut medicine. Mon–Fri 8–4. Free. ⅍ (South)

U.S. ARMY MEDICAL MUSEUM
Fort Sam Houston
Harry Wurzbach and Stanley Rd.
San Antonio
210/221-6358
The entire history of U.S. Army medicine is in the spotlight at this fascinating museum. Photographs and displays document military healing practices through times of war and peace since the nation's birth, and research efforts to meet the medical needs of America's troops. Particularly interesting—and sobering—are displays of U.S. and captured enemy medical equipment and supplies, including the makeshift instruments used by heroic Capt. Thomas Hewlett to treat his fellow prisoners of war in Japan during WWII. Lectures are provided on a regular schedule, so call to find out what will be available during your visit. Wed–Sun 10–4. Free. ⅍ (Northeast)

GALLERIES

BLUE STAR ART SPACE
1400 block of S. Alamo St.
San Antonio

Museums That Started Out as Something Else

- *San Antonio Museum of Art—Lone Star Brewery*
- *Buckhorn Museums—Lone Star Brewery*
- *McNay Art Museum—Private home of Marion Koogler McNay*
- *Hertzberg Circus Museum—San Antonio's first public library*
- *Institute of Texan Cultures—Texas Pavilion for the 1968 World's Fair*

Places to Find Unusual Art

ArtPace
  445 N. Main St.
  210/212-4900

Center for Spirituality and the Arts
  707 Broadway
  210/829-5980

Nueva Street Gallery
  507 E. Nueva St.
  210/229-9810

One9Zero6 Gallery
  1906 S. Flores St.
  210/227-5718

San Antonio Art League Museum
  130 King William St.
  210/223-1140

Wong Spot
  1502 S. Flores St.
  210/475-0771

210/227-6960

The proverbial silk purse from a sow's ear, the Blue Star complex took a decrepit handful of warehouse spaces, updated them, and filled them with galleries, studios, a brewpub, and a theater. The offerings of the lofty, utilitarian gallery/studios are predominantly contemporary, often cutting-edge. Throughout the year, tenants collaborate to provide artsy activities, many of them family-oriented. Call ahead for a schedule or just show up and browse. A tribute to the success of the Blue Star is the fact that some non-tenant artists have relocated their studios to the surrounding area, turning a crumbling industrial neighborhood into San Antonio's liveliest contemporary art center. Each July, Blue Star is one of the Contemporary Art Month headquarters. See www.bluestar.net for more information. Partially wheelchair accessible. (Downtown)

CARVER COMMUNITY CULTURAL CENTER
226 N. Hackberry St.
San Antonio
210/207-2234

Primarily a performance venue (see Chapter 11, Performing Arts), the Carver also frequently features art exhibits in its lobby space. Works by some of the city's finest artists, African American and otherwise, may be found here. Call for current exhibitions. Mon–Fri 9–6 (evening and weekend events vary). & (Northeast)

GALERIA ORTIZ
El Mercado St.
102 S. Concho St.
San Antonio
210/225-0731

A standout among the several galleries in Market Square, Ortiz specializes in quality pieces that reflect the Latino spirit of San Antonio. Sculpture, jewelry, paintings, and folk art by some of the finest artists of South

Texas and North Mexico are represented, most with contemporary flair. Daily 10–8. (Downtown)

**GREENHOUSE
GALLERY OF FINE ART
2218 Breezewood St.
San Antonio
210/828-6491**

This Alamo Heights gallery offers original oils and bronzes, fine art glass, and antique etchings and engravings. A subspecialty is nature art, including wildlife stamps and prints, and old and new botanical and watercolor paintings. Call for hours. For more information see www.greenhousegallery.com. ᕫ (Northeast)

One Not-So-Notable Sculpture

American Federation of Labor founder Samuel Gompers wasn't born in San Antonio. In fact, he probably visited only once, passing through by train from a rally in Mexico in 1924. What was to have been an overnight stay at the St. Anthony Hotel, however, instead became Gompers' eternal layover—he died during the visit.

To commemorate that singular salute from their hero, the Texas/San Antonio chapter of the AFL-CIO commissioned a statue of Gompers from sculptor Betty Gene Alden in 1982. The resulting concrete and plastic stucco tribute, which stands on Market Street across from the Henry B. Gonzalez Convention Center, is widely regarded as the ugliest piece of art in town. In fact, while the Fairmount Hotel was being moved down Market Street in 1985, spectating locals shouted encouragement to workers to divert the hotel's route slightly and give Gompers his second San Antonio demise.

Bluebonnet Paintings

South Texas's enviable array of wildflowers might be expected to conjure the painting muse for aspiring and accomplished artists. Indeed, next to renderings of the Alamo from every conceivable angle (some fictional), wildflower paintings are probably San Antonio's most prevalent art form. These are often disparagingly dismissed by jaded locals as "bluebonnet paintings," after the ubiquitous state flower.

Granted, bluebonnets are a tempting, cooperative subject for less accomplished paletteers. If your route to San Antonio takes you through International Airport's Terminal 2, you may see some lesser efforts on your short walk from the concourse to the luggage carousel. But some very talented painters have found inspiration in the fields surrounding the city, and their oils and watercolors can be found in many of the city's galleries. If the beauty of South Texas wildflowers speaks to you, by all means, take one of these paintings home. Long after our bluebonnets have disappeared under gray winter skies, they'll still be in your living room. And they look good with any sofa.

GUADALUPE CULTURAL ARTS CENTER
1300 Guadalupe St.
San Antonio
210/271-3151

While the indoor and outdoor theaters at the Guadalupe are its primary attractions (see Chapter 11, Performing Arts), exhibitions showcasing Latino art are frequent and fascinating. In fact, the Guadalupe is nationally recognized as a Hispanic arts mecca. Classes are also offered in various forms of contemporary and traditional Mexican and Chicano art. Call for current exhibitions.

Mon–Fri 8:30–6 (evening and weekend events vary). ♿ (Northwest)

SOUTHWEST SCHOOL OF ART AND CRAFT
300 Augusta St.
San Antonio
210/224-1848

This Catholic girls' academy turned art school/gallery/downtown oasis sits on one of the River Walk's loveliest bits of property (see Chapter 5, Sights and Attractions). Airy galleries continually offer outstanding shows of visiting and resident artists. The French-influenced architecture on the grounds, dating to

1851, is a work of art in itself, including an elegant chapel rich in stained glass. Stay for lunch at the Copper Kitchen restaurant and dine riverside. If the length of your stay allows, you can study with one of several staff teachers, with special programs offered for children. Mon–Sat 10–4. ♿ (Downtown)

TEXAS TRAILS GALLERY
245 Losoya St.
San Antonio
210/224-7865

The name says it all. TT is the place to find traditional Lone Star and neighboring state flatworks and bronzes, including contributions by Native American artists. A visit to the gallery offers a nostalgic, though sometimes romanticized, look back at the Old West. A fascinating contrast can be found by first visiting either Texas Trails or the Keene Gallery, then strolling across the street to the other. Call for hours. ♿ (Downtown)

WILLIAMS SCULPTURE
WORKS & STUDIO
712-C S. St. Mary's St.

San Antonio Museum of Art, p. 112

San Antonio
210/354-0155

The Sculpture Works is the only studio in town where you can browse a collection of the artist's sculptures while waiting to see what's next in or out of the kiln. Don Williams' specialty is contemporary bronze. Call for hours. (Downtown)

Natural Bridge Wildlife Park

7

Much of San Antonio's appeal is rooted in its vivid history. After all, the birth of the Great State of Texas made the city a tourist destination in the first place. But face it: You can spend only so much time at the Alamo and the other missions, in San Fernando Cathedral and the King William Historic District, before your offspring are subtly squirming in their seats, or outright hollering in protest. That's the time to lighten up and avail yourself of less educational but (admit it, you think so, too) far-more-fun attractions. Best of all, several of San Antonio's family-oriented attractions present both education and fun. Those, of course, are the best and most memorable.

ANIMALS AND THE GREAT OUTDOORS

FORT SAM HOUSTON QUADRANGLE
N. New Braunfels Ave.
at Grayson St.
San Antonio
210/221-1886
Fort Sam is full of history but none of it as colorful as the quadrangle's. This stone enclosure was home to the Apache chief Geronimo when he and 30 of his warriors were held prisoner in 1886. While they were here,

camped in army-issue tents, they were surrounded by free-roaming, semi-tame deer, rabbits, and other Texas fauna. The Chief is gone, but the offspring of that wildlife remain, and feeding them by hand is a popular family outing. Wed–Sun 10–4. Free. (Northeast)

HEMISFAIR PARK
Bowie and Durango Sts.
San Antonio
210/207-8615
The park's 92 acres contain several attractions for young people, including the following: the Downtown All

Armadillos

San Antonio doesn't hold a trademark on the armadillo, the reclusive, armored citizen affectionately called the unofficial mascot of the Lone Star State. But enter a tourist-oriented gift shop in the Alamo City and you can't swing a plush, stuffed armadillo without hitting . . . lots and lots of plush, stuffed armadillos.

The Texas variety of this mammal, found throughout the southeast United States and Central and South America, is the nine-banded or long-nosed armadillo (Dasypus novemcinctus to those in the armadillo know). The "bands" are separations in the 'dillo's shell that allow it to move. Unlike some varieties, D. nov. can't roll completely into a ball when threatened. Instead, when in 'dillo danger, it pulls its legs and head in tight and sits close to the ground.

Armadillos are nocturnal and shy and have powerful front legs with which they dig up small invertebrates and insects very rapidly. Loose dirt is scattered by the hind legs, while wiggly delectables are pulled in by a sticky tongue—up to 40,000 ants at a sitting.

'Dillos harm no one larger than themselves. Sadly, their gentle nature has led to their abuse by people who ought to have better things to do. And their nocturnal habits often result in ill-advised ventures onto Texas roads. In fact, the only place you're likely to see the Texas mascot during your visit (aside from the San Antonio Zoo) is on the highway shoulder. 'Dillos are also a part of some people's diets, particularly in Mexico.

Ironically, though armadillos have suffered at the hands—and under the wheels—of man, they have been of enormous benefit to mankind. Their species is the only other, besides homo sapiens, prone to Hansen's disease, better known as leprosy. Research on armadillos has led to the near eradication of this once-dreaded disease in most countries. However, a San Antonio clinician has demonstrated a link between contact with infected, wild armadillos and Hansen's in humans. Best advice? Leave 'em alone. That's the way the gentle 'dillo wants it anyway.

Around Playground with kid-designed wooden playsets; the Tower of the Americas; a number of fountains (including a flowing set of terraces that feed the sprawling "water garden"), and lots of room in which to run around and get worn out. Sun–Thu 9 a.m.–10 p.m. Free. (Downtown)

MILAM PARK PLAYGROUND
Commerce St.
across from Market Square
San Antonio
210/207-8480
This popular and free playsite is named after Texan patriot "Ol'" Ben Milam. The colorful play equipment and open spaces offer the kids a great place to unwind. It's up to you whether or not to tell the kids that the park was created on top of a burial ground for San Antonio's original Canary Island settlers. Daily dawn–9 p.m. Free. ♿ (Downtown)

NATURAL BRIDGE CAVERNS
AND WILDLIFE PARK
26495 Natural Bridge Caverns Rd.
210/651-6101 (caverns)
210/438-7400 (park)
The underground partner of this pair is a rarity: a living cavern (still forming after 140 million years) open for tours. Among more than 10,000 notable formations on the 80-minute tour are the Castle of the White Giants, the Chandelier, the Bombburst, Purgatory Creek, and the namesake limestone bridge over the entrance. Aboveground to the north is the Wildlife Park, a drive-through taste of the veldt with dozens of species, including some vanishing ones. Food for the critters is available at the entrance gate for a couple of bucks, and most visitors drive through the park with their windows open to distribute it. Note: The animals are very tame,

and the ostriches, antelope, and zebras have no fear of sticking their heads in your window to ask for a bite. Very small children may be frightened, and bison saliva is difficult to wash off. Cavern tours depart 9–4 daily (9–6 June–August). Wildlife Park open 9–5 (9–6:30 in summer). Closed Thanksgiving, Christmas, and New Year's Day. Call for admission prices. No credit cards. Cave is not wheelchair accessible. (Northeast)

SAN ANTONIO
BOTANICAL GARDENS
555 Funston Pl.
San Antonio
210/207-3250
While they may not initially be interested in the huge variety of native and non-native flora, kids will be fascinated by moving from one enclosed biosphere to the next. Also on the 33-acre site are formal gardens, a Japanese garden (with traditional eye-fooling perspective tricks), and areas and activities created with young ones in mind. Tue–Sun 9–6 (except Christmas and New Year's Day).

Six Flags Fiesta Texas, p. 131

Six Flags Fiesta Texas

Magic Time Machine

If the kids want to eat in a place they'll enjoy, but you want more than a burger next to a noisy play area, Magic Time Machine has a perfect alternative. All of the waitstaff in this maze-like, bubble-topped eatery dress as fictional characters—from Snow White to the Mad Hatter to Sinbad the Sailor. And they love kids. The food is good, though a bit overpriced. Adults' meals such as steaks and prime rib run between $10 and $20, but kids' meals (chicken fingers are favorites) are around $5. Start off healthy with a visit to the Salad Car—a 1953 MG sports car filled with ice and garden bounty. Or go for the purely hedonistic, $14.99-per-person Roman Orgy. (Good luck explaining the title to the kids.) A good drink selection is available for grownups, and kids can enjoy a fizzy, lime-green, dry-ice concoction in a collectible glass. It's at 902 NE Loop 410, San Antonio. Open for dinner seven days. 210/828-1470 ⅃

$3 adults, $2 seniors, $1 children 3–13. ⅃ (Northeast)

SAN ANTONIO ZOOLOGICAL GARDENS AND AQUARIUM
Brackenridge Park
3903 N. St. Mary's St.
San Antonio
210/734-7183
With 3,400 animals representing 700 species, the San Antonio Zoo has Texas's third-largest collection, including many of the weird and dangerous varieties that the kids like so much. The beautifully xeriscaped grounds offer shady spots to rest and enjoy many new exhibits. The new Conservation Research Center features many amazing animals. Zoo docents along the walks allow your children to pet animals that might send *you* screaming toward the car. Memorial Day–Labor Day daily 9–6, rest of the year daily 9–5. Note: You can stay in the park past closing time, until 8 p.m., in the summer. $7 adults, $5 children 3–11. ⅃ (Northeast)

SCOBEE PLANETARIUM
San Antonio College
1300 San Pedro Ave.
San Antonio
210/733-2910
This unassuming little dome on the SAC campus, though surrounded by city lights and sounds, is a window on the universe. The 30-to-40-minute star projection show with easy-to-follow narration and lively music makes the silver bubble a popular field trip destination during the

school year. Star shows Fri at 6:30 and 8 p.m. Observatory open to the public at 9 p.m. Admission is free. & (Northwest)

MUSIC AND ENTERTAINMENT

IMAX THEATRE
Rivercenter
849 E. Commerce St.
San Antonio
210/225-IMAX
Suggested IMAX agenda: 1) Make the kids sit through the 45-minute documentary *Alamo: The Price of Freedom*, then 2) buy them another ticket for whatever thrill-instiller they'd like to see, such as *Speed* or *Roller Coaster!* or *Flight*. Don't change the order of the agenda. After the latter high-tech, high-speed stressfests, the siege and cannon battle that gave birth to Texas will seem tame. 9 a.m.–10:20 p.m. (last show) every day. $6.95 adults, $6.75 seniors, $4.75 children 3–11. (Discount for two-show packages.) & (Downtown)

MAGIK THEATRE
HemisFair Park
420 S. Alamo St.
San Antonio
210/227-2751
Richard Rosen's dream of a professional theater company in San Antonio resulted in Magik Theatre, which truly offers fun for all ages. The kids will sit on the floor munching popcorn and interacting with the cast while you relax in a director's chair. Recent shows include originals such as *When Dinosaurs Rocked the World*, with music of the Beatles, and adaptations such as *The Grinch* and *Willy Wonka*. $5 adults, $3 children. (Downtown)

SAN ANTONIO SYMPHONY
222 E. Houston St., Ste. 200
San Antonio
210/554-1000
The symphony's 24 Young People's Concerts, presented every year in Trinity University's Laurie Auditorium, feature the full orchestra in bargain-priced programs tailored for ages 3 to 6. For all ages, the symphony created the Interactive Family Classics

Heroes and Fantasies

Heroes and Fantasies, the city's most popular comic book, card, and kids' collectibles chain, has become a local phenomenon. Various evenings are devoted to "trade nights" in several genres, leading to parking lots packed with parents listening to their car radios. All of the hot items your teen or preteen looks for at home can be found here, with the help of a very knowledgeable staff. If the kids are using words you don't understand, take them to somebody who does. Open daily, hours vary by store.

Institute of Texan Cultures

which allow you and your children to meet the musicians and the conductor, try to play an instrument, and ask questions (in the middle of the concert!). Ticket prices and schedules vary, so call for information. (See also Chapter 11, Performing Arts.) & (Downtown)

THE TEXAS ADVENTURE
307 Alamo Plaza
San Antonio
210/227-8224

This might be a good place to start introducing the kids to the Alamo story (and legends), although the ghostly stars of this Encountarium F/X Theatre have to vie with those at *Alamo: The Price of Freedom* at the IMAX Theatre. If you opt for the Adventure, you'll appreciate the history lesson and the kids will love the special effects—a sort of educational version of Disney's Haunted Mansion, with the Alamo defenders telling their tales. Shows begin every 30 minutes 10–10 daily. $6.50 adults, $5.90 seniors and military personnel, $4.50 children 3–11. & (Downtown)

MUSEUMS AND LIBRARIES

HERTZBERG CIRCUS MUSEUM
210 Market St.
San Antonio
210/207-7810

You'll enjoy the 20,000 bits of circus memorabilia. But "circus" also means "weird stuff," so let the kids look for photos of the Hilton Siamese twins; life-size cutouts of giant Jack Earle, fat lady Jolly Fielder, and Lentini, the three-legged man; and heirlooms such as midget Tom Thumb's coach, violin, and rifle. You'll want to keep them out of the blade box used by contortionist and cut-up Marvin Smith. One Saturday each month, storytellers, puppeteers, magicians, and clowns visit. Call for schedule. Mon–Sat 10–5, Sun and holidays noon–5. $2.50 adults, $2 seniors, $1 children 3–12, free to active military. One-hour free parking across Market Street in River Bend Garage. (Downtown)

INSTITUTE OF TEXAN CULTURES
HemisFair Park

San Antonio's Five Best Roller Coasters

1. **The Rattler** (Fiesta Texas)
2. **Great White** (Sea World)
3. **Steel Eel Hypercoaster** (Sea World)
4. **Roadrunner Express** (Fiesta Texas)
5. **Joker's Revenge** (Fiesta Texas)

Bowie and Durango Sts.
San Antonio
210/458-2300
This low-slung, turtle-like building housed the Texas Pavilion during the 1968 World's Fair. Today it's home to the University of Texas system's vast collection of Texana. For kids, however, the best time of year to go is late July/early August for the Texas Folklife Festival. With food, music, games, and a chance to try their hands at traditional crafts, they'll learn about the more than 30 cultures that created the Lone Star State without even knowing they're being educated. Tue–Sun 9–5 (except Thanksgiving and Christmas). $4 adults, $2 seniors and children 3–12. (Prices do not include Folklife Festival.) & (Downtown)

RIPLEY'S BELIEVE IT OR NOT!/
PLAZA THEATRE OF WAX
301 Alamo Plaza
San Antonio
210/224-WAXX
You might have to explain who Marilyn Monroe and Mae West were, but the kids will love even the lifelike wax figures they don't recognize. Ripley's exhibits of authentic dinosaur eggs and the man with double pupils in each eye are surefire

kid pleasers. But if your little ones have trouble staying in their own beds, stop and think before descending into the cellar Theatre of Horrors. Daily 9 a.m.–10 p.m. Combination ticket $11.95 adults, $7.95 children 4–12. & (Downtown)

SAN ANTONIO CENTRAL LIBRARY
600 Soledad St.
San Antonio
210/207-2500
Here's a joke for your kids: Why is the Central Library the tallest building in San Antonio? Because it has the most stories. Actually, it's not the tallest. But it is the most colorful, and the vibrant exterior palette carries through to the third-floor children's library. Next to the six-story atrium, young ones will find shelf upon shelf upon shelf of age-appropriate books, along with cozy seating (close to the floor, of course) for reading them. Interactive, educational computer games are also on hand. Mon–Thu 9–9, Fri–Sat 9–5, Sun 11–5. Free. & (Downtown)

SAN ANTONIO
CHILDREN'S MUSEUM
305 E. Houston St.
San Antonio
210/212-4453
Tell them you're taking them to a

museum, just to see their long faces brighten when they walk through the doors of 305 E. Houston. The Children's Museum is about as far from a museum as you can get. In fact, it's three floors of perpetual educational chaos. Every exhibit, whether it involves the sciences, history, economics, or the arts, is very definitely hands-on. Favorites include the bubble room; the two-story, kid-powered elevator; and the scale-model airplane. Toddler and infant spaces available, too. Tue–Sat 9–6, Sun noon–5. $4, children under 2 free. One-hour free parking at Mid-City Garage, across the street at Navarro and College. ♿ (Downtown)

SAN ANTONIO MUSEUM OF ART
200 W. Jones Ave.
San Antonio
210/829-7262

SAMA's outstanding art collections are complemented by outstanding educational programs for kids. The schedule varies throughout the year, so call for information. Mon–Sat 10–5 (Tue 10–9), Sun noon–5. $4 adults, $2 seniors and students (with I.D.), $1.75 children 4–11; free Tue 3–9. ♿ (Downtown)

TEXAS TRANSPORTATION MUSEUM
11731 Wetmore Rd.
San Antonio
210/490-3554

This small, out-of-the-way, mostly outdoors museum is a kid favorite for one special reason: train rides. Before you get to the depot, stroll past other modes of transport from Texas's past. Train cars not wheelchair accessible. Thu, Sat, Sun 9–4. Trains run 12:30–3:30, leaving every 45 minutes. $3 adults, $1 children 12 and under. (Northeast)

WITTE MUSEUM
Brackenridge Park
3801 Broadway
San Antonio
210/820-2111

One of the best-attended exhibits at the Witte (WIT-ee) in recent years was "Back Yard Monsters"—a lovely little promenade lined with giant insects, some of them robotically mobile, large enough to snatch the little ones up if they were so inclined. They didn't, and the entomological hit left town on friendly terms, to be followed by several equally creative and attractive science shows. Kids love the Witte—particularly since the addition of the new four-story Science Treehouse. June–Aug Mon–Sat 10–6, Tue 10–9, Sun noon–5; rest of the year Mon–Sat 10–5, Sun noon–5. $5 adults, $3 children. ♿ (Northeast)

STORES KIDS LOVE

HARD ROCK CAFÉ
111 W. Crockett St.

There's something for everyone at Market Square.

Al Rendon

San Antonio
210/224-ROCK

If you have preteens, be a hero: Take 'em to Hard Rock and buy 'em a T-shirt. Their classmates will be impressed, and you'll move up a few notches. Sun–Thu 11 a.m.–11:30 p.m., Fri–Sat 11 a.m.–1 a.m. (Downtown)

MARKET SQUARE (EL MERCADO)
514 W. Commerce St.
San Antonio
210/207-8600

El Mercado offers at least one interesting shop for every age of shopper, widely varied levels of price and quality, interesting eateries for handy snacking, and stuffed armadillos. Hardly a weekend goes by without some kind of celebration. This is the ideal place to find inexpensive souvenirs for the kids and unique party favors for the next young 'un's birthday celebration (preferably not the bullwhips). (See also Chapter 5, Sights and Attractions.) (Downtown)

WITTE MUSEUM GIFT SHOP
Brackenridge Park
3801 Broadway
San Antonio
210/820-2111

Fascinating, science-oriented gifts await you at the end of your trip through the Witte. From dinosaurs to kites to ant farms to kaleidoscopes, the Witte's mercantile offers something for every budding scientist. A great place to shop for gifts. Mon–Sat 10–6 (Tue 10–9), Sun noon–6. (Northeast)

THEME PARKS

DISCOVERY ZONE
5751 NW Loop 410

San Antonio
210/681-3300

These local branches of the DZ chain aren't any different from the ones you might find at home. But they do offer you a place to sit down while the kids work off the energy they built up looking at things you wanted them to look at. Let 'em be rowdy—they've earned it. Mon–Thu 10–8, Fri and Sat 10–9, Sun 11–7. $5.99 ages 4–12, $3.99 ages 1–3, over 13 and adults free with a paid child. Some activities are wheelchair accessible. There's an additional location at 13722 Embassy Row, 210/494-1226. (Northwest)

KIDDIE PARK
3015 Broadway
San Antonio
210/824-4351

Located near the zoo, Kiddie Park claims to be the oldest children's amusement park in America. The newly restored carousel was hand-carved in 1918. The 1950 Little Dipper roller coaster isn't Fiesta Texas's Rattler, but younger riders will find sufficient thrills. Also on the park's grounds are a Ferris wheel; boat, plane, and kiddy-car rides; and a game room with old-fashioned Skee-ball, pinball, and newfangled video games. A snack bar offers all of those treats neither you nor your kids should be eating. Daily 10–dusk. $5.95 unlimited ride passes. ♿ (Northeast)

SEA WORLD OF TEXAS
10500 Sea World Dr.
San Antonio
210/523-3611

Visitors to Sea World who are of the shorter, younger persuasion will enjoy Shamu's Happy Harbor—a playground with lots of splashing-type activities in addition to the swings and slides. Swim- or easily dried-wear is recommended for participants. Also, some lucky youngster is selected during every Shamu show to pet one of the elegant carnivores, which may include rubbing their tongues. The whales love it and are usually considerate enough to keep their mouths open. Open at 10 a.m.; days and closing times vary with the season, so call ahead. $29.95 adults (10 percent off for seniors), $19.95 children 3–11. ♿ (Northwest)

SIX FLAGS FIESTA TEXAS
17000 I-10 W.
San Antonio
210/697-5050
When the Six Flags amusement park chain bought Fiesta Texas in 1995, it added some kid-oriented shows and attractions to its stable of musical entertainment. You'll find the ubiquitous superhero and cartoon-character shows and some rowdy rides, including the Joker's Revenge roller coaster.

A water park is on-site, so dress for mess. 10–10; days vary with season. $32 adults (48 inches and taller), $22.50 seniors, children (under 48 inches), and physically challenged. Parking $5. ♿ (Northwest)

SPLASHTOWN
3600 I-35 N.
San Antonio
210/227-1400
The sight of Splashtown on the horizon will definitely catch a young eye, with the tubes 'n' tunnels of several waterslides towering over its 18 acres. At ground level are more sedate liquid attractions such as the wave pool, lazy river, and "dive-in movies." But if you stay on the ground, wear sunglasses to keep an eye on your offspring in line high in the air. Sun–Thu 11–9, Fri–Sat 11–11. $17.99 adults, $12.99 children under 48 inches. ♿ (Northeast)

8

PARKS, GARDENS, AND RECREATION AREAS

The San Antonio Department of Parks and Recreation has done yeoman work in providing nature preserves and greenbelt areas throughout the city. Many of these preserves are cut from the same cloth: urban/suburban oases of live oak forests sheltering hiking and biking trails, picnic tables, and sturdy climbing sets for kids. Others have unique features to recommend them. No matter where you are, there is a city park near you. For information, call the Parks and Recreation Department at 210/207-3000.

More specialized parks and gardens, some just steps from the downtown bustle, encourage contemplation rather than recreation. And the Mission Trail, a linear stretch of National Park land linking the four most beautiful of San Antonio's five historic missions, adds historical perspective to the mix.

BRACKENRIDGE PARK
3800 N. St. Mary's St.
San Antonio
210/207-3000

Brackenridge is the flagship of San Antonio parks. The 350 acres were handed to the city in 1899 by George Brackenridge, who had operated a waterworks there on the banks of the San Antonio River. A likeness of George B. stands at the Broadway entrance to the park. Many of the buildings and bridges he built for his

company remain and have been joined by several lovely and lively attractions. (Northeast)

FRIEDRICH PARK
Milsa Rd. north of Loop 1604
San Antonio
210/698-1057

This remarkable, 250-acre nature preserve to the northwest of the city offers an opportunity to hike through the Hill Country and observe its wildlife and vegetation. Trails are

Brackenridge Park Attractions

Carousel: *A favorite of kids of all ages, this antique merry-go-round twirls in the zoo parking lot for a small charge.*

San Antonio Zoo: *See Chapter 5, Sights and Attractions, and Chapter 7, Kids' Stuff.*

Driving Range: *Across from the stables and bridle trail, this range gives you a chance to warm up for the big links just down the park road. See Chapter 10, Sports and Recreation.*

Fishing: *A common pastime along the river in the park, particularly for kids. Call Parks and Recreation for permit information.*

Golf Course: *Dating to 1917, the park's 6,500-yard course was the original home of—and the last public course to be used for—the Texas Open. See Chapter 10, Sports and Recreation.*

Horseback Riding: *Brackenridge has a bridle trail and a rent-a-horse service. The horses are very gentle, and ponies are provided for the youngest cowpokes. See Chapter 10, Sports and Recreation.*

Japanese Tea Garden: *One of San Antonio's most contemplative spots, the tea garden was crafted against the wall of a used-up rock quarry in 1919. Native and non-native fauna shade meandering walks and stone bridges. Towering above it all is a 60-foot waterfall that plunges into pools filled with traditional Oriental carp and water lilies. You'll have to take your own tea, but there is a snack bar. Some areas are wheelchair accessible.*

Sky Ride: *A cable-borne tram gives a marvelous view of the city as it spans the park from the zoo to the Japanese Tea Garden. There is a small charge, and the ride is wheelchair accessible.*

Sunken Garden Amphitheatre: *An ingenious use for an old rock quarry. See Chapter 11, Performing Arts.*

Brackenridge Eagle Railroad: *Miniature trains circumnavigate 3.5 miles of the park. These replicas of an 1893 Huntington were built by Chance Manufacturing, the Wichita, Kansas, company that created the Alamo City streetcars found downtown. There is a small charge, and the railroad is wheelchair accessible.*

Witte Museum: *See Chapter 6, Museums and Galleries.*

The Brackenridge Eagle in Brackenridge Park, p. 132

clearly marked, and rope-lined and wheelchair trails are provided so that the visually and mobility impaired don't miss out on the beautiful surroundings. Hikes last anywhere from 30 minutes to an hour and can be guided with a reservation. Wed–Sun 8–5 (winter), 8–8 (summer). Free. ♿ (Northwest)

HEMISFAIR PARK
Bowie and Durango Sts.
San Antonio
210/207-8615

These 92 downtown acres were the site of the 1968 World's Fair, Hemis-Fair. Many of the original pavilions are gone, but historical buildings remain, surrounded by relaxing landscaping and fountains. (Sadly, some of both are being sacrificed for the new Convention Center hotel.) There's a delightful playground for kids, as well as picnic areas. See it all from the top of the park's 750-foot centerpiece, the Tower of the Americas. Sun–Thu 9 a.m.–10 p.m. Park is free, but there's a charge for the tower. ♿ (Downtown)

MCALLISTER PARK
Jones Maltsberger St.
south of Thousand Oaks
San Antonio
210/821-3000

Of all of San Antonio's parks, these 850 acres on the northeast are best suited for the active visitor. Hiking trails, biking trails, soccer fields, and softball diamonds are very popular, and sturdy climbing equipment is provided for the limber and fearless. Covered picnic

TRIVIA

San Antonio's frequent water shortages have led the San Antonio Water System to offer rebates to residents who use cacti, succulents, and other low–water-use species for water-conscious landscaping, known as xeriscaping.

Watch Where You Step

San Antonio wouldn't be the city it is without immigration from the south. But there is one visitor locals would rather had never showed up: the fire ant. Found in nearly every grassy or bare patch of ground around town, the ants will pour out of their mounds at the slightest provocation, such as your shadow falling over them. Once on you, they establish a grip with tiny pincers and then jab you with rear-mounted stingers, injecting an acidic venom.

A fire ant sting doesn't really hurt that much. Problem is, you never get just one. The ants attack in swarms and can be all over your legs before you know it. (Grown men and women have been known to remove their pants on crowded golf courses upon realizing that fire ants have invaded them.) The stings leave small, fluid-filled blisters that lasts a few days.

You don't really have anything to fear from fire ants, but children may not think fast enough to brush the bugs off once attacked. And some people may be slightly allergic to the venom. Swarms of the ants have been known to kill newborn animals—even fawns—in the wild.

Watch out for loose mounds of dirt anywhere between a few inches to a foot or so wide, and a few inches high. Those are probably fire-ant casas. If you want to make sure, disturb the mound slightly with a twig or your finger. You'll know soon enough. (But be prepared to vacate the premises—immediately!)

shelters offer a place to cool off. McAllister also allows camping, but only with a reservation and permit available through the Parks and Rec office. ⅃ (Northeast)

MILAM PARK PLAYGROUND
Commerce St. across from
El Mercado
San Antonio

210/207-8480
This tidy little park downtown is better suited to brief stopovers during sightseeing so the kids can unwind on the playsite. It's also a relaxing downtown lunch spot. Named after Texan patriot Ben Milam, the park was once a cemetery for San Antonio's original Canary Island settlers. Open daily to 9 p.m. Free. ⅃ (Downtown)

MISSION TRAIL
San Antonio Missions National
Historical Park
Beginning on Mission Rd.
at S. St. Mary's St.
San Antonio
210/229-5701
This driving tour takes you through
the four Spanish missions south of
the Alamo: Concepción, San José,
San Juan Capistrano, and San Francisco de la Espada. Visitors center at
2202 Roosevelt Ave. Visitors center

hours: fall/winter daily 8–5, spring/
summer daily 9–6; closed Thanksgiving, Christmas, and New Year's Day.
Free. (South)

SAN ANTONIO
BOTANICAL GARDENS
555 Funston Pl.
San Antonio
210/207-3250
On the border of Fort Sam Houston
are 33 elysian acres of native plants,
formal gardens (including one of the

San Antonio Wildflowers

*If you're driving to San Antonio in the spring, your path—or at least
the highway medians and shoulders—will be blanketed with broad
stretches of several brilliant varieties of wildflowers. Look for these:*
Bluebonnet—*The Texas state flower is a violet-hued lupine with
tall clumps of cupped petals.*
Coreopsis—*Reddish-brown centers create round yellow flowers almost all year.*
Cutleaf daisy—*This one- to three-foot plant bears clusters of yellow blooms that open in the daylight.*
Gaura—*A truly unique flower with an asparagus-like stalk dan-
gling pure white blooms with bright red tendrils.*
Indian blanket—*Also called firewheel, for its brilliant red petals
that jut spoke-like from the center and turn yellow toward their tips.*
Indian paintbrush—*The most visible parts of the flower, its red-
orange leaves, hide cream-colored blossoms beneath.*
Pink evening primrose—*Delicate, nearly translucent pink petals
form a bowl with a yellow center.*
Rose verbena—*Butterflies congregate around the clusters of tiny
purple petals on this creeping flower.*
Wild mustard—*These three-foot stalks are early harbingers of
spring, producing bright yellow blooms in February.*

Ten Interesting Facts about San Pedro Park

1. The Spanish missionaries who discovered the spring in the middle of the park in 1709 named it San Pedro Spring.

2. In 1729 King Philip V of Spain declared the land around the spring *elido* (public land), making San Pedro Park the second-oldest park in America (next to Boston Common).

3. The Spanish were latecomers. Around 9000 B.C. the land around the spring was home to a tribe of seven-foot aborigines, whose skeletons were found in caves on the north end of the park.

4. Native Americans used what is now the park as an intertribal center for trading and recreation. Tribes who visited included Payaya, Comanche, Apache, Aztec, and Coahuilteca (for which Texas is named).

5. During the Civil War the land was used as a prisoner-of-war camp for Union soldiers.

6. The park once contained a spring-fed swimming/boating lake. Renovations currently underway will restore it.

7. In the early 1900s the park contained the city's first zoo and branch library. Popular activities included horse racing (on a track) and balloon rides.

8. The San Pedro Playhouse, built in the park in 1929, is one of America's oldest public theaters.

9. The branch library in the park was designed by local architectural superstar Atlee Ayres.

10. On Tuesdays and Thursdays, the intertribal Native American dance troupe Teokalli performs sunset ceremonies in the park.

Japanese discipline), and fascinating recreations of 1800s farmhouses and lands. Strolling among the gardens guarantees a lovely afternoon. But the most striking features are the glistening glass biospheres of the Lucille Halsell Conservatory, which contain vegetation from all corners and climates of Texas. October brings the lovely and popular Gardens by Moonlight celebration, which extends the gardens' hours and provides live entertainment and snacks. Educational programs are available for all ages. Tue–Sun 9–6 (except Christmas and New Year's Day). $3 adults, $2 seniors, $1 children 3–13. & (Northeast)

TRIVIA

The Japanese Tea Garden in Brackenridge Park was called exactly that from its 1919 christening. But during World War II, when hostilities overseas forced the garden to change its ancestry, it became the Chinese Tea Garden. After wartime sentiments cooled down, the name changed back.

SAN PEDRO PARK
San Pedro Ave. at Ashby Pl.
San Antonio
210/207-8480

In 1729, when Spain's King Philip V declared the land surrounding the San Pedro Spring *elido*—public land—he created the second-oldest public park in America, predated only by Boston Common. In the late nineteenth and early twentieth centuries, the spring fed a lake-like swimming pool (the city's first). On the shore was the first San Antonio zoo, a horse-racing track, and a branch library. The zoo moved to Brackenridge Park, the lake was replaced by a standard pool in the

Japanese Tea Garden

© Leo de Wys, Inc./Bob Thomason

1950s, and the park declined over the years. But a $4.5-million restoration currently underway will return the lake, and much of the park, to its pristine condition—with old-fashioned lighting along promenade walkways. The first phase is completed. Also in the park is the McFarlin Tennis Center, which has hosted all-star exhibition matches; and the San Pedro Playhouse, one of the oldest publicly owned theaters in the nation. Hours: Always open (though not always safe). Admission is free. & (Downtown)

TRAVIS PARK
Travis St. at Pecan St.
San Antonio
210/207-8480

San Pedro Park is America's second oldest, and Travis Park is the third. This tidy little square across the street from the St. Anthony Hotel was once an orchard owned by the only surviving Alamo defender, Samuel Maverick. Maverick, who was out of town during the Alamo siege, had a habit of not branding his cattle. Hence the popular term for strays. Center stage in the park, a statue of a Confederate soldier stands atop a pillar with a cannon below. Most of the year the park is a popular brown-bag destination for downtown lunchers and codependent pigeons. But outdoor concerts and festivals are

Know Your San Antonio Trees

Live oak—The most common tree in town, these short, broad growers have small oval leaves. The more ancient of these trees can reach astonishing diameters. An excellent example of a venerable live oak is found on the Alamo grounds, the immense weight of its horizontally zealous branches supported by braces and cables.

Mesquite—From a distance, mesquites may appear similar to live oaks. On close inspection, the most obvious difference is the mesquite's wispy, nearly feathery foliage and pea plant–like bean pods in season. In fact, mesquites are part of the legume family. The beans were used as a food source by local Native Americans. Mesquite wood is prized in other parts of the country for the character it adds to barbecue. Ironically, most hard-core grillmeisters in the Alamo City prefer imported woods such as hickory and oak, believing that mesquite imparts an oily flavor.

Bald cypress—These tall trees that grow in clumps (not true members of the cypress clan) add a touch of the Everglades along the river. If, as you walk, you look up admiringly into their handsome umbrellas, you'll soon find yourself prone on the ground. All around the base of the cypress are "knees"—knobby protuberances that look as if they wanted to be trunks, then thought better of it after reaching a height ideal for tripping over. Some bald cypresses have lived as long as 1,200 years.

Prickly pear—Saguaros may be the most common cactus in kitschy San Antonio souvenir shops, often with lonesome, bandana-sporting coyotes howling mournfully beneath. But don't waste your time looking for these favorites in the wild—they don't grow here. The paddle-laden prickly pear is nature's cactus of choice for South Texas. Some varieties live up to the name "prickly," with spines approaching threatening lengths. Others have tiny filaments within their paddles that will happily disappear into your thumb. The spiny types sport globular blooms in season, most commonly in red and purple hues.

frequently held here, including the highly successful September festival Jazz'SAlive. Open daily 24 hours. Free ♿ (Downtown)

WOODLAWN PARK
1100 Cincinnati Ave.
San Antonio
210/207-8480

The centerpiece of Woodlawn Park is a pretty little lake, surrounding an island that bears a lighthouse. The lighthouse isn't really necessary—until a proposed clean-up frees the lake from choking weeds, the inland water isn't really usable for anything but looking at. That in itself is relaxing, however, and hordes of pigeons and ducks will keep you company as they relieve you of whatever tidbits you might bring along. The park is a center of activity for the surrounding neighborhood, and includes large children's play areas and picnic spots. You need a reservation for the pavilions. Be sure and visit one of the always-present stands that sell *raspas*—a uniquely Tex-Mex variation on the sno-cone—and roasted ears of corn, served hot on sticks. Slather these with butter and sprinkle with chili powder. You can work off the butter on the jogging trail that circumnavigates the lake. Free. ♿ (Downtown)

9

SHOPPING

Wherever there are tourists, there are souvenir shops. Every major attraction has one, and most of them offer too much of the same thing: items for you to take home that prove you were here, such as imitation 'coonskin caps and Colonel Travis–autographed swords made in Taiwan. You can't avoid these places, so don't bother looking for them in this chapter. Instead, here you'll find an array of shops that brim with el espíritu de San Antonio—antique stores with real South Texas memorabilia and craft shops where many of the items are made by San Antonio hands. These are the places to find gifts that you'll find nowhere else and keepsakes that will help you remember your trip to the Alamo City for many years to come.

And because you always forget something when you leave home (or maybe you do it deliberately just because you like shopping), also look here for the better, more accessible department stores and malls that can provide your day-to-day needs.

SHOPPING DISTRICTS

Downtown

Most of the easiest to find, on-the-beaten-tourist-path shops down-town think they know what you want: souvenirs. And the plush, stuffed armadillos are awfully cute. But downtown is also the place to find quality merchandise that is uniquely San Antonian. In fact, it seems that the farther you go north of the city center, the farther you get from the Alamo City's heart and history. Most of the northerly tourist attractions offer only merchandise of the generic, "you-could-get-this-anywhere" variety. Speaking of history, downtown is also the place to shop if you are a lover of all things antique and collectible. Look *carefully and you'll find the ideal memento of your River City visit.*

ALAMO ANTIQUE MALL
125 Broadway
San Antonio
210/224-4354
With three stories of shops filled floor-to-ceiling, the AAM is billed as the largest such mall downtown. The stock in the more than 40 individually owned boutiques ranges from standard and common to unique and irresistible, and some of the proprietors offer shipping. The AAM is two blocks from the Alamo, next to the St. Anthony Hotel. Partially wheelchair accessible. (Downtown)

ANTIQUES DOWNTOWN MALL
515 E. Houston St.
San Antonio
210/224-8845
Around the corner from the Alamo is this delightful emporium of all things old. Each of the tenant shops is staffed by helpful, informative antique buffs, and most of their wares are

Paris Hatters

Paris Hatters

high quality, with an occasional outstanding find. Shipping is usually available. Partially wheelchair accessible. (Downtown)

CHAMADE JEWELERS
504 Villita St.
San Antonio
210/224-7753
Distinguished from its jeweler neighbors in La Villita and all over town, Chamade's specialty is custom jewelry made to order. Gold, silver, and platinum designs are always exquisite, as is Chamade's selection of new and old pieces from France and Italy. (Downtown)

KALLISON'S WESTERN WEAR
123 S. Flores St.
San Antonio
210/222-1364
Dudes and city slickers, stay home. Kallison's is one of San Antonio's oldest Western-wear shops, and it's serious about all things cowpoke. Major boot and hat lines are carried, with a smattering of shirts, skirts, and accessories to help you fit in when you finally get around to taking those country-western line-dancing lessons. But rugged workwear is a specialty. &
(Downtown)

MARKET SQUARE (EL MERCADO)
514 W. Commerce St.
San Antonio
210/207-8600
Market Square is the ideal tourist souvenir shop. Merchandise ranges from knickknacks of dubious quality to outstanding imports, and most items are priced reasonably. The best feature of the Mercado, however, is that there is nearly always a party of one kind or another going on in the courtyard. Follow the mariachis and you'll be there. & (Downtown)

There is perhaps no more accurate retail reflection of San Antonio past and present than that found in La Villita. The original San Antonio settlement is now a craft, jewelry, clothing, and art must-see, particularly during Fiesta, when craftspeople put out their finest and most vibrant wares.

PARIS HATTERS
119 Broadway
San Antonio
210/223-3453

If you can't leave Texas without the appropriate headgear, you can't do better than Paris Hatters. In business since the early part of this century, Paris carries all the major brands such as Stetson and Resistol, and also does custom fittings and repair. & (Downtown)

THE RESERVATION
Rivercenter
San Antonio
210/226-0935

The name may not be quite politically correct in the opinion of Native Americans, but the wares found in these Southwestern galleries reflect the most beautiful crafts of their cultures. The Reservation features museum-quality pottery, weaving, and jewelry, the likes of which you might find in the finer shops of Santa Fe. Repairs and custom work are also available. A second location is found at Central Park Mall. & (Downtown)

Alamo Heights

Alamo Heights, one of San Antonio's "suburban cities," is also one of its tonier areas. It's no surprise that the shops that have sprung up over decades along the main drag through "09" (short for the Heights's zip code
and sometimes used disparagingly by non-09ers) reflect the good—and sometimes expensive—tastes of their residential neighbors. Shops include art galleries, Oriental-rug dealers, jewelry shops, bookstores, garden shops, and others far too numerous to list. Two mini-malls particularly deserve a look for their small, tasteful shops: The Collection at Broadway and Sunset and Lincoln Heights at Broadway and Basse. Driving up Broadway is a great way to spend an afternoon (and perhaps a lot of money) just browsing. But if you succumb to one temptation, resist another: the speed limit is 30 mph, and they mean it. Below are other notable Alamo Heights shops.

AZIZ ORIENTAL RUG GALLERY
5200 Broadway
San Antonio
210/822-1410

Whether or not you're ready to buy an Oriental rug, Aziz is worth a look. Featured beside excellent modern (and thus reasonably priced) reproductions are the beautifully aged varieties you see on those British dramas on PBS. Some of these cost more than a first home. & (Northeast)

NOMADIC NOTIONS
5214 Broadway
San Antonio
210/828-6270

Beads are the sole stock at this ultra-hip boutique in Alamo Heights. Choose from thousands of beads, many of them hand-carved, and string them yourself on your choice of stringers. (Keep track of each bead's price on the provided notepads as you go, or you'll regret it later.) It's great therapy, it's fun for kids, and you end up with an enviable piece of jewelry at an excellent price. & (Northeast)

RELAX THE BACK
5800 Broadway
San Antonio
210/822-1228
If you drove to San Antonio and your back hasn't recovered (or if you hurt it trying to load an Oriental rug onto the car), stop in Relax the Back. The shop specializes in all things dorsal, including a staggering variety of massagers, pads, pillows, seat covers,

and motorized massage chairs that would look at home on the space shuttle. & (Northeast)

Los Patios

This small enclave of women's clothing stores, craft boutiques, and a garden shop is a welcome relief from more crowded shopping areas. Located off Loop 410 (at the Starcrest exit), the live oak–shaded Los Patios also has a couple of very good restaurants. You won't be visiting the patios if there's been a recent heavy rain, however. As lovely as it is, the low-lying area is prone to flooding. Here are two favorites.

INCA BOUTIQUE
2015 NE Loop 410
San Antonio

The Twig Bookshop's Favorite Books about San Antonio by Local Authors

San Antonio is home to several well-known authors, including Sandra Cisneros and Naomi Nye. Here are a few more local recommendations from the Twig Bookshop (5005 Broadway, 210/826-6411 or 800/729-8944).

- **Jay Brandon:** Loose Among the Lambs *and* Fade into the Heat, *two novels*
- **Robert Flynn:** When I Was Just Your Age, *a collection of interviews with people around San Antonio*
- **James Michener** *(a transplant who was fondly claimed as a local):* The Eagle and the Raven, *a novel about the Alamo*
- **Rick Riordan:** The Big Red Tequila, *a mystery set in San Antonio*
- **Whitley Strieber:** The Secret School, *a book about a UFO landing near San Antonio*

210/599-2904

Another historically themed gift store, this one reaches a bit further back into history. Yes, there were Inca—or branches of them—in San Antonio thousands of years ago. Their heritage is preserved, tastefully, in this shop of Native American and related arts, crafts, and jewelry. ♿ (Northeast)

TEJAS GIFTS
2015 NE Loop 410
San Antonio
210/655-6171

"Tejas" comes from Coahuiltecas, one of the Native American tribes that lived in the area. As you might expect, a shop that bears the old name of Texas carries gifts with an old-Texas theme. Think of it as the South Texas equivalent of Santa Fe's pottery and art shops. An excellent souvenir stop. ♿ (Northeast)

ARTISAN'S ALLEY
555 W. Bitters Rd.
San Antonio
210/494-3226

If you can find it, you won't forget it. And you won't leave without buying something. This off-the-beaten-path enclave of crafters and gift dealers is particularly busy near the holidays, when locals are looking for unique gifts. Inside the mazelike complex of 20 oak-shaded shops is an astonishing collection of wares.

Trumpeting "A Bountiful Collection of Tea Garden Delights," the **English Ivy** deals in Crownford china teapots, hand-painted trompe l'oeil tables, garden markers, flowerpots, feeders, bird houses, and floral designs.

The **Stamping Factory** anticipated the current stamped paper craze and was ready with a phenomenal collection of rubber stamps, pens, embossing powders and accessories, and a large selection of handmade papers; classes and a catalogue are available.

At **Back Alley Antiques**, the variety says, "flea market," while the quality says, "antique specialist." Actually, Back Alley is an 8,000-square-foot cooperative of more than one antique specialist, and their varied interests and expertise show in their many fascinating offerings.

Be sure to check out **Sunrise Pottery**. How can you go home without a hand-thrown tortilla warmer? Or chips-and-salsa set? Or honey jar, tea pitcher, lamp, piggybank, candle holder, fountain, and any of hundreds of other family-made items? Personalized items are available, but you'll have to order them (well in advance, if they're for Christmas).

And, finally, don't miss the sawdust pie at **Apple Annie's** restaurant. Limited wheelchair access. (Northwest)

NOTABLE BOOKSTORES AND NEWSSTANDS

Bookcities Barnes & Noble and Borders have relegated the popular chain BookStop to the history books. But two local book stops remain local favorites, primarily because they offer things the giants don't.

HALFPRICE BOOKS,
RECORDS & MAGAZINES
3207 Broadway
San Antonio
210/822-4597

Gleefully downscale, Halfprice's four locations are local favorites for their combination of new and used books. Most of these are marked at half the manufacturers' price or less. The selection is as extensive as it is eclectic, featuring new and used titles. Cassettes, LPs, CDs, and videos are also among the offerings. Browsing here always yields surprises, and you'll probably yield more money than you intended to. Other locations (all NW): 7959 Fredericksburg Rd., 210/692-8868; 4919 NW Loop 410, 210/647-1103; 2106 NW Military, 210/349-1429. See www.halfpricebooks.com for more information. ♿ (Northeast)

THE TWIG BOOKSHOP/
THE RED BALLOON
5005 Broadway
San Antonio
210/826-6411 or 800/729-8944

Independently owned, the Twig has made a niche for itself among the city's book giants. Service is instantaneous, knowledgeable, and exceedingly friendly, helping you make your way through a selection of popular releases and lesser known, more artsy works. Authors of local and national stature are frequent visitors for signings and conversation. A particular specialty is books on the state and the South Texas region. If your photography skills are not quite in Ansel Adams's league, you might opt for one of several gorgeously illustrated books on San Antonio. Next door to the Twig is its children's branch, The Red Balloon, which is very popular with local literary young 'uns and school librarians. ♿ (Northeast)

OTHER NOTABLE STORES

ANTIQUE CENTER
11345 West Ave.
San Antonio
210/344-4131

Americana is the theme of this tidy, recently relocated collection two miles north of Loop 410. The collectibles include primitive offerings, vintage jewelry, china and glassware, furniture, slot machines and jukeboxes, and nostalgic advertising. Call for hours. ♿ (Northwest)

GARDEN RIDGE
I-35 N. at Schertz Rd.
210/599-5700

This sizable complex used to be called

Aziz Oriental Rug Gallery, p. 143

Aziz Oriental Rug Gallery

St. Joske's

One of San Antonio's most beloved department stores, Joske's (JAH-skees) is no longer around. Julius Joske started a retail empire in 1873 with his tiny, one-room adobe store on Austin Street. The family business grew until seven more stores were built throughout Texas, and its one-block headquarters store on Alamo Plaza dwarfed a neighboring Catholic church that became widely known as St. Joske's. When Dillard's bought out Joske's, the building was incorporated into Rivercenter.

Garden Ridge Pottery, but its inventory expanded way beyond the clay-pot and lawn-ornament field, and it has become a regional favorite for all kinds of home and garden decorating needs. Silk and dried flowers, holiday decorations, pictures and frames, party supplies, and mirrors span seven acres of indoor and outdoor aisles, but even these departments are dwarfed by the selection of pots, planters, and baskets. And do-it-yourselfers use Garden Ridge as their crafts HQ. &. (Northeast)

JAMES AVERY CRAFTSMAN
7120 Blanco Rd. (at Loop 410)
San Antonio
210/342-3412

Avery's shops are local favorites. The silversmith for whom the stores are named is still at work in a Hill Country enclave in Kerrville, where he and his apprentices turn out elegant silver and gold jewelry with a variety of themes—Southwestern and Texana, special occasion (particularly graduation), and just plain dress-up. They do a remarkable job of combining an old-Americana look with contemporary cues. You'll have to see it to

understand. Avery's religious jewelry is particularly attractive. Other locations are found in Ingram Park, Rolling Oaks, and Windsor Park Malls. &. (Northwest)

LEBMAN'S LEATHER
8701 Perrin Beitel Rd.
(at Loop 410)
San Antonio
210/655-7553

After you have your Stetson or Resistol hat from Paris Hatters and your full-quill ostrich-hide boots from Lucchese, you'll need a custom leather vest to complete your ensemble. Lebman's is the place to go. If it can be made of leather, you'll find it at Lebman's. All of the work is done on-site by some of the region's finest hide artists, and the prices reflect this. But it's well worth a look. &. (Northeast)

LUCCHESE BOOTS
4025 Broadway
San Antonio
210/828-9419

With the arrival in San Antonio of Salvatore ("Sam") Lucchese (loo-KAY-zee) in 1883, San Antonio footwear took a giant step forward.

Selena's, Etc.

The shooting death of rising Tejano music star Selena Quintanilla Perez came and went in much of the country, but here in the Tejano Capital of the World it was akin to a presidential assassination. Not long before a deranged one-time fan-club president killed her, the lovely songstress had fulfilled another of her young dreams and opened a shop and salon called Selena's, Etc. at 3703 Broadway in San Antonio. Thousands of Selena's fans have visited—and still visit—the site to pay homage to the 23-year-old singer, so that Selena's, Etc. has become as much a shrine as a boutique.

The immigrant from Palermo, Italy, brought with him generations of bootmaking expertise. The business is now corporately owned, but the boots are still the best. You'll find standard as well as exotic hides, such as ostrich, lizard, and snake. Warning to the tenderfoot: While Lucchese boots are the finest, wear them to Sea World on your first day at your feet's peril. Just like any horse worth havin', good boots need to be broke. Note: Lucchese boots look great topped with something from Paris Hatters. (Northeast)

PAPA JIM'S BOTANICA
5630 S. Flores St.
San Antonio
210/922-6665
A San Antonio institution, Papa Jim's can take you for a walk on the weird side. The mysticism of some religious practices indigenous to the San Antonio area is never far below the surface, so Papa's found a home here. His southside emporium stocks every product you could possibly need for forays into paranormal realms: tarot cards, herbs, powders, oils, amulets, candles, incense, floor washes, talismans, crystals, religious statuary, deer hooves, black-cat bones, voodoo dolls, wolf skulls, lion teeth, and just about anything smelly or spooky. Papa Jim also has a mail-order catalog. Call for hours. ♿ (South)

TOO GOOD TO BE THREW
7115 Blanco Rd.
San Antonio
210/340-2422
One of San Antonio's most popular vintage clothing stores (and undoubtedly the most cleverly named), TGTBT carries an extensive selection of high-quality, well-preserved clothes in women's, men's, and children's lines, and accessories for all. Since the clothes are on consignment, the stock changes frequently. This is an ideal shop stop if your fashion taste is more than your wallet can stomach. Mon–Sat 10–6, Thu to 8. There are steps to the second floor, but salespeople will bring items down to customers with disabilities. ♿ (Northwest)

DEPARTMENT STORES

You already know Sears, JC Penney, Montgomery Ward, and a few other national chain stores. Here are a few that may be less familiar.

BEALL'S
Central Park Mall
Loop 410 at Blanco Rd.
San Antonio
210/341-8216
This friendly regional chain (pronounced "bells") offers clothes not quite ready for the fashion-show runways but nonetheless of good quality and at very good prices. Mon–Sat 10–9, Sun noon–6. Other locations at Ingram Park Mall (NW), 210/684-7870; and Rolling Oaks Mall (NE), 210/651-4085. ♿ (Northwest)

BURLINGTON COAT FACTORY
Crossroads of San Antonio
4522 Frederickburg Rd.
San Antonio
210/735-9595
BCF is not really a factory, and it sells more than coats. In addition to the out-

Tejas Gifts, p. 145

Los Patios

erwear in the name (including a huge selection of leather), you'll find sportswear, baby needs, and bedding, most at substantial discounts. (Northwest)

DILLARD'S
North Star Mall
Loop 410 at San Pedro Ave.
San Antonio
210/341-6666
An upscale store much like Macy's, Dillard's features pricey name and house brands in clothing, jewelry, watches, fragrances, and homewares. Other locations at Central Park (NW), 210/341-5151; Ingram Park Mall (NW), 210/681-7970; Rivercenter (DT), 210/227-4343; and Rolling Oaks Mall (NE), 210/651-5033. ♿ (Northwest)

FOLEY'S
North Star Mall
Loop 410 at San Pedro Ave.
San Antonio
210/340-4266
Houston-born Foley's is much like Dillard's, though it moves aside some of the New York labels for its own, more affordable brand. Other locations at Ingram Park Mall (NW), 210/647-2496; Rivercenter (DT), 210/554-6914; and Rolling Oaks Mall (NE), 210/651-8984. ♿ (Northwest)

MACY'S
North Star Mall
Loop 410 at San Pedro Ave.
San Antonio
210/979-0333
There was much thanksgiving in San Antonio when the New York–based parademeisters moved into North Star Mall in 1997. The Macy's folk were happy to be coming to San Antonio, too, spending huge amounts on a floor-to-ceiling redesign of a space that had been occupied by Marshall Fields. Since then, the shiny

The corporate types who run Saks Fifth Avenue out of New York probably weren't too pleased when negotiating their North Star Mall location to learn that outside their potential doors was a distinctly non—Big Apple sculpture—a 40-foot-high pair of ostrich-skin cowboy boots by sculptor Robert Wade. They let the gargantuan footwear stay to become a trademark.

new store has claimed a niche for itself among its similar neighbors, Dillard's and Foley's. & (Northwest)

SAKS FIFTH AVENUE
North Star Mall
Loop 410 at San Pedro Ave.
San Antonio
210/341-4111
If you have lots of money (or powerful plastic) and an equal portion of fashion sense, you're in the right place. & (Northwest)

SOLO SERVE
118 Soledad St.
San Antonio
210/225-6738
Solo Serve is similar to Beall's, but the savings come largely from irregularities rather than seasonality. You may have to look for a while to find what you want. But a frequently heard comment from locals is, "You found that at Solo Serve?!" It's worth a look. Other locations at 12233 Nacogdoches Rd. (NE), 210/590-4219; 114 SW Military Dr. (S), 210/924-5941; and 7000 San Pedro (NW), 210/828-0641. & (Downtown)

STEIN MART
Crossroads of San Antonio
Loop 410 at Fredericksburg Rd.
San Antonio
210/734-7012

Not an emporium for beer mugs, Stein Mart is instead a clever bit of retail marketing. If that little number with the designer label you fell in love with last spring was just out of your price range, you'll probably find it this year at Stein Mart—without the hoity-toity price tag. Other locations at 999 E. Basse Rd. (NW), 210/829-7198; and 18134 San Pedro (NE), 210/499-5561. & (Northwest)

SHOPPING MALLS

CENTRAL PARK MALL
Loop 410 at Blanco Rd.
San Antonio
210/344-2236
Central Park is a mall in search of a mission. Just across San Pedro Avenue is the newer, flashier North Star Mall, which has devastated the customer base of the more established Central Park. Nonetheless, Central Park offers some things the Star doesn't, including reasonable prices at its anchor stores, Sears and Beall's, and a far-less-crowded Dillard's. Besides the mandatory boutiques, Central Park also boasts a very fine—though reasonable—Italian restaurant, Aldino's, and the Park Place mega-nightclub. Kids like Central Park for the two-level carousel in the middle of the mall. & (Northwest)

CROSSROADS OF SAN ANTONIO
Loop 410 and Fredericksburg Rd.
San Antonio
210/735-9137

Though not the equal in selection to North Star, Crossroads offers a variety of large and small stores orbiting around Montgomery Ward, Stein Mart, and the Burlington Coat Factory outlet. Its theater is topflight and is usually the only place in town to see "art house" flicks. & (Northwest)

INGRAM PARK MALL
Loop 410 and Ingram Rd.
San Antonio
210/684-9570

Dillard's, Foley's, JC Penney, and Sears anchor this complex, with the requisite specialty stores. Not as elaborate or well stocked as North Star but not nearly as crowded, either, it's a handy stop between most points of origin and Sea World. & (Northwest)

NORTH STAR MALL
Loop 410 between San Pedro Ave.
and McCullough
San Antonio
210/340-6627

North Star is the city's flagship mall. Anchor stores are Dillard's, Foley's, Macy's, Mervyn's, and Saks Fifth Avenue, with 200 shoes-to-software specialty shops. Along your stroll are gift carts/traffic impediments, some with Alamo City–related merchandise. Services include child care, stroller rentals, ATMs, wheelchairs, and an enticing food court. The holiday season at North Star is delightful, with round-the-clock holiday music around the central fountain. It's also phenomenally crowded—the best of times, the worst of times—and you may not get home until Easter. (Note: Check out the landmark sculpture outside Saks—a pair of 40-foot-tall cowboy boots, lighted for the holidays.) & (Northwest)

Five Rules for Shopping at Rivercenter

1. *Two hours of parking are free with any purchase in the mall—even just a taco in the food court—but you have to remember to take your parking ticket in with you. As you park . . .*

2. *Remember which side of the mall your garage is on. There are two, they're identical, and security guards get tired of telling people, "No, your car hasn't been stolen."*

3. *Rivercenter is a good place to start strolling the River Walk or to catch a barge cruise.*

4. *During holidays and peak tourist season, the lagoon in the center of the mall hosts nearly constant entertainment.*

5. *If you're going to catch the evening show at the Rivercenter Comedy Club, come in the afternoon, make your reservation, then shop until showtime. You'll have a much easier time parking.*

QUARRY MARKET
U.S. 281 N. at Basse Rd.
San Antonio

There was great anticipation to see what stores would end up finding a home at this mall in time for its 1998 opening, and it's been a hot property ever since. Not exactly a mall, the Quarry features a wide variety of trendy shops scattered on an immense, strangely laid-out parking lot. The reason for the latter is that the Quarry Market is an out-of-business cement plant and quarry. Some of the buildings, particularly the large central facility, are original to the site, and four huge smokestacks have been reinforced and painted to serve as the new mall's trademark. Here you'll find Borders Books and Music; Bed, Bath & Beyond; Whole Earth Provision Co.; Airlume Candles; and many other boutiques for outfitting home and body. Because of the Quarry's proximity to Alamo Heights and some of the priciest property in town, most of these are mid- to upper-price stores. There is also a wide selection of very interesting, very good, or both, restaurants, and an industrially inspired theater that redefines the word "theater." ♿ (Northeast)

RIVERCENTER
849 E. Commerce St.
San Antonio
210/225-0000

Between Dillard's and Foley's at this shopping mecca are 130 gift, clothing, and knickknack boutiques; restaurants, bars, and a comedy club; an IMAX Theatre; and a food court. Beyond the towering glass walls and fountain on the river side of the mall is a lagoon—actually an extension of the river—bordered by a large patio with an "island" stage. This is the venue for constant music and dance performances during tourist and holiday seasons. Rivercenter seems to be nearly always crowded. So if you need to get away for a while, a ticket station for barge cruises is nearby at the water's edge. In fact, with two

---

Five Rules for Shopping at North Star Mall

1. *Access off McCullough is faster than off San Pedro.*
2. *If you go anytime between Thanksgiving and Christmas, set aside lots of time. But . . .*
3. *Stop and enjoy the holiday music. Some of the city's finest musicians (including moonlighting San Antonio Symphony members) carol around the mid-mall fountain.*
4. *There are two parking garages that look remarkably similar, and each has levels painted like the other's, so remember where you entered the mall.*
5. *A quality child-care center is provided for little ones tired of shopping.*

---

hours' free parking with any purchase, Rivercenter is a great place to start your river exploration. Just remember to take your ticket with you. ♿ (Downtown)

ROLLING OAKS MALL
6909 N. Loop 1604
San Antonio
210/651-5513
Far from the madding crowd downtown, Rolling Oaks houses two of the same major stores—Dillard's and Foley's—with far fewer people. Rolling Oak's developers gambled that San Antonio would expand to the northeast faster than it has. They lost, but the very attractive mall is still here, and many local shoppers see it as a welcome relief from North Star. ♿ (Northeast)

FACTORY OUTLET CENTERS

A.I. ROOT CO.
537 Flores St.
San Antonio
210/223-5475
One step (with your eyes closed) inside this quaint shop and you'll know immediately what they sell: candles. The importance of candles to Southwestern Catholicism helps maintain this store's huge market segment, and Root is one of the best suppliers in the field. Choose from candles in glass or not, in 44 designer fragrances, a spectrum of colors, and a world of sizes, all offered at a large discount. (Downtown)

NEW BRAUNFELS FACTORY STORES
I-35 N. at Exit 188
New Braunfels
888/SHOP-333
"Shop like crazy, save like mad!" is

Market Square, p. 142

the slogan of this outlet nirvana in the little community of New Braunfels (BRAWN-fehls), 30 minutes northeast of San Antonio. Among the 50 factory outlets for fashions, accessories, and homewares are Bass, Bugle Boy, Van Heusen, Easy Spirit, Oneida, Royal Doulton, L'Eggs, American Tourister, Carter's, and WestPoint Pepperell, all claiming 20 to 70 percent savings over retail. The factory stores are frequently the last stop of San Antonio visitors driving north on I-35. ♿ (Northeast)

SAN MARCOS FACTORY STORES
I-35 N. at Exit 200
San Marcos
800/628-9465
Of course, some of those visitors get as far as San Marcos, 10 minutes north of New Braunfels, and stop again. That's because the San Marcos outlet mall, Texas's largest, adds a number of name outlets to New Braunfels's roster, such as Nike, Liz Claiborne, and Coach leather goods. ♿ (Northeast)

Corey LeVar Brookshire—Blue Skies

10

SPORTS AND RECREATION

San Antonians want a professional football team so badly they can hear the cheering. High-school and college football have always been very big in Texas, and the husky neighbors to the north, the Dallas Cowboys (and, to the near east—until recently—the Houston Oilers), have a rabid Alamo City following.

But despite city leaders holding out the lease to the football-friendly Alamodome, the NFL isn't knocking on their doors. So San Antonians have to be content with an on-again, off-again NBA team and a constantly shifting roster of minor-league clubs in other sports.

Many local sports take matters into their own hands to manage their spectator disgruntlement on the softball field. Softball is a way of life for thousands of the city's residents, and the relatively mild winters and accessible parks make year-round practice an option. Others sweat their frustrations away in the many gyms around town. And owing to San Antonio's hardy frontier roots, outdoor pursuits are very popular. Deer season is granted a reverence akin to religious holidays (leave your antler hat at home), runners abound (so watch out while driving), and major thoroughfares lead past many golf courses (so watch out while driving). In fact, nearly every sweaty enterprise short of tobogganing has a devoted local following. Whatever your athletic predilection, the Alamo City has a way for you to act on it—unless your favorite form of exercise is hefting a hot dog and a beer before a kickoff.

PROFESSIONAL SPORTS

Rackets, Gunslingers, Force, Toros, Wings, Riders, Texans, Iguanas, Tejanos—the litany of professional sports organizations that have tried to make a go of it and instead gone belly-up in the Alamo City continues to grow, with the loss of a hockey team as recently as 1997. Even Red

McCombs, legendary car dealer and civic leader, gave up trying to win a new team for San Antonio and bought the Minnesota Vikings (whom he says he's not going to move south).

Still, other athletic entrepreneurs keep trying, and every new club develops a loyal, if small, following. If you're inclined to use part of your vacation watching others do the sweating instead of doing it yourself, here's who's left.

Auto Racing

The San Antonio Gran Prix, an IMSA-GTP race weekend that each year closed the streets between Rivercenter and the Institute of Texan Cultures to all traffic except thundering prototype cars, died about a decade ago due to lack of interest and profits. So far, CART and Formula 1 haven't sent any scouts, and if they did they would likely encounter disinterest. San Antonio is a Southern town, after all, so oval tracks are given priority over street courses in the minds of local live-racing fans. Those who realize that steering wheels turn two directions have to be content with ESPN, FOX, and ABC.

ALAMO DRAGWAY
Off Hwy. 16 at Watson Rd.
210/923-8801
For race fans who believe steering wheels shouldn't turn at all, the dragway's quarter-mile heats up every Saturday except during the Christmas holidays. (South)

SAN ANTONIO SPEEDWAY
State Hwy. 16, 5 miles south of Loop 410
210/695-8550
Not far from the Dragway, this NASCAR-sanctioned track is part of the annual Winston Cup circuit, and also runs sprints and modifieds. Call for a schedule of the season, which runs March through October. (South)

Baseball

SAN ANTONIO MISSIONS
Nelson Wolff Stadium
5757 U.S. 90 W. at Callaghan Rd.
San Antonio
210/675-7275
The Missions is a Texas League, Los Angeles Dodgers AA farm club with a tradition of winning seasons in the Texas League (which includes more than just Texas). But another tradition almost as popular is the Missions' hospitality to families, which includes very reasonable admission prices. And every game, at the seventh-inning stretch, the Puffy Taco takes the field. This rather unsettling looking entrée on legs invites one child out of the stands to chase it around the bases. If the child catches and tackles the Taco (which always happens somewhere between second and third—the Taco doesn't have the legs it used to), prizes result. Missions games are a refreshing return to old-time baseball. Call for schedule and prices (usually $2–$7). (Northwest)

Basketball

SAN ANTONIO SPURS
Alamodome
100 Montana St.
San Antonio
210/554-7787
Though the Spurs have exhibited a tendency to choke under late-season pressure, yielding a few lukewarm seasons, they reached the finals in 1999, winning against the Knicks. Spurs-mania is widespread and noisy, due in no small part to the

charismatic, intelligent Admiral, David Robinson. David's leadership and performance have both been bolstered by newcomer and number-one NBA draft pick Tim Duncan.

Everyone knows the Spurs will be moving out of the Alamodome as soon as city leaders can find a way to convince voters that maybe the dome wasn't such a good idea after all, and could they please pay for yet another facility, please? But for now, a Spurs game at the dome is great fun for the family. Call for prices and schedule. (Downtown)

Golf

WESTIN TEXAS OPEN
La Cantera Golf Club
16401 La Cantera Pkwy.
(by Fiesta Texas)
San Antonio
800/TEX-OPEN
The first Texas Open was held on the Brackenridge Park course in 1922. The PGA returns to San Antonio every year to a large and enthusiastic crowd. Since 1995, La Cantera Golf Club has gotten the nod, and winners have included Duffy Waldorf, David Ogrin, and Tim Herron. Call early for ticket information. Also check into a Park and Ride service to avoid the very heavy traffic. (Northwest)

Hockey

SAN ANTONIO DRAGONS
Freeman Coliseum
6201 E. Houston St.
San Antonio
210/7-DRAGON
Don't believe in hockey teams in South Texas? Until 1997, San Antonio had two: the International Hockey League Dragons and the Central

Hockey League Iguanas. The Dragons proved to be the bigger lizards, and the Iguanas slithered away. Considering their home is a place where practically nobody plays ice hockey (though the inline-skate street variety is gaining momentum), the Dragons have a respectable following. Call for schedule and prices. (Northeast)

Horse Racing

RETAMA PARK
I-35 N.
Selma
210/651-7000
The joke a few years back was that the only things running faster than the horses at Retama Park were the track's owners trying to outrun their creditors. Fortunately, track management did a miraculous job of pulling Retama back from bankruptcy and ruination, and the crowds have never been better at this not-yet-a-decade-old facility just north of the city.

Retama features live racing Wed–Sat, with post time at 7 p.m. Seasons include thoroughbred and quarter-horse. General admission is $2.50, and bettors must be at least 21 years old. Minimum wager is $2. Call for shuttle-bus information. When the flesh-and-blood horses are wintering in Kentucky, pony players can satisfy their cravings with simulcast racing, shown daily throughout the year beginning at 10:30 a.m. (Northeast)

Rodeo

SAN ANTONIO STOCK SHOW AND RODEO
Freeman Coliseum
6201 E. Houston St.

San Antonio
210/225-5851
San Antonio returns to its ranching roots early each February with this two-week series of events and concerts featuring top-flight rodeo athletes and country and Tejano music stars. To really get the spirit, arrive in time for the massive Cowboy Breakfast that kicks off the rodeo from the parking lot of Central Park Mall. Call for dates and prices. (Northeast)

Soccer

SAN ANTONIO PUMAS
11924 Vance-Jackson Rd.
San Antonio
210/696-4952
Soccer is a huge sport among San Antonio kids, many of whom seem to be kicking before they're walking. But grown-up players receive considerably less support. The Pumas have no field of their own and no

Fun Facts about the Alamodome

- *The dome was a pet project of former mayor and former HUD secretary Henry Cisneros.*
- *It sits on the former site of Alamo Iron Works, so . . .*
- *Much of the soil that was excavated for the dome was contaminated. No one seems to know where the soil ended up.*
- *It's not a dome. Cables suspend the roof over 72,000 seats.*
- *Remarking that the cable towers make the building look like an upended armadillo, some citizens suggested the name "'Dillodome."*
- *It cost $190 million, financed through an ingenious (some say insidious) sales tax levied through VIA Metropolitan Transit. VIA's taxing authority could be used only if the project was public transit–related—hence the huge bus lots on the north side and the lack of parking ease—but . . .*
- *The tax allowed the dome to be built with no debt.*
- *The dome has the world's largest movable seating system and is the only place on the continent with two permanent Olympic skating rinks.*
- *It hosted the 1993 U.S. Olympic Festival.*
- *It doesn't have an NFL football team (much to the city's consternation), and the Spurs are trying to move out.*

It's ironically appropriate that a city that's seen so many professional and semipro sports franchises come to tragic ends is also the home of KENS-TV 5 sportscaster and *San Antonio Express-News* columnist Dan Cook. Don't recognize the name? You'll recognize this: According to *Bartlett's Familiar Quotations*, Cook was the guy who, in April 1978, first spouted the immortal observation, "The opera ain't over till the fat lady sings."

major corporate sponsorship. If you want to see them play, call before arrival to make sure they're still here. Tickets are usually at $3 for adults and $1 for children. (Northwest)

RECREATION

Baseball and Softball

Several city parks contain diamonds. You'll need a reservation for the better ones. Call Parks and Rec (210/207-8480) for information on: Fischer, 10700 Nacogdoches Rd. (NE); Kennedy, 3101 Roselawn Ave. (S); Koger Stokes, Brackenridge Park (NE); Lambert Beach, 400 N. St. Mary's St. (DT); Polo Field, Brackenridge Park (NE); and Rusty Lyons, 5200 McCullough Ave. (NW).

Bicycling

Until federal transportation guidelines that provide for bicycles take effect, serious cycling in San Antonio will continue to be impractical due to narrow road shoulders and few paths. The public parks are an option, particularly for mild mountain biking.

But local cyclists are eagerly anticipating the Mission Trail. To be completed in 2000, this combination

of parks and greenbelt areas will connect the Alamo downtown with the other four missions in the chain along the San Antonio River. A bike path will run the length of the trail. Much of that path exists now, but in disconnected and unfinished form. The final product will be much better.

If you're intent on roadside pedaling, the local cycling community does have regular get-togethers, particularly outside Loops 410 and 1604. Call the San Antonio Wheelmen (210/826-5015) cycling club for information. Some of the local bike shops organize rides as well, including B & J Bicycle Shop, 8800 Broadway (NE), 210/826-0405; and Broadway Bicycle Show, 8306 Broadway (NE), 210/805-0805.

Boating, Fishing, and Sailing

For anything bigger than bass, you'll have to head east to the coast. Locally you'll find the three very fine lakes that follow. Others, such as Medina Lake (50 miles northwest, past the town of Bandera), are equally popular but farther.

CALAVERAS LAKE
Off U.S. 181, 15 miles southeast
San Antonio
The best nearby fishing, particularly

for bass and cat, is found in this 3,500-acre lake. (That large industrial complex is a City Public Service coal and gas power plant.) (Northeast)

CANYON LAKE
FM 306 off I-35 N.
San Antonio
Trout is a specialty at this very scenic lake. Its 8,500 acres were formed by a Corps of Engineers dam on the Guadalupe River, and they house several yacht clubs. Skiing and jet-skiing are also popular, and many inlets are good for swimming. (Northeast)

LAKE MCQUEENY
FM 78 off I-35 N.
New Braunfels
A small (400-acre) lake where skiing is the hot ticket. Ski shows are frequently presented in season, and comfortable swimming areas are favorites. (Northeast)

Bowling

UNIVERSITY BOWL
12332 I-10 W.
San Antonio
210/699-6235
Far and away the city's most popular pin spot, despite its northwest corner location, is University Bowl. The 32-lane center's recent renovation includes a state-of-the-art scoring system with 36-inch displays, sound effects, and other cool bells and whistles, as well as an out-of-this-world video arcade for those wishing to mow down bug-eyed monsters rather than pins. But UB was popular before it rolled into the twenty-first century, and local celebrities such as David Robinson and George Strait have been patrons. Daily 9 a.m.–midnight. $1.90 per game. ♿ (Northwest)

Canoeing, Tubing, and Rafting

GUADALUPE RIVER
I-35 N.
New Braunfels
210/625-2385 (New Braunfels Visitors Center)
In summer the Guadalupe River around New Braunfels often has more tubers than fish. Several outfitters are found along the Guadalupe's banks. For more information, call the New Braunfels Visitors Center, 210/625-2385. If you're up to a three-hour raft trip, call the Gruene River Co., 210/625-2800. Prices are around

Strike Factory

Though few people are aware of it, the Alamo City is an important landmark in the history of bowling. The city is the headquarters of Columbia 300, one of the world's largest manufacturers of bowling balls. Columbia's stock-in-trade is supplying balls to bowling alleys and pro shops. Its factory at 5005 West Avenue on the city's north side was nearly destroyed in an explosion and fire in summer 1997 but will be rebuilt.

Brackenridge Stables, p. 165

$15 for adults, and reservations are recommended. (Northeast)

Fitness Clubs

If you have a membership at your hometown YMCA or YWCA, it's reciprocal with the seven San Antonio YMCA branches and one YWCA. Call to make arrangements and to determine what equipment is available. There are several outstanding private health clubs, both independent and chains. Two of the best are:

BALLY TOTAL FITNESS
5819 NW Loop 410
San Antonio
210/647-9600

This popular national chain has four San Antonio locations. Most feature cardiovascular equipment, aerobics, swimming pool, child care, circuit training, and free weights. Call the Bally closest to where you're staying and check the amenities: 255 E. Basse Rd. in the Quarry Market (NE), 210/930-6282; 12311 Nacogdoches (NE), 210/646-6262; 8725 Marbach (NW), 210/674-2244. Use your Bally membership, or ask for the one-time nonmember visit. (Northwest)

CONCORD ATHLETIC CLUB
7700 Jones Maltsberger Rd.
San Antonio
210/828-8880

The Lexus of San Antonio fitness clubs, the Concord is located along U.S. 281 just inside Loop 410. Its highrise facility has huge glass windows looking out on the downtown San Antonio skyline. Inside those windows are three racquetball courts, three squash courts, a 25-meter pool, weight machines, stationary bikes, a full basketball court, and two exercise studios offering 80 classes each week. After your workout, enjoy the sauna, steam room, and a massage. $10 guest fee. & (Northwest)

Golf

San Antonio's temperate climate makes golf a near-religion here. Visiting linksters have some outstanding public courses to choose from.

(Descriptions courtesy of San Antonio Convention & Visitors Bureau.)

BRACKENRIDGE
Brackenridge Park
San Antonio
210/226-5612

The oldest 18-hole public course in the state, Brackenridge was designed by the legendary A. W. Tillinghast. The course opened in 1916 and hosted the first Texas Open in 1922. The front nine is lined by ancient oaks and pecans, requiring accurate tee shots. The back nine is more open, but the wind comes into play. Par 72, 6,185 yards (men), 5,216 yards (women), rating 67, slope 122. $14 on weekdays, $16 on weekends and holidays, $16.50 for cart. (Northeast)

CEDAR CREEK
8250 Vista Colina Rd.
San Antonio
210/695-5050

Set in the picturesque Hill Country, Cedar Creek has been ranked the top municipal course in South Texas in numerous surveys. As demanding as it is beautiful, the course winds through limestone hillsides, taking golfers up and down steep elevation changes, through oak thickets, and around and over several waterfalls and meandering creeks. Fairways are generous, but multitiered greens demand accurate iron work and put a premium on the short game. Par 72, 7,150 yards (men), 5,525 yards (women), rating 73.4, slope 132. $18 on weekdays, $20 on weekends and holidays, $16 for cart. (Northwest)

HILL COUNTRY GOLF CLUB
9800 Hyatt Resort Dr. (in the Hyatt Regency Hill Country Resort)
San Antonio
210/647-1234

From the veranda of the ranch-style clubhouse, the Hyatt Regency Resort's championship course seems to have been here forever, not just since

---

Ike and Proud (St.) Mary

In 1916, when Dwight D. Eisenhower was a newly commissioned lieutenant posted to Fort Sam Houston, he was approached by priests from St. Louis College (which would later become St. Mary's) who had heard of his prowess on his college gridiron. St. Louis hadn't won a football game in five years, and the faculty felt Eisenhower was an obvious, if somewhat unconventional, choice for coach. With the blessing of—and under pressure from—his commanding officer, Ike took over the team and led them to a 5–1–1 season his first year. Ike's new wife, Mamie, attended and cheered at every game. She holds the distinction of being the only woman in St. Mary's history ever awarded a football letter.

1993—a testament to designer Arthur Hill's subtle style. With plenty of cacti, native oaks, and Texas wildflowers, the course blends naturally with its surroundings. Three par-4s are less than 340 yards—a reprieve from the three that are over 445. And a huge double green serves both the ninth and 18th holes. This is an authentic Texas Hill Country Golf experience. Just keep the ball on the fairway or you'll see more of the countryside than you bargained for! Par 72, 6,913 yards (men), 4,781 yards (women), rating 73.9, slope 136. $90 on weekdays, $100 on weekends (both fees include cart). $55 twilight rate (all the holes you can hit after 3 p.m. Mon–Sat and after noon on Sun). Reservations always required. Call 48 hours in advance. (Northwest)

LA CANTERA GOLF CLUB
16401 La Cantera Pkwy.
(by Fiesta Texas)
San Antonio
800/4-GOLFUS
Carved from the walls of a limestone quarry and nestled amid the live oak

trees, streams, and wildlife of the Hill Country, La Cantera is a visual stunner. The thrills include a tee shot from atop an 80-foot quarry wall, where you take aim at Fiesta Texas's famous roller coaster, the Rattler. But don't be fooled by the dramatic scenery—this beauty can be a beast. Elevated tees help the shorter hitter, but accurate second shots are a must. This is one of the final courses designed by the renowned team of Jay Morrish and Tom Weiskopf. As proof of their success, the course has been selected to host the PGA Tour's Westin Texas Open at La Cantera. Par 72, 7,155 yards (men), 4,940 yards (women), rating 72, slope 132. Call for times and prices. (Northwest)

MISSION DEL LAGO
1130 Mission Grande Rd.
San Antonio
210/627-2522
Built at the same time as Cedar Creek, Mission del Lago couldn't be more different from its sister course. Here the land is flatter, making the Texas wind a

Retama Park, p. 156

Retama Park

Pooling Resources

If it's just fun and splashing you're after during the outdoor swim-
ming season, visit one of the following parks. All are within an easy
trip of downtown, but call to check individual pool hours.

Cassiano, *1440 S. Zarzamora St., San Antonio, 210/434-7482, NW*

Concepción, *600 E. Theo Ave., San Antonio, 210/532-3473, S*

Cuellar, *503 SW 36th St., San Antonio, 210/434-8028, NW*

Dellview, *500 Basswood Dr., San Antonio, 210/349-0570, NW*

Elmendorf, *4400 W. Commerce St., San Antonio, 210/434-7380, NW*

Fairchild, *1214 E. Crockett St., San Antonio, 210/226-6722, NE*

Garza, *5800 Hemphill Dr., San Antonio, 210/434-8122, NW*

Kennedy, *3101 Roselawn Ave., San Antonio, 210/436-7009, S*

Kingsborough, *350 Felps Blvd., San Antonio, 210/924-6761, S*

Lincoln, *2803 E. Commerce St., San Antonio, 210/224-7590, NE*

Monterrey, *5919 W. Commerce St., San Antonio, 210/432-2727, NW*

Normoyle, *700 Culberson Ave., San Antonio, 210/923-2442, S*

Roosevelt, *300 Roosevelt Dr., San Antonio, 210/532-6091, S*

San Pedro, *2200 N. Flores St., San Antonio, 210/732-2778, NW*

Southcross, *819 W. Southcross Blvd., San Antonio, 210/927-2001, S*

Southside Lions, *900 Hiawatha St., San Antonio, 210/532-2027, S*

Sunset, *103 Chesswood Dr., San Antonio, 210/435-4011, NW*

Ward, *435 E. Sunshine Dr., San Antonio, 210/732-7350, NW*

Westwood, *7601 W. Military Dr., San Antonio, 210/673-3382, NW*

Woodlawn, *1100 Cincinnati Ave., San Antonio, 210/732-5789, NW*

real factor. And for a municipal course, Mission del Lago is superbly bunkered. Hit a shot off-line and one of the 124 bunkers waits in anticipation. Add the water that comes into play on ten holes and subtle greens, and you have a course that will test every part of your game. A good score from the back tees at Mission del Lago is something to be proud of. Par 72, 7,208 yards (men), 5,291 yards (women), rating 72, slope 129. Call for greens fees and tee times. (South)

OLMOS BASIN
7022 N. McCullough Ave.
San Antonio
210/826-4041
One of the city's most popular courses, Olmos Basin has hosted the

San Antonio Stock Show and Rodeo, p. 156

Men's City Championship 27 times. Highlighted by a collection of par-3 holes, this course is an honest test of golf. There's nothing too tricky—good shots are rewarded and you pay a price for bad ones. The greens are straightforward, with no severe undulations, but their size demands accurate iron shots or a sure, firm touch with your putter. Par 72, 6,894 yards (men), 5,805 yards (women), rating 71.2, slope 123. $16, plus $18 for cart. After 1 p.m., $22 for two players and cart. (Northwest)

PECAN VALLEY GOLF CLUB
4700 Pecan Valley Dr.
San Antonio
210/333-9018
This majestic course was the site of the 50th PGA Championship in 1968, when Julius Boros edged Arnold Palmer on the 18th hole. Huge old pecans and oaks line the fairways and frame the greens. Rated in *Golf Digest's* Top 50 Public Courses in America, Pecan Valley will test every part of your game—as a championship course should. But for most

people, the real attractions are the beauty of the course and the chance to play this piece of history. Par 71, 7,116 yards (men), 5,621 yards (women), rating 73.9, slope 136. $57 (includes cart). (South)

THE QUARRY GOLF CLUB
444 E. Basse Rd.
San Antonio
210/824-4500
Keith Foster designed this very new course, part of the ambitious quarry reclamation project west of Alamo Heights, while under the influence of Great Britain. Like a British Open course, the front nine has no trees, a deep heather rough, and a constant bedeviling breeze. But it's the back nine that amazes most golfers. All nine holes are set within the 86-acre limestone quarry, winding around its 100-foot-tall perimeter and challenging the golfer to carry shots over imposing chasms. The Quarry was recently named Best Public Golf Course in Texas by the *Dallas Morning News*. Par 72, 6,740 yards (men), 4,897 yards (women), rating 71.8,

slope 122. $75 Mon–Thu, $85 Fri–Sun (both fees include cart). (Northeast)

RIVERSIDE
203 McDonald St.
San Antonio
210/533-8371

Located on the site where Teddy Roosevelt and his Rough Riders trained, Riverside opened in 1929 as a nine-hole course. In 1961 an additional 11 holes were added, all par-3s. Today the par-3 course still exists, and a full-size 18-hole championship course offers 6,602 yards of fun. Huge, old trees (particularly the ornery one blocking the right side of the fairway on the seventh hole) give straight hitters an advantage on the front nine. The back nine is more open, letting long hitters cut loose. Par 72, 6,602 yards (men), 5,730 yards (women), rating 72, slope 128. $13 on weekdays, $16 on weekends and holidays. $18 for cart. $4 for nine holes of par-3. (South)

WILLOW SPRINGS
202 Coliseum Rd.
San Antonio
210/226-6721

Opened in 1923, Willow Springs has hosted the Texas Open numerous times, with Ben Hogan, Sam Snead, and Byron Nelson all headlining. The course was redesigned in 1975, but the small, well-guarded greens and tough par-4s remain. Willow Springs also features the longest hole in the city—its 663-yard, par-5 second hole. Two creeks and numerous ponds come into play on seven holes, but they're more of a visual accent than an actual hazard. This is a great course if you like to walk. Par 72, 6,407 yards (men), 5,792 yards (women), rating 73.7, slope 115. $14 on weekdays, $16 on weekends and holidays. $16.70 for cart. (Northeast)

Hiking

Unless you want to set off into the Hill Country and blaze your own trail north or start across the flatlands to the south, San Antonio hiking is confined to the city parks. Many of these have more-than-adequate trails, and some are particularly suited to hikers with short legs and attention spans to match.

The finest nature trails are found in the 250 acres of Friedrich Park in the far northwest zone. It's a bit of a drive to the park from downtown, but once you get up into the wildflower-clad hills, you'll forget how you got there.

Horseback Riding

BRACKENRIDGE STABLES
840 E. Mulberry St.
San Antonio
210/732-8881

Maybe it's because of San Antonio's ranching history, when people owned their own horses, that it's hard for you to rent one. In fact, Brackenridge is the only place to rent horses anywhere in town. Don't expect to go galloping across the prairie. The beautiful wooded trails are as gentle as the mounts. Riding on your own (no guide) $23 per hour. Guided trail rides (ages 4 and up) $15 for 20–30 minutes, $20 for 45 minutes. Pony rides $6 for 15 minutes, $11 for 30 minutes. (Northeast)

Scuba Diving and Snorkeling

TROPICAL DIVERS
12241 San Pedro Ave.
San Antonio
210/490-3483

This equipment shop and dive school is the local headquarters for bubble-blowers. In addition to teaching scuba

San Antonio Dragons, p. 156

technique and renting and selling the requisite equipment, TD arranges diving outings to Canyon Lake, to a couple of rivers, and—for the more ambitious—to the Gulf Coasts of Texas and Mexico. If you're part of the wet set, call ahead to see if such an excursion coincides with your visit. (Northwest)

Skating

CRYSTAL ICE PALACE
I-10 W. and De Zavala Rd.
San Antonio
210/696-0006
Ice is in short supply in South Texas, so there's only one rink. Afternoon Mon–Fri noon–5:30, Sat and Sun 1–5. Evening Sun–Thu 7–9, Fri and Sat 7:30–midnight. $4.50 adults, $3.50 ages 12 and under, seniors, and military personnel. Sun and Mon are "Cheap Skate" nights: $2 for everyone. Skate rental $2. (Northwest)

EMBASSY SKATE CENTER
606 Embassy Oaks Dr.
San Antonio
210/495-2525
Of the half-dozen roller rinks in town, Embassy is the local favorite. Birthday parties are a specialty. Tue–Fri 4–6, Sat and Sun 1–5, Tue and Wed 7:30–9:30 p.m., Fri and Sat 7:30–11 p.m. $3 weekday afternoons, $5 evenings and weekends. Rent skates or bring your own (inlines are welcome). (Northwest)

Skeet and Target Shooting

A PLACE TO SHOOT
Moursund Blvd., 2 miles outside
Loop 410 S.
San Antonio
210/628-1888
APTS has everything you could possibly need for target practice: pistol and rifle ranges, skeet and trap, and a complete line of supplies. If you didn't bring your "shootin' arn" with you, you can rent one here. An HK 40-caliber semiautomatic pistol runs around $15 for the day (on-site only). Ammo is extra. (South)

Skydiving

BLUE SKIES SKYDIVING ADVENTURES
14965 Cassiano Rd.
Elmendorf
210/635-7013, 800/801-JUMP
The Alamo City looks even sweeter as it's rushing toward your face at 120 mph. At Blue Skies, strap yourself to a "tandem master" skydiver, fly two miles above the city, and enjoy a 40-second plummet before a parachute blossoms above you (Lord willing) and glides you gently to earth four minutes later. Free T-shirt included. $140 per person. (South)

Swimming

The Department of Parks and Recreation maintains more than 20 park pools and one indoor pool, the Natatorium, at 1430 W. Durango, 210/226-8541 (NW). But if you're a serious lap swimmer you won't have much luck with the public pools, as the crowds of kids rarely yield the right-of-way. Your surest bet for uninterrupted lapping is the Palo Alto College Natatorium, 1400 Villa Real, 210/921-5234 (S), which is open to the public after 5 p.m.

Tennis

Parks and Recreation has a couple of court options. The nicest is McFarlin Tennis Center in San Pedro Park (DT), 210/732-1223. Another good choice is the Fairchild Tennis Center at 1214 E. Crockett St., 210/226-6912.

Volleyball

GUNN SPORTS PARK
12001 Wetmore Rd.
San Antonio
210/545-2700
What you'll see from the road is an admirable complex of ball diamonds. But this park's 18 sand courts and two traditional courts make it San Antonio's volleyball headquarters. Concession stands and all the required amenities are part of the central structure. Fees and times vary for non-league play, so call ahead. (Northeast)

Harlequin Dinner Theatre

11

PERFORMING ARTS

A special license plate recently began popping up on highways statewide. It reads, "Texas: State of the Arts." That's debatable. Despite having a huge population with a host of ethnic origins from which to draw artistic activities, the state woefully underfunds its artists. For the past several years, in nationwide rankings of state support for home-grown arts, Texas has ranked 53—behind Guam.

Perhaps that explains why San Antonio has no full-time professional theater company, no professional ballet, and no professional opera. And while the San Antonio Symphony is highly regarded within the classical music world for its creativity and quality, the orchestra is perpetually cash-strapped and on the verge of permanent decrescendo.

Nonetheless, San Antonio has a thriving arts community. Amateur troupes take the stage and do praiseworthy jobs. And the city's multicultural heritage is well represented; some of the most memorable arts events in the city, such as the symphony's sold-out, bilingual performances of A Midsummer Night's Dream a few years back, combine the best of familiar European fine arts and lively, south-of-the-border folk traditions. You'll also find a strong representation of the avant garde, particularly in theater, where a few companies commission and perform regional works with a universal impact.

Maybe the license plate is right after all. The state won't pay to ensure the survival of high-quality arts, so San Antonio's arts community has drawn a line in the sand, set up footlights along it, and invites you to sit down and enjoy.

THEATER

Until recently, San Antonio's theater scene has been dominated by volun-

teer, civic theater–style productions. But recent successes by paying companies have upped the ante—and the quality—for everyone in the thespian community. Three relatively new professional companies, San Antonio Public Theater (210/829-PLAY), the New Playwright's Theatre (210/826-2616), and the Shoestring Shakespeare Company (210/732-7058), do not yet have their own venues for staging their high-quality shows, so call for schedules and locations.

Laudable productions are also fielded during the school year by the theater departments of Trinity University (715 Stadium Dr., 210/736-8511), the University of the Incarnate Word (4301 Broadway, 210/829-3810), and San Antonio College (1300 San Pedro Ave., 210/733-2715).

ALAMO STREET RESTAURANT & THEATRE
1150 S. Alamo St.
San Antonio
210/271-7791
This dinner theater is unique for a number of reasons. First, the performance hall is actually the sanctuary of a church built in 1912. Second, dinner is not in the theater, but in the former choir-rehearsal room. And third, the shows may be familiar musical chestnuts or Texas originals. ASR&T offers a very affordable, very enjoyable evening's entertainment by a professional cast. ♿ (Downtown)

HARLEQUIN DINNER THEATRE
Harney Rd., Bldg. 2652
Fort Sam Houston
210/221-5953
A professional company provides a popular, continuously running series of musicals and murder mysteries in Fort Sam's delightful base theater. Expect both golden-age standards and refreshingly new originals. ♿ (Northeast)

JOSEPHINE THEATRE
339 W. Josephine St.
San Antonio
210/734-4646
This tidy little theater is home to locally produced, predominantly musical shows that are regularly recognized with Alamo Theater Arts Council Globe Awards. Inside is a full-service bar that provides refreshment before the show and a not-to-be-missed "aftershow" following the last curtain call. ♿ (Downtown)

JUMP-START PERFORMANCE COMPANY
108 Blue Star St.
San Antonio
210/227-5867
As you might expect from a theater company making its home in the very contemporary Blue Star Art Space (see Chapter 6, Museums and Galleries), Jump-Start's productions are cutting edge. Usually original, by turns disturbing and hilarious, and always memorable, Jump-Start shows have won numerous local and—while on the road—national awards. A relatively new company, the Firelight Players, have been singled out for local honors. ♿ (Downtown)

MAGIK THEATRE
420 S. Alamo St.
San Antonio
210/227-2751
Outstanding, award-winning family fare is par for the course. For more information, see Chapter 7, Kids' Stuff, page 126 (Downtown)

SAN PEDRO PLAYHOUSE
San Pedro Park at Ashby
San Antonio
210/733-7258
Located on the edge of San Pedro Park is one of the oldest publicly owned playhouses in America and San Antonio's longest-operating

community theater company. Limited budgets often impose restrictions on the quality of sets and costumes and the size of the live orchestra, but the players are often some of the city's finest. Expect mostly musical favorites from Broadway's golden age and a few more up-to-date offerings. Downstairs in the Cellar Theatre (formerly the SALT Cellar, before the company abandoned the moniker San Antonio Little Theatre) are found intimate, slightly more adventurous productions. ⑤ (Northwest)

STEVEN STOLI'S PLAYHOUSE
11838 Wurzbach Rd.
San Antonio
210/408-0116
Stoli consistently provides quality productions of popular favorites and Texas originals in his mall-based theater. The Playhouse is the home of *Hang 'Em High in the Selma Sky*, San Antonio's longest-running comedy murder mystery, set in the little burg of Selma, just north on I-35. Stoli also directed a lauded live re-creation of Orson Welles's *War of the Worlds* broadcast on its 60th anniversary.

Children's theater is offered on select weekends. (Northwest)

CLASSICAL MUSIC AND OPERA

¡ARTS! SAN ANTONIO
222 E. Houston St., Ste. 630
San Antonio
210/226-2891
This presenting organization fields a full season of top-flight artsy entertainment from around the globe, including chamber music, classical ballet and contemporary dance, and the annual free Shakespeare in the Park productions. Call for schedule, venues, and prices. (zone varies with venue)

SAN ANTONIO OPERA COMPANY
10100 Reunion Pl.
San Antonio
210/227-6863
San Antonio was once a center for grand opera, with the Symphony Grand Opera Festival bringing luminary performers from the world's finest stages from the 1940s through

Buying Tickets

Tickets for nearly every major event in town are available through the omnipresent TicketMaster, 210/224-9600, which has a lock on ticket services for San Antonio. The San Antonio Symphony, ¡Arts! San Antonio, the Majestic Theatre, and Laurie Auditorium also sell tickets to their own events, allowing you to bypass the rather substantial service charge tacked onto each ticket's price by the TM monopoly. Smaller theaters and dinner theaters usually handle their own tickets. Call the number listed for each.

the '60s. But because of the declining popularity of the form and the high cost of presenting it, those days are past. Just don't tell the San Antonio Opera Company. This dedicated handful of volunteers is working to revive local opera through small-scale shows and visiting companies. Performances are sporadic, though usually well-received, in various venues. (zone varies with venue)

SAN ANTONIO SYMPHONY
222 E. Houston St., Ste. 200
San Antonio
210/554-1010

Perennially in dire financial straits, the symphony very nearly died in fall 1998, at the dawn of its 60th season. This would have been a tragedy, because the Alamo City's hometown band is truly unique among American orchestras. While standard heavy-weight fare is regularly performed to excellent reviews, the symphony really shines in a genre it pioneered and champions: programs commingling the classical traditions of western Europe with folk music and dance influences of South Texas and northern Mexico.

New works commissioned from regional composers have hung several national awards for adventuresome programming on the symphony office walls. Even the traditional concerts in the Majestic Theatre are hardly stuffy, since young and effervescent Music Director Christopher Wilkins

delights in talking to the audience—particularly during the very popular Interactive Classics family concerts (see Chapter 7, Kids' Stuff). If the San Antonio Symphony can survive, it is well worth a listen during your visit. ♿ (zone varies with venue)

DANCE

Professional dance companies regularly pass through town, most often presented by ¡Arts! San Antonio. The Carver cultural center imports some more adventurous shows, and though the Carver's roots are in African American culture, its offerings are more eclectic. An annual professional Nutcracker, *produced by the symphony and ¡Arts! San Antonio with an out-of-town company (Fort Worth Dallas Ballet, lately), recruits a horde of local ballet students as mice and such. But with no home-grown professional hoofers, dance in San Antonio is predominantly regional in nature.*

That's not to say visiting dance fans should write off Terpsichore in South Texas. Folklorico, or Mexican folk dance, is a fascinating spectacle of swirling skirts, flying feet, and intoxicating rhythm. And some folk dance companies reach farther back in South Texas/Mexico history—all the way across the Atlantic—to present flamenco. The groups listed here present an always-changing menu of dance, most of it worth seeing.

Sunken Garden Amphitheatre, p. 179

BALLET SAN ANTONIO
4335 Vance Jackson Rd.
San Antonio
210/340-0607
This school for up-and-coming dancers features regular, rewarding recitals by its standout students. Ballet San Antonio is also the leading purveyor of mice for the annual *Nutcracker*. Call for a schedule of recitals and venues. (zone varies with venue)

DEPARTMENT OF
PARKS AND RECREATION
950 E. Hildebrand Ave.
San Antonio
210/821-3130
Parks and Rec has a vibrant dance program. In fact, some of its dancers started in the program as children and stayed into adulthood. Emphasis is on *folklorico*, but clogging, square dance, and flamenco are represented as well. The easiest time to enjoy everything the program has to offer is mid- to late summer, when Parks and Rec troupes dance every night of the week at the Arneson River Theatre

during Fiesta Noche del Rio and Fiesta Flamenca. Call for performance schedules and additional venues. (Northwest)

GUADALUPE CULTURAL
ARTS CENTER
1300 Guadalupe St.
San Antonio
210/271-3151
The Guadalupe has a dance school, and it adds flamenco to the *folklorico*. The best place to experience the GCAC's programs is at the on-site amphitheater—particularly since tamale and fajita stands are usually part of summer evenings there. (Northwest)

URBAN 15
829 N. Alamo St.
San Antonio
210/222-1408
Of all of San Antonio's dance companies, Urban 15 is the most difficult to pigeonhole—and the most fun to watch. The all-volunteer organization demands high levels of commitment and perspiration from its Caribbean-style dancers and drummers, and it

shows. Urban 15 provides spicy performances throughout the year, but it is at its best in February when its Carnaval de San Anto Mardi Gras Fiesta Masquerade brings a bit of Rio to the River City. Call for performance schedules, and while you're at it, ask if you can drop in for a rehearsal. U-15 is a friendly bunch. (Downtown)

CONCERT VENUES

ALAMEDA THEATRE
318 W. Houston St.
San Antonio
210/299-4300
The Alameda has recently been restored into a multivenue performance hall for Latino arts (see Chapter 5, Sights and Attractions). Before long, it should be returning to its former stature as a Hispanic entertainment capital. Call for a schedule of perfor-

mances that might coincide with your visit. & (Downtown)

ALAMODOME
Durango St. and I-37
San Antonio
210/223-DOME
For stadium-style concerts, the dome is the only choice in town. The acoustics are, of course, abysmal—just what you would expect when listening to music in a football arena. But with the gigawatt sound systems, wide-screen video, and often-frightening pyrotechnics available to today's rock artists, the 72,000-seat Alamodome is remarkably successful as a concert hall. Hint: Don't drive to the dome. Parking is limited, expensive, and distant. Walk from a downtown hotel, or opt for one of VIA Metropolitan Transit's well-managed Park and Ride shuttles. Call 210/227-2020 for VIA information and

---

San Antonio Sounds

San Antonio is renowned as the Tejano Capital of the World. For those unacquainted with the word, Tejano (Teh-HAH-noh, Spanish for "Texan") is a rhythmic, Tex-Mex/country-western style featuring a button accordion and lyrics in Spanish.

Tejano itself is an outgrowth of conjunto *(kohn-HOON-toh), a blend of Mexican-based folk music and the polkas and waltzes brought to Texas by European immigrants in the late nineteenth and early twentieth centuries.*

Neither Tejano nor conjunto *is the same as mariachi (mah-ree-AH-chee), which is much closer to traditional south-of-the-border folk music, though* conjunto *uses many of the same horns, and Tejano is a sort of "mariachi meets Nashville."*

the location of the nearest Park and Ride lot. ♿ (Downtown)

ARNESON RIVER THEATRE
La Villita (on the River Walk)
San Antonio
210/207-8610
This lovely little 800-seat amphitheater on the river was part of the original 1939 Paseo del Rio project, designed by River Walk creator Robert H. Hugman himself and named after project engineer Edwin Arneson. River barges pass between the audience and the cozy stage and mission-style stage house, with its trademark church bells. Throughout the warm months the Arneson hosts countless free community performances. Summer evenings bring the Fiesta Noche del Rio music and dance variety shows (Thu–Sat), Fiesta Flamenca (Sun–Tue), and Fandango music and dance (Wed). Take a blanket or lawn chair. ♿ (Downtown)

BEETHOVEN HALL
420 S. Alamo St.
San Antonio
210/207-3412
Though the grand turn-of-the-century facade of this concert hall was lost to the expansion of Alamo Street in the 1920s, the building still contains a very fine little auditorium hosting various events. It is perhaps the finest medium-size hall in town for solo piano performances, and is also the home of the wonderful Magik Theatre. ♿ (Downtown)

CARVER COMMUNITY CULTURAL CENTER
226 N. Hackberry St.
San Antonio
210/225-6516
It's ironic—and fitting—that a building born of segregation should be reborn into one of the city's finest small performance halls and an arts center for all San Antonians. Built as a "colored" library to discourage African Americans from using other downtown branches, the Carver has been transformed into a several-hundred-seat theater and studio

Carnaval de San Anto Dancers, a part of Urban 15, p. 172

The Urban 15 Group

Majestic Theatre

Architect John Eberson is legendary as the father of the "atmospheric theater" concept. In the first quarter of this century, before the questionable improvements offered by today's cinema megaplexes, a theater was a place to spend an entire evening. The 1929 Majestic was one of Eberson's last and finest creations, restored to its former glory in 1989 with significant acoustic and accessibility enhancements.

The interior architecture is an intriguing amalgam of Moorish points and Baroque swirls and doodads. Arches, rough-hewn woodwork (most of which is actually cast plaster), walls, seats, carpet, and light fixtures all glow with only-in–San Antonio colors, reflecting Eberson's fondness for the Alamo City. Inside the massive wooden entry doors—uniquely located at the side of the auditorium—is a demure, life-size nude statue that was reportedly nicknamed "Sweet Grapes" by construction workers for the cluster she holds over one bare shoulder. Just beyond, a large aquarium is built into the wall.

But it's inside the hall where magic is really found. To make evenings in the Majestic pleasant, even unforgettable, Eberson moved the outdoors in. The asymmetric side walls re-create a Mediterranean village at evening, complete with climbing vines and real exotic birds (though not as real as they once were), some circling above the massive proscenium. The latter is intricately cast with sculpture and filigree, and other fine sculpture and tapestry are found throughout.

Above it all, in a deep blue Texas sky, twinkling stars are occasionally obscured by wispy, drifting clouds (really!). In a tribute to the theater's 1929 opening—and his own perfectionism—Eberson obtained a celestial map of where the stars would be over San Antonio on opening night and had his own stars placed exactly there.

complex presenting outstanding touring entertainment throughout the year. Call for a roster of the topflight jazz, dance, and theatrical presentations that are guaranteed to be here when you are. ఉ (Northeast)

FREEMAN COLISEUM
3201 E. Houston St.
San Antonio
210/224-1374
This massive structure is often called into use for rock concerts but is bet-

---

Municipal Auditorium

Gifted San Antonio architect Atlee Ayres hit a home run in 1926 with this Moorish-inspired auditorium. In fact, the immense, $1.5 million structure erected as a World War I memorial garnered Ayres an award from the American Institute of Architects.

Legendary entertainers from movie to music greats (Al Jolson, Bob Hope, Louis Armstrong, Will Rogers, and Elvis) all graced the Municipal's stage, as did visiting dignitaries such as Lyndon B. Johnson and Richard Nixon. The auditorium was also home to the late, lamented San Antonio Symphony Grand Opera Festival, which for several decades was one of America's most highly regarded operatic series.

By the 1960s Municipal had fallen into disrepair and disrepute—the latter due in part to Mayor Maury Maverick's decision to allow a few local Communist sympathizers to host a rally there in 1939. The 100 or so Socialists were greeted by 5,000 or so anti-Socialists, who took over the hall and largely destroyed the interior.

The auditorium's ignominy was complete in 1979, when fire destroyed the grand pipe organ, seats, and roof, leaving only a gutted shell. City leaders ignored advice to tear the structure down and instead restored it. A 1996 Broadway touring production of Phantom of the Opera *packed the hall and renewed its prominent place in the minds of locals (though many attendees loudly criticized the distance between some seats and the stage, and boomy acoustics that obscured the dialogue). But for events such as rock concerts that are not quite large enough for the Alamodome, Municipal is still Queen of San Antonio.*

ter suited for visiting circuses and as the home base of the San Antonio Dragons hockey team. (Northeast)

GUADALUPE CULTURAL ARTS CENTER
1300 Guadalupe St.
San Antonio
210/271-3151

While the Carver doesn't limit itself to African American arts, the Guadalupe has focused its attentions on things Latino, with admirable results. Events such as the Tejano Conjunto Festival, the Cine Festival film series, and presentations of visiting artists have made the Guadalupe one of the United States's most important centers of Hispanic arts. The center has two performance venues. The intimate indoor theater offers contemporary Latino theater productions, often in world premieres. An outdoor amphitheater is surrounded with tantalizing food booths during colorful festivals of music and dance. ♿ (Northwest)

LAURIE AUDITORIUM
Trinity University
715 Stadium Dr.
San Antonio
210/736-8117

With seating for nearly 3,000 and very dry acoustics, Laurie is ideally suited for amplified concerts, dance performances, lectures, and comedy. It presents all of these throughout the year,

The Tejano Conjunto Festival at Guadalupe Cultural Arts Center

including an outstanding visiting-speaker series featuring high-profile newsmakers and noisemakers. Laurie is also home to the Symphony's Young People's Concert Series. The very wide "pie slice" configuration and floor-level stage mean that patrons seated near the side walls may have difficulty seeing action near the wings, but the seating is otherwise excellent. ♿ (Northwest)

LEEPER AUDITORIUM
McNay Art Museum
6000 N. New Braunfels Ave.
San Antonio

T I P

Traffic around any of the downtown performance venues gets thick. If you're driving there, go a bit early and find a nearby place for a nice dinner. Also, check the Spurs's basketball schedule. If there's a home game that night, allow even more time.

Sunken Garden Amphitheatre

This quarry-turned-concert venue, the first Portland Cement factory west of the Mississippi, has been a San Antonio favorite since its rebirth in 1917. Most of this popularity is due to its pastoral location in the middle of Brackenridge Park, next to the Japanese Tea Garden that gives the amphitheater its name. Today many of the music events held in Sunken Garden venture into triple-digit decibel territory (bringing regular complaints from the park's neighbors), though theatrical productions are also featured. Several of the Garden's offerings are of the all-day or weekend festival variety. Rain, of course, is a risk in spring and fall.

210/824-5368

Leeper has become a second home to musicians of the San Antonio Symphony for their small-ensemble performances. (Northeast)

LILA COCKRELL THEATRE
Henry B. Gonzalez
Convention Center
200 E. Market St.
San Antonio
210/207-8500

Named for a former San Antonio mayor, Lila (as both the theater and the mayor are affectionately called) is the only venue in town with a full orchestra pit. Consequently, it's the hall of choice for touring ballet and opera companies—but not often. The convention-center location makes it far more lucrative for the city to reserve Lila for conferences, trade shows, etc. For music and large-scale performances, however, it's a very fine hall, with excellent sightlines, comfortable seating, and admirable acoustics. ♿ (Downtown)

MAJESTIC THEATRE
230 E. Houston St.
San Antonio
210/226-3333

You've never seen a theater like the Majestic. One of the last, great "atmospheric" theaters to be built, the Majestic is home to the San Antonio Symphony, the Majestic Broadway series of touring musicals and plays, and the annual Tejano Music Awards. Seating and sound are excellent throughout, but the long-of-leg should avoid the balcony section above the mezzanine. Behind (and sharing) the backstage wall is the smaller, less fantastical Empire Theatre. More intimate and stately, the Empire has only recently opened as a home for chamber music, comedy, small dance, and folk performances. ♿ (Downtown)

MCALLISTER AUDITORIUM
San Antonio College
1300 San Pedro Ave.
San Antonio

210/733-2000

A recently renovated, acoustically fine hall on the campus of San Antonio College, McAllister is called into service for many community events and concerts. (Downtown)

MUNICIPAL AUDITORIUM
100 Auditorium Circle
San Antonio
210/207-8511

This grand old hall at the northern terminus of the River Walk has seen some tough times, including fire and a riot sparked by San Antonio's last—and only—Communist rally (see sidebar). It has recovered nicely from both, and while the barnlike acoustics leave much to be desired from some types of shows, it's ideal for large-scale events with substantial sound boost. ♿ (Downtown)

SCOTTISH RITE CATHEDRAL
308 Avenue E
San Antonio
210/222-0133

Scottish Rite isn't the permanent home of any performing group, though it's often called into service if the Majestic is booked or too expen-

sive for a local group. And it needs some work—particularly in the wheelchair-accessibility department. But the massive 1928 building is amazing. Like the Majestic, it has a starry sky, with the constellations outlined in gold. The stage can go from standard to immense (thanks to a large moving floor) and is wide enough to accommodate nearly anything. The cathedral is often used for touring opera performances that don't need the orchestra pits of the Majestic or Lila Cockrell. (Downtown)

SUNKEN GARDEN AMPHITHEATRE
Brackenridge Park
3875 N. St. Mary's St.
San Antonio
210/735-0663

San Antonio's only large outdoor venue (see sidebar) is in need of renovation, but that doesn't stop it from hosting a wide variety of events throughout the year, including the very popular Reggae Fest. Sunken Garden is operated by the Parks and Recreation Department, which can clue you in to what's happening when. Call 210/821-3130. ♿ (Northeast)

Boardwalk Bistro

12

NIGHTLIFE

San Antonio has a lively and remarkably varied night scene. In fact, short of Fiesta, no facet of San Antonio is more reflective of the city's multicultural roots than the fun that starts after the sun goes down.

If you're a Yankee planning a San Antonio vacation far enough in advance, take some country-western line-dancing classes. Then, upon your arrival, hit one of the Western-wear stores like Kallison's to pick up your dancing duds. There's a hometown, all-American feel to country dance halls that you can't find anywhere else.

Wherever you go for fun, remember: The Driving While Intoxicated laws in Texas are stiff and unforgiving, so don't risk spending part of your time sampling the hospitality of the Bexar County hoosegow. Dance a lot, laugh a lot, drink a little.

One more note: While the night scene is lively, it can also be transitory. Clubs may come and go without a ripple, so be sure to call before setting out for a night of dancing and fun.

DANCE CLUBS

AFTERSHOX
13307-A San Pedro Ave.
San Antonio
210/495-SHOX
Describing their after-hours place as an "industrial-strength nightclub," the folks at Aftershox provide recorded, high-energy techno music

for your dancing pleasure. Wed 8 p.m.–2 a.m., Fri–Sat 9 p.m.–4 a.m., Sun 9 p.m.–3 a.m. Cover charge: $1 Wed, $5 Fri–Sun. ⅄ (Northwest)

AVALON
8779 Wurzbach Rd.
San Antonio
210/696-7748
This eclectic little club serves up live

jazz on Tuesday, reggae on Thursday, and more jazz and oldies on Friday; all for dancing. Tue and Fri 5 p.m.–3 a.m., Thu and Sat 8 p.m.–3 a.m. No cover. ♿ (Northwest)

BONHAM EXCHANGE
411 Bonham St.
San Antonio
210/271-3811

The Bonham is San Antonio's most popular gay bar, a favorite with the straight crowd, too. The DJed music is techno, industrial, and irresistible. The club is partially wheelchair accessible. Mon–Fri 4 p.m.–2 a.m., Sat 8 p.m.–4 a.m. Cover charge: $5 Wed and Sat, $2 Thu, $3 Fri. (Downtown)

CIBOLO CREEK COUNTRY CLUB
8640 E. Evans Rd.
San Antonio
210/651-6652

Don't expect golf carts and debutantes. The emphasis at this country club is on country. A trip around the floor of the CCCC is a trip around Texas, to the accompaniment of Texas swing, zydeco, Cajun, and rockabilly tunes. Dinner is available to accompany that Texas staple, the longneck. Wed, Thu, Sun 3–11 p.m.; Fri–Sat 3 p.m.–2 a.m. Cover charge: $5–$15. No credit cards. ♿ (Northeast)

JOE'S VOLCANO
6844 Ingram Rd.
San Antonio
210/680-7225

Joe's blows seventies to nineties rock in this large and popular dance club. Wednesday night is Ladies' Night, with a complimentary prime rib buffet. Wed–Sun 7 p.m.–2 a.m. Cover charge: $5–10. ♿ (Northwest)

KRAMER'S
9323 Perrin Beitel Rd., No. 201

San Antonio
210/590-9662

Kramer's has a unique approach to nightlife—at least for San Antonio. Jukebox dance music from the sixties to the nineties shares the bill with celebrity impersonators, dance routines, and skits. Snacks are available. Tue–Fri 6 p.m.–2 a.m., Sat 7 p.m.–2 a.m. Cover charge: $3 Fri and Sat. ♿ (Northeast)

ODYSSEY
11431 Perrin Beitel Rd.
San Antonio
210/653-9176

One of San Antonio's newest night spots offers hi-tech music as well as yesterday's hits for dancing. Four full-service bars will cool you down in Odyssey's "space-age" environment. Finger foods will build up your energy for the next set. Open Tue–Sun to 2 a.m. (Northwest)

MARTINI'S
8507 McCullough Ave.
San Antonio
210/344-4747

Tapping into two current crazes—martinis and swing dancing—Martini's calls itself a great place to have fun or just relax. Contemporary dance music is joined by live shows some nights. Snacks provided. Mon–Fri 3 p.m.–2 a.m., Sat 8 p.m.–2 a.m. (Northwest)

PARK PLACE
622 NW Loop 410
(in Central Park Mall)
San Antonio
210/349-3801

If you and your companion can't make up your minds what your nightlife experience should be, pick Park Place. Here, under one roof, you'll find no fewer than five separate clubs: Cactus Moon (gambling/video games), Cheers (karaoke), Bell Bottoms (disco, '70s/'80s retro, pool), Denim and Diamonds (country, pool, mechanical bull), and Kokomo's (Top 40 and retro rock, cigars, premium liquors, shadowbox dancers, and an airplane sticking out of the wall). Nightly drink specials are unencumbered by food. Wed–Sun 7 p.m.–2 a.m. Cover charge: $5 Fri and Sat, $2 weeknights for any or all of the clubs. ♿ (Northwest)

PETTICOAT JUNCTION
1818 N. Main Ave.
San Antonio
210/737-2344
Relatively new, the Junction is a gay/lesbian country dance club. Tue–Sun 7 p.m.–2 a.m., Fri 5 p.m.–2 a.m. Cover charge: $2 Fri, $3 Sat. ♿ (Northwest)

ROARING '20S
13445 Old Blanco Rd.
San Antonio
210/492-1353
Craig Herman's place is unique not only because it maintains much of the look it had when built in 1926 but also because it is San Antonio's only night spot for dancing to live, big-band jazz. Dinner and hors d'oeuvres are available when you need a break from the Lindy and jitterbug. Tue, Fri, Sat, Sun 6:30–midnight. Cover charge: $7–$8. ♿ (Northwest)

THE SAINT
1430 N. Main Ave.
San Antonio
210/225-7330
The Saint is a gay club featuring dancing and the city's longest-running drag show. Mon–Thu 9 p.m.–2:30 a.m., Fri–Sun 9 p.m.–4 a.m. Weekend cover charge: $4 adults, $7 minors. (Northwest)

JAZZ CLUBS

BERRINGERS
11874 Wurzbach Rd.
San Antonio
210/493-1900
This comfortable, upscale club features live jazz on Thursdays and recorded music other nights. Finger

The crowd at Dick's Last Resort

Dick's Last Resort

Far West Rodeo

If you have only one night to spend in San Antonio, and you want to cram all the Texas into it you can, there's only one place to go: Far West Rodeo. FWR isn't so much a nightspot as it is Texas in a box. A really big box. Under the roof of the two-story "Texas town"-looking building, you'll find:

- *68,000 square feet of entertainment space for 3,800 guests*
- *A restaurant serving mesquite-smoked barbecue, steaks, and Mexican food*
- *Two Texas-size dance floors for the two-step, shottische, Western waltz, Cotton-Eyed Joe, and line dancing (lessons available)*
- *Live country-western and Tejano bands, including national touring stars*
- *Billiards and video games*
- *A mechanical bull (for you to ride)*
- *A 1,500-seat arena*

In this last, after you've finished your steak, you can sit back with a drink and watch somebody ride steak-on-the-hoof. FWR has brought indoors a real pro rodeo, complete with the opening pageant, bull-riding, and clowns. Only Texas could create a place like Far West Rodeo, and Texas is the only place you'll find it. Intersection of Loop 410 E. and I-35 S. (NE), 210/646-WEST.

foods are available. Mon–Fri 2 p.m.–2 a.m., Sat 11 a.m.–2 a.m., Sun noon–10 p.m. (Northwest)

BOARDWALK BISTRO
4011 Broadway
San Antonio
210/824-0100
The live acoustic jazz provided most nights is excellent, particularly when drummer Kyle Keener and guitarist Polly Harrison perform as Small World. Also excellent is the mar-

velously varied light nouveau menu. Mon 11 a.m.–4 p.m., Tue–Thu 11 a.m.–10:30 p.m., Fri–Sat 11 a.m.–11:30 p.m. No cover. (Northeast)

DICK'S LAST RESORT
406 Navarro St.
San Antonio
210/224-0026
This rowdy restaurant on the River Walk features live music every night, including some of the city's best jazz and blues artists. There's no room for

dancing, but the buckets of fiery crawdads will keep you busy reaching for your cold drink. Daily 11 a.m.–2 a.m. No cover. & (Downtown)

JAZZ, A LOUISIANA KITCHEN
2632 Broadway
San Antonio
210/472-2520
A taste of N'Awlins on Broadway, Jazz serves up live acts (both local and touring), along with Louisiana cuisine. Dine and listen on the patio or inside. If you're a player, bring your ax and sit in on the Sunday night jazz jam. Sun–Thu 11 a.m.–midnight, Fri–Sat 11 a.m.–1 a.m. (Northeast)

JIM CULLUM'S LANDING
123 Losoya St.
(in the Hyatt Regency)
San Antonio
210/223-7266
Opened in 1963, Cullum's cozy little jazz club on the River Walk occasionally originates "River Walk: Live from the Landing," carried on over 200 National Public Radio stations nationwide. On weekends, Cullum and his band play

some of the finest traditional Dixieland jazz in America. If you live to hear Bix Beiderbeck, Jack Teagarden, Jelly Roll Morton, and early Satchmo, you have to stop in. Lunch, dinner, and snacks are available. Mon–Fri 11:30 a.m.–1 a.m., Sat–Sun noon–1 a.m. Cover charge: $5. & (Downtown)

SWIG MARTINI BAR
111 W. Crockett St., Ste. 205
San Antonio
210/476-0005
One of the newest pubs in town, Swig was also one of the first places to jump on the martini/cigar bandwagon. Fortunately, the club eschews actual lounge music for live jazz on Mon and Sat. Swing dancing some nights. Daily 2 p.m.–2 a.m. No cover. & (Downtown)

BLUES CLUBS

CARLSBAD TAVERN
11407 West Ave.
San Antonio
210/341-0716
The name may be cute but the blues

Cibolo Creek Country Club, p. 181

Ben Thorn

are serious, particularly on Tuesdays at the live blues jam. Other nights enjoy acoustic and folk, rock, Cajun parties, karaoke, and more. Daily noon–2 a.m. (Northwest)

HOUSTON STREET ALEHOUSE
420 E. Houston St.
San Antonio
210/354-4694
This relative newcomer to the local nightlife scene quickly built a loyal following. The Alehouse serves dinner, but that's a sidelight to its increasingly famous martinis. Live blues and rock are featured most nights. Mon–Fri 4 p.m.–2 a.m., Sat–Sun noon–2 a.m. Cover charge: $2 (Fri and Sat only). & (Downtown)

ROCK CLUBS

DMZ
1318 Cupples Rd.
San Antonio
210/431-3004
DMZ offers only metal music from live local bands and touring groups, and offers it only to teens. Actually, older folks can get in, too, but there's no alcohol once you do. DMZ's hours and cover charges vary with events, so call to find who's on deck and when. (Northwest)

GREEN ONION LOUNGE
1033 Avenue B
San Antonio
210/224-4334
Owner Rudy Abad is very specific: The Onion is very cool but not trendy. It is a small club for ages 21 and up with a maximum occupancy of 80. All of the live music—alternative, garage, punk—is original. (Rudy, the drummer for local punk heroes Sons of Hercules, doesn't like cover

bands.) The beer is cheap, but eat before you come. Tue–Sun 8 p.m.–2 a.m. Cover charge: $3–$5. Rudy also dislikes credit cards. & (Downtown)

HILL'S AND DALE'S
15403 White Fawn Dr.
San Antonio
210/695-2307
At Hill's and Dale's you'll hear a little bit of everything—rock, blue, oldies, R&B—and meet people from all walks of life, young and old. And you'll be able to sample between 300 and 400 beers. If you return to San Antonio often, you might even get a plaque on the ceiling with your name on it . . . for trying each one of the beers they have on tap. Sun–Thu noon–midnight, Fri and Sat 11:30 a.m.–2 a.m. Never a cover. & (Northwest)

WHITE RABBIT
2410 N. St. Mary's St.
San Antonio
210/737-2221
San Antonio's most successful (and perhaps loudest) live rock club, the Rabbit brings in big names and big crowds. All ages are welcome, but the local curfew is observed. (Owner/manager Jordan Silber looks as if he too should be in before dark, but his shrewd business acumen has brought new nightlife to the "St. Mary's Strip.") Usually open daily 8 p.m.–2 a.m., but hours and cover charges vary with bands. So does seating, which can affect wheelchair accessibility, so call to verify. (Northwest)

COUNTRY AND WESTERN CLUBS

BLUE BONNET PALACE
16842 I-35 N.

San Antonio
210/651-6702
This good ol' Texas roadhouse is open for kickin' back with live music and line dances. Fri–Sat 7 p.m.–2 a.m. Cover charges vary. ⅃ (Northeast)

COWBOY BAR
12952 Bandera Rd.
San Antonio
210/695-8049
What's in a name? Everything, at the Cowboy Bar. This not-too-big country-western dance hall is a great place to experience your first Texas two-steppin'. Finger foods are available, as is a happy-hour buffet during the week, and live and recorded music provide the rhythms. Mon–Fri 4 p.m.–2 a.m., Sat–Sun 6 p.m.–2 a.m. (Northwest)

DALLAS
2335 NW Military Dr.
San Antonio
210/344-9469
With its hard oak dance floor, hot country music, and pairs of two-steppers, this is a true country bar (despite the advertised $50,000 bikini contest). Appetizer-style and finger foods are served, sometimes accompanied by live music. If you get good enough, you can enter the two-step contest. Tue–Sun, 5 p.m.–2 a.m. (Northwest)

FLOORE COUNTRY STORE
14464 Old Bandera Hwy.
San Antonio
210/695-8827
It really is a store, right down to the sawdust-strewn floor. It's also the favorite local haunt of Willie Nelson. The Red-Headed Stranger got his San Antonio start here longer ago than he'd like to remember, but he makes it a point to stop in to hear the bands—sometimes unannounced—when he's

in the neighborhood. Mon–Thu 11 a.m.–8 p.m., Fri 11 a.m.–midnight, Sat 3 p.m.–1 a.m., Sun 3 p.m.– 10 p.m. Cover charge varies. (Northwest)

GRUENE HALL
1281 Gruene Rd.
New Braunfels
830/606-1281
The Texas pronunciation—"green"— is close to the original German, but the hall itself is pure Texas, and pure roadhouse. Gruene Hall is one of the most popular old-style country music venues in South Texas. Mon–Fri 11 a.m.–midnight, Sat 10 a.m.–1 a.m., Sun 10 a.m.–9 p.m. Cover charge: $6 and up. No credit cards. ⅃ (Northeast)

TEJANO, SALSA, AND LATIN CLUBS

ARJON'S INTERNATIONAL CLUB
8736 Tesoro Dr.
San Antonio
210/804-1409
Arjon's brings the world to San Antonio. Live music every night features salsa, *cumbia*, Tejano, merengue, and some other forms of hot dance music you may not even have heard of. The appetizer-type food is equally eclectic, with a free buffet during happy hour on weekdays. Valet parking is available at no charge. Mon–Fri 4 p.m.–2 a.m., Sat–Sun 7 p.m.–2 a.m. ⅃ (Northeast)

EL CARIBE
2611 Wagon Wheel Dr.
San Antonio
210/826-8818
As the name implies, El Caribe delights in all things Caribbean. Both food and music come from Cuba, Puerto Rico, and Mexico, the former including salsa and merengue (live on

Sunset Station

One structure in San Antonio succinctly links San Antonio's past with its present and future: the Sunset Depot, now called Sunset Station. Built in 1903, the Sunset Depot was the train station that welcomed settlers, including European immigrants, to San Antonio (see Chapter 5, Sights and Attractions). Now, the city hopes Sunset Station will bring even more visitors to town, and more residents back to downtown.

The space where arriving and departing passengers once waited for their trains is becoming a rollicking entertainment destination, containing at least six clubs. These include (or will include) a Top 40 club, a retro disco, a blues and jazz room, a karaoke bar, and the Sunset Saloon. The latter will offer live entertainment with a house band and local talent in a country-and-western ambience. Outside will be the Lone Star Pavilion, whose seating capacity of nearly 3,000 will accommodate big shows that won't fit inside.

The concept is that the Station will be family friendly, with jugglers, clowns, and mariachis in the areas between the clubs. Eating spots will also be found within.

Sunset Station is a work in progress, but some of the businesses are now open. And while the function of the beautiful, historic depot has been drastically changed, much of the original architecture and detail remains. Drop in and see where San Antonio has been, and where it's going. Open nightly at 1174 E. Commerce St., just northeast of downtown. Call 210/227-5371 for information.

Fri and Sat). Buffet Mon–Fri 11 a.m.–2 p.m. Open Mon–Wed 11 a.m.–9 p.m., Thu 11 a.m.–10 p.m., Fri–Sat 11 a.m.–midnight. (Northeast)

HACIENDA SALAS PARTY HOUSE
3127 Mission Rd.
San Antonio

210/923-1879
The Hacienda was honored by the local daily paper as the Number One Nightclub in San Antonio in 1992. From nearby Mission San José, you can hear the live Tejano and *conjunto* dance tunes. Wed, Fri, Sat, Sun 5 p.m.–2 a.m. Cover charge: Fri $2, Sat

$3 for caballeros only. No credit cards, *por favor.* ♿ (South)

TEJANO OPRY HOUSE
110 Produce Row
(in Market Square)
San Antonio
210/476-0100
Located in historic El Mercado, the TOH brings together the best of north and south of the border. Tejano acts include locals and national stars. Tired of dancing? Take your drink out on the balcony that overlooks the marketplace. Fri–Sun 6 p.m.–2 a.m. (Downtown)

OTHER CLUBS

ALL STARS
9440 I-10 W.
San Antonio
210/593-0576
All Stars is primarily a place for guys—a combination sports bar and what Texans refer to as a gentleman's club. That means the entertainment takes the form of wide-screen telecast sports and half-clad women. Over 200 of them, according to the management. All Stars offers a full, if standard, menu. Daily 11 a.m.–2 a.m. ♿ (Northwest)

CLUB W
820 San Pedro Ave.
San Antonio
210/271-9663
The crowd at Club W is mixed, but cabaret-style shows featuring male dancers are gay-oriented. Dance music is primarily techno. Daily 9 p.m.–2 a.m. (Northwest)

FATSO'S SPORTS GARDEN
1704 Bandera Rd.
San Antonio
210/432-0121
Wisconsin visitors, take note: Fatso's is your official San Antonio Cheese-headquarters. It's also a sports bar—listed, in fact, in the 1997 edition of *Best Sports Bars in America*—with 15 satellite receivers and eight large-screen TVs. The full and very filling

The Jim Cullum Jazz Band, p. 184

The Jim Cullum Jazz Band

Esquire Tavern

On Commerce Street, just above the River Walk, is the oldest continually operating saloon in Texas, the Esquire Tavern. It ain't fancy, but it is historic. For instance, the Esquire opened for business on December 3, 1933—the day Prohibition was repealed. It has the longest bar in the state, over which have passed more than 33 million beers. Many of those sat on the bar simultaneously when the Esquire earned a listing in Ripley's Believe It Or Not! for "289 rednecks drinking 5,973 longnecks." Perhaps more respectable is the title bestowed by Texas Monthly: "The best-looking bar in Texas." The magazine went on to say, "The hand-shaken margaritas are even better than those in the border towns." Add to that a Wurlitzer that plays everything from Bob Wills to Glenn Miller, and waitresses who will call you by name, and you have more than enough reasons to visit. 155 E. Commerce St. (on the River Walk), San Antonio, 210/222-2521. Mon–Sat 9 a.m.–midnight, Sun noon–midnight.

barbecue menu is available for lunch and dinner, and a party deck and four sand volleyball courts stand ready to help you work up an appetite or work off a meal. Daily 11 a.m.–2 a.m. No cover. & (Northwest)

MI TIERRA MARIACHI BAR
218 Produce Row (in El Mercado)
San Antonio
210/225-1262

Dining while being serenaded by mariachis takes some getting used to, but it's worth the experience. (Note: It's also worth money. The tableside performers aren't in it for the *cabrito*.) Mi Tierra is a very popular spot after the other clubs close, since it's open seven days, 24 hours. & (Downtown)

OLLY'S BEEF & LOBSTER
3117 NW Loop 410
San Antonio
210/341-1500

In addition to excellent surf-and-turf dinners, Olly Otten serves up live dance music from the fifties to the eighties. If you're too stuffed to dance, sit back and enjoy the only live, Las Vegas–style shows in San Antonio. Olly opens his doors Mon 4 p.m.–midnight, Tue 4 p.m.–1 a.m., Wed–Fri 4 p.m.–2 a.m., Sat 5 p.m.–2 a.m. Amazingly, there's no cover. (Northwest)

O'NEILL'S IRISH HOUSE
302 E. Commerce St.
San Antonio
210/222-8550

Gruene Hall, p. 186

Emerald Isle lunch and dinner fare is served up with Celtic music on various nights, although the wearin' of the green is as often accompanied by the playin' of the blues. So if your heart's set on "Danny Boy," call first. Mon–Sat 3 p.m.–2 a.m. No cover. & (Downtown)

ONE-O-SIX
106 Pershing Ave.
San Antonio
210/820-0906
A cozy neighborhood gay bar whose jukebox is fully stocked with all styles. Appetizer-style snacks are available. Daily noon– 2 a.m. (Northeast)

PUBS AND BARS

BLUE STAR BREWING COMPANY
1414 S. Alamo St., No. 105
San Antonio
210/212-5506
San Antonio's favorite and hippest brewpub, the Blue Star is located in the arts complex of the same name. All beers served are made on the premises to accompany lunch and dinner six days, and brunch on Saturday. The Blue Star also boasts a large wine list and features live acoustic music. Mon–Sat 11 a.m.–2 a.m. (Downtown)

BREW MOON CAFÉ AND PUB
16350 Blanco Rd.
San Antonio
210/479-0066
In addition to very good food in this full-service restaurant, Brew Moon offers nearly 400 beers, all of them micro-brewed or imported. Wine is represented as well. The atmosphere is casual, surrounded by recorded music. Brew Moon was voted Best Beer Selection in the *San Antonio Current*'s 1997 readers' poll. (Northwest)

CADILLAC BAR
AND RESTAURANT
212 S. Flores St.
San Antonio
210/223-5533
A San Antonio tradition for nearly two decades, this Cadillac of bars offers several party rooms serving good food and great music. Recorded and

live artists represent Texas, Tejano, and more. The Cadillac is in the *Guinness Book of World Records* for World's Largest Margarita. Mon–Fri 11 a.m.–11 p.m. (Fri to 2 a.m.), Sat 5 p.m.–2 a.m. (Downtown)

HILL'S & DALE'S
15403 White Fawn Dr.
San Antonio
210/695-2307
It's not close to downtown, but if a huge selection of cereal malt beverages is what you seek, make the drive. Hills & Dales offers 54 on-tap beers and over 400 bottled varieties, accompanied by oldies rock and country (live, Thursday–Saturday). In business for a quarter of a century, H&D is open Sun–Thu noon–midnight, Fri–Sat 11:30 a.m.–2 a.m. Neither wheelchair nor credit-card accessible. (Northwest)

THE LABORATORY
BREWING COMPANY
7310 Jones Maltsberger Rd.
San Antonio
210/824-1997
This trendy new spot is located next to the trendy new Quarry Market. Beers are hand-crafted to accompany a full lunch and dinner menu. Live music is provided Thu–Sun, with a Vegas-style lounge show on Wed. Every Sun brings swing dancing. Daily 11 a.m.–2 a.m. ♿ (Northeast)

COMEDY CLUBS

MAIN AVENUE STUDIO
1608 N. Main Ave.
San Antonio
210/227-ATSA
San Antonio's version of the Second City comedy troupe is the Oxymorons—a truly inspired bunch of lunatics who perform improvisational comedy at the MAS on Friday at 10:45 p.m. Some of the humor is locally topical, but all of it's funny. $6. ♿ (Northwest)

RIVERCENTER COMEDY CLUB
Rivercenter, fourth level
across from AMC Theater
San Antonio
210/229-1420
The premier local comedy venue presents nationally recognized "A-list" comedians seven days a week, plus the best of the local crop. The location is A-list, too—the fourth level of Rivercenter makes RCC an ideal finish to an evening of downtown sightseeing and shopping. The club is open nightly for drinks and dinner or just appetizers. Hours and prices vary. Call for lineup and reservations. Note: Parking just before showtime is a problem, so arrive early and park in the Rivercenter garage, then stroll the River Walk. ♿ (Downtown)

POETRY SPOTS

BORDERS BOOKS & MUSIC
255 E. Basse Rd.
(in the Quarry Market)
San Antonio
210/828-9496
The book mega-chain's San Antonio spots offer frequent poetry readings, as well as lectures and discussion groups. The café serves light fare, including sandwiches, soups, desserts, and, of course, coffee. Live music plays in the café Thu–Sat evenings. A second location is in the Huebner Oaks Center at 11745 I-10 W. (NW), 210/561-0022. ♿ (Northeast)

CLIPPER SHIP BOOKSTORE
722 Balcones Heights Blvd.

San Antonio
210/734-5409
The most in-your-face of the local poetry venues, Clipper Ship holds a mike open (perhaps for you?) on Monday from 8–10 p.m. The bookstore is also open Tue–Fri 2–8 p.m., Sat noon–6 p.m., Sun noon–5 p.m. (Northwest)

FREEDOM COFFEE HOUSE & DELI
2407 N. St. Mary's St.
San Antonio
210/737-3363
Freedom's good coffee and sandwich fare is accompanied by mostly good poetry on open-mike Wednesday night. Deli open Tue–Sat noon–midnight. ♿ (Northwest)

MULLIGAN'S LAGOON
3000 N. St. Mary's St.
San Antonio
210/737-8734
Mulligan's has a little of everything: game room, beer and wine, ice-cream bar, coffee bar, full-service Caribbean restaurant, live music, and poetry. Mon–Thu 11:30 a.m.–midnight, Fri–Sat to 2 a.m. (Northwest)

MOVIE HOUSES OF NOTE

For a decade or so, San Antonio has been the site of a bitterly contested struggle between competing theater chains. The names of each chain's management may have changed. Regal Cinemas currently rules the roost with 14 movieplexes (www. regalcinemas.com). Runner-up is trendsetter AMC, with two valuable properties (www.amctheatres.com). Cinemark Theatres limits itself to two discount movie houses (www. cinemark.com).

All of the competition has been positive for San Antonio filmgoers.

Several San Antonio theaters now feature "stadium seating"—steeply inclined floors bearing wide, high-backed seats with movable "love-seat" armrests—in non-stadium-size screening rooms, with large screens and state-of-the-art sound systems. Highly hyped movies are shown on two or three screens simultaneously in most of these. Handy, though less-impressive theaters are found in nearly every shopping mall. One exception is the IMAX theater in downtown's Rivercenter, which screens both educational and feature films in mega-screen format. (See Chapter 5, Sights and Attractions.)

Most local theaters inflict 10 to 15 minutes of commercials beginning at film-starting time, so as long as you have your ticket, there may be no hurry to catch the opening credits.

CROSSROADS
4522 Fredericksburg Rd.
(In Crossroads Mall)
San Antonio
210/737-0291
Crossroads has found its niche as the closest thing San Antonio has to an art-film house. This persona led to the Crossroads's designation at the Best Intimate Theater in San Antonio. Don't expect cutting-edge flicks that you might find in Greenwich Village, though you will find some films you won't find anywhere else in town. Do expect seven screens, with no duplication of the hottest releases from screen to screen. (Northwest)

EMBASSY 14 THEATER
13707 Embassy Row
San Antonio
210/496-4940
This is a quibble, but if you want to find out what's playing at Embassy, buy a paper. The marquee on U.S. 281

is often broken, unreadable, or filled with indecipherable abbreviations. This place is crying out for a new sign. That aside, Embassy does feature stadium seats in all auditoriums and good sound, and restaurants EZ's, Mama's, and Alamo Café are nearby. Credit cards are accepted. Allow for traffic, as Embassy is off the very busy Bitters Rd./U.S. 281 intersection. (Northwest)

HUEBNER OAKS 24
100 75 W. I-10
San Antonio
210/558-9988
Huebner (HEEB-ner) Oaks is the San Antonio theater that started the move toward stadium seating—not to mention being the first and only one to break the 20-screen barrier. So far. As Huebner is the newest cinema in town, it was designed with stadium seating in all screening rooms, and topflight audio, resulting in a Best Theater in San Antonio title in a recent poll. It's also taken a small step toward partial art-house status by offering "gourmet movies" at selected times. HO-24 is not close to the city center, but you can stop in after a day at Fiesta Texas before returning to downtown. (Northwest)

MOVIES 16
5063 NW Loop 410
San Antonio
210/523-1294
One of Cinemark's two discount theaters, Movies 16 offers films a few months old for several dollars less. Matinees are $1, and after 6 p.m. all tickets are $1.50. The sound is usually provided in "Ultra Stereo," a less-pricey relation of THX and Dolby. But the audience is still listening. Seating is of the familiar, non-stadium variety, and snacks are, of course, available.

The other Cinemark discount house, Movies 9 in McCreless Mall (South), offers all shows at $1.50 except on Super Tuesdays, when the price is a buck. Accommodations are similar, and both theaters are handicapped accessible. & (Northwest)

NAKOMA THEATER
11603 W. Coker Loop
San Antonio
210/496-9560
Nakoma is another discount theater, this one operated by Regal Cinemas. All shows are $1.50. Nakoma is very popular with parents who use it to catch up on all the family Christmas and summer fare they didn't catch with the young 'uns the first time around. Lots of restaurants are nearby. (Northeast)

NORTHWOODS 14
17640 Henderson Pass
San Antonio
210/402-7369
The newest San Antonio theater, Northwoods gleams like a purple, neon Xanadu in the far north-central region. The neo-deco architecture outside is something to behold. An enormous lobby is pseudoindustrial, with factory-inspired photos that don't appear to have anything to do with the theater. No matter. Movies are first-run, accommodations are first rate, and credit cards are welcome. An excellent movie house. (Northeast)

QUARRY THEATER
255 E. Basse Rd.
(in the Quarry Market)
San Antonio
210/804-1115
The Quarry Theater is even entertaining before the movies start. Located in the rock-crushing building on the

former digs of the Alamo Cement plant, the theater takes it architectural cues from the past. The immense diesel engine that powered the rock crusher hovers above the lobby, emitting steam and industrial noises at appropriate times. Photos of the plant and its personnel dominate the industrial architecture, which must have inspired the Northwoods 14. All screening rooms have stadium seating and excellent sound, and credit cards are valid. The Quarry is very popular, so a good plan is to pick up your tickets early, then eat at Joe's Crab Shack or one of the other fine restaurants in the Market. (Northeast)

Lyndon B. Johnson N.H.P.

13

Day Trip: Lyndon B. Johnson National Historical Park

Distance from San Antonio: 60 miles or about a one-hour drive

The boyhood home of the 36th president of the United States is the centerpiece of this trip, which comprises two parks (one state and one national) and a small Texas town. Your first stop should be the latter, **Johnson City**, where you'll find a visitors center on the corner of G and 9th Streets. Pick up information brochures and then walk across the street to the **Boyhood Home** of LBJ. A lengthy walking trail will lead you to **Johnson Settlement**, where LBJ's grandfather, Sam Ealy Johnson, started his ranching and farming operation. The complex of restored buildings and an exhibit center trace the evolution of ranching in the Texas Hill Country, from open range to local spreads.

Return to your car and drive 14 miles west on U.S. 290 to the **Lyndon B. Johnson State Historical Park Visitor Center**. There you'll find exhibits and programs, a swimming pool, tennis courts, a baseball field, hiking trails, and picnic areas. Also near the visitors center is the **Sauer-Beckmann Living Historical Farm**, with facilities for outdoor recreation and nature study.

Board a bus back at the visitors center for a tour of **Lyndon B. Johnson National Historical Park**, which includes **LBJ's Birthplace**, the one-room **Junction School** he attended, the **LBJ Ranch** (also known as "The Texas White House"), and the **Johnson Family Cemetery**, where the president lies under the shade of his beloved live oaks.

SAN ANTONIO REGION

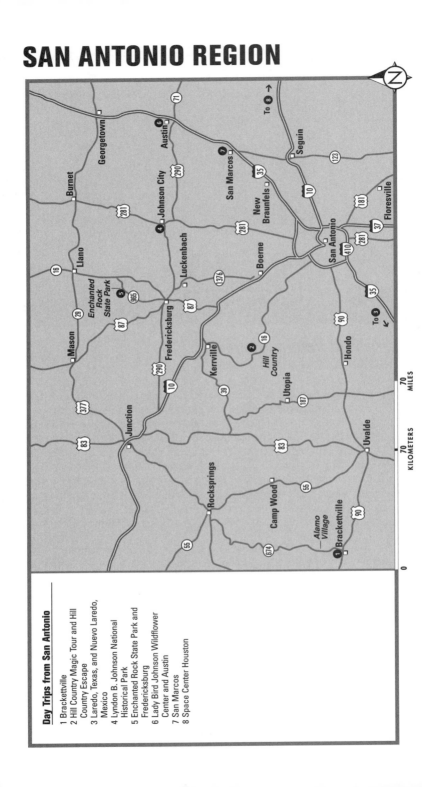

Day Trips from San Antonio

1 Brackettville
2 Hill Country Magic Tour and Hill Country Escape
3 Laredo, Texas, and Nuevo Laredo, Mexico
4 Lyndon B. Johnson National Historical Park
5 Enchanted Rock State Park and Fredericksburg
6 Lady Bird Johnson Wildflower Center and Austin
7 San Marcos
8 Space Center Houston

The visitors centers, LBJ's Birthplace, and Ranch tour buses are all wheelchair accessible, and written scripts of the tour narration are available for the hearing impaired.

A couple of notable shopping/stopping attractions are along the way: the **Feed Mill** on U.S. 290, a restored agricultural terminal that now houses an unexpectedly delightful smattering of antique, import, and art emporiums, restaurants, and a wine shop; and a collection of antique and craft dealers called **Horse Feathers Mall**.

If you'd like to extend your stay in the attractive little burg of Johnson City, call the office of Johnson City Bed & Breakfast at 210/868-4548 and select from several very different restored homes and buildings where you can spend the night. This is an attractive option if you intend to proceed with the next-day trip to Enchanted Rock State Park.

Getting There from San Antonio: *Take U.S. 281 north 60 miles to Johnson City.*

Day Trip: Enchanted Rock State Park and Fredericksburg

Distance from San Antonio: 105 miles or about a two-hour drive

The breathtaking geological artifact for which this park is named has long been a favorite destination of San Antonians wanting a quick one-day getaway. **Enchanted Rock** is an enormous, 650-acre outcropping of granite, the second largest stone formation in the nation. Only Georgia's Stone Mountain is larger. For many visitors, the attraction of the park is its Hill Country naturalism and the lovely picnic grounds. For other souls who

Hikers at Enchanted Rock State Park

FCVB/Al Rendon

wish to combine communing with nature and heavy breathing, a trail leading up the rock beckons.

Actually, anyone in fair physical condition can conquer the rock in an hour or so and reach the summit, which offers a stunning view of the surrounding Hill Country. Some smaller formations around the Enchanted one provide experienced, equipped climbers with additional challenges.

The park is intentionally maintained in a pristine state, so don't expect a handy Coke machine. If you forget to take your own food and drink, backtrack to **Fredericksburg**, where, as you try to decide whether to quench your thirst and appetite at **Altdorf German Biergarten and Restaurant** (301 W. Main St.) or the **Peach Tree Tea Room** (210 S. Adams St.), you'll encounter a number of equally interesting attractions. These include the following:

Pioneer Museum—1850s-era church, homes, and other buildings looking back to Fredericksburg's (and Texas's) roots; **Admiral Nimitz State Historical Park**—two museums (including the new George Bush Gallery) and two parks dedicated to Fredericksburg resident and WWII Pacific Commander Chester W. Nimitz; **Bauer Toy Museum**—3,500 vintage toys from the nineteenth and twentieth centuries; and **Fort Martin Scott Historic Site**—the first military installation on the Texas frontier.

Information on these major (and other minor) stops is available at the office of the **Fredericksburg Convention and Visitor Bureau** at 106 N. Adams, which is open daily. Call 830/997-6523 for advance tips.

Getting There from San Antonio: *Take U.S. 281 north 60 miles to Johnson City. Take Hwy. 290 west 30 miles to Fredericksburg. Turn north on Route 965 and go 15 miles to the park.*

Luckenbach

M. L. Abbott

Day Trip: Hill Country Magic Tour and Hill Country Escape

The easiest day trip is undoubtedly the one in which you don't have to drive. Two local tour-bus companies know this and so offer packages that include some of the most attractive day-trip destinations. (Note: Neither tour is wheelchair accessible.)

San Antonio City Tours' day-trip offering is the **Hill Country Magic Tour**. Make your reservation in advance (anytime night or day) by calling 210/228-9776, then pick up your ticket at the Alamo Visitor Center on Alamo Plaza just before you meet your air-conditioned motor coach.

Leaving at 9 a.m., the bus heads first for **Fredericksburg** along main and back roads. (Wildflower alert! Go in spring.) The Fredericksburg stop allows time for lunch, shopping, and a browse through the **Nimitz Museum and Gardens**. (See the previous Day Trip. Lunch and museum admission not included in price.)

After lunch, the bus continues to the picturesque **Pedernales River** and a guided tour of the **LBJ Ranch**, then returns to Alamo Plaza at 5 p.m. $39 adults, $19.50 children 5–10; seniors receive a 10 percent discount.

Gray Line Tours' **Texas Hill Country Escape** offers an identical route but leaves Alamo Plaza at 8:30 a.m. to allow for a return trip stop in **Lukenbach**. Immortalized by a country-western song ("Let's go to Lukenbach, Texas, with Waylon and Willie and the boys . . . "), the tiny, historic town "where everybody is somebody" is home to Willie Nelson's annual Fourth of July Festival and Picnic. At the center of town are the **General Store** and a shop or two. Lukenbach mementos are available in the restored **Post Office**. The Gray Line returns at 5:30 p.m.

Tickets are available by calling 210/226-1706. Tours operate every day except Easter, Thanksgiving, Christmas, and New Year's Day. $39 adults, $19.50 children 5–12.

Day Trip: Lady Bird Johnson Wildflower Center and Austin

Distance from San Antonio: 70 miles or about a 1.5-hour drive

There are many reasons to visit the Texas capital: history, music, and art are only three. But all of Austin's attractions combined can't compete with the beauty of the Lady Bird Johnson Wildflower Center on the city's west side; the dream come true of former First Lady and wildflower fanatic Lady Bird Johnson.

The 42-acre center, which is open year-round, is at its best in spring. A stroll along the meadow's trail will let you forget about the job you left behind. But first stop in the **Visitors Gallery** and get a lesson in backyard agriculture from **Ralph, the Talking Lawnmower**. (Ralph's not allowed in the meadow.) The gallery also gives you access to the three-story stone **Observation Tower** with its spectacular view of the surrounding natural bounty and one of North America's largest rooftop rainwater-harvesting system, which replenishes the grounds.

From the gallery, step out into 23 stunning **Display Gardens** filled with theme-flower beds. Take a break for a light lunch and cappuccino at the **Wildflower Café** or picnic in the shade.

If you're a gardener and the guided tour of the grounds inspires you to learn more about the staggering variety of North American wildflowers and how you can plant them at your own home, browse the **Research Library** (Wed, Thu 2–4). When the kids get tired of waiting for you, take them to a space reserved just for them: the **Children's Little House** (Sat 10–noon, 1–4; Sun 1–4). Then select your souvenir from **Wild Ideas: The Store**. But before leaving this heaven on earth behind and braving the decidedly unheavenly traffic on I-35 through Austin, sit beside the stone pool, watch the birds, and stop and smell the primroses.

Oh, yes—then there's Austin itself. There are far too many historical and commercial attractions in the star of the Lone Star State to list in this chapter (much less to absorb in the course of a reasonable day), but they include the **State Capitol**, the **Governor's Mansion**, **Zilker Park**, the **Umlauf Sculpture Garden and Museum**, **Town Lake**, the **Austin Children's Museum**, and the **Jourdan-Bachman Pioneer Farm**. For information on the wildflower center, stop by at 4801 LaCross Ave., 512/292-4100. Or stop by the **Visitor Information Center** at 300 Bouldin Ave., or call 512/478-0098. Open daily.

Getting There from San Antonio: *Take I-35 north 70 miles to the Austin metroplex. Take the Slaughter Lane exit and go left on Slaughter 5.8 miles to Loop 1, also called Mopac. Turn left and go the short distance to La Crosse Avenue. Turn left on La Crosse to the Center. The wildflower center charges $4 adults; $2.50 students and seniors; free for 4 and under and members.*

Day Trip: San Marcos

Distance from San Antonio: 50 miles or about a one-hour drive

This is an ideal day trip for families: animals, caves, and boats for the kids; shopping for the parents.

Located just west of San Marcos on I-35 is a complex of attractions called **Wonder World**. Its premier attraction is **Wonder Cave**, formed 30 million years ago when central Texas was still an ocean. A cataclysmic earthquake along the Balcones Fault opened up a 160-foot-deep cavern, which would become the state's most-visited cave. Tour guides will lead you along the well-lit, handrail-bordered walkways in the cave's year-round 71 degrees. Along the walls are clearly visible fossils of creatures and plants from millions of years ago, and photography is encouraged.

Those walls are actually the borders of the two enormous land masses that make up much of Texas, but don't worry—they haven't moved in a while.

Aboveground, Wonder World also boasts the **Tejas Tower**, which gives you a view of the Balcones Fault from 110 feet in the air. With your feet back on the ground, walk through the ever-popular **Anti-Gravity House** and then to the train depot for a ride through **Mystery Mountain** and **Crystal Falls** to **Texas Wildlife Park**—the state's largest petting zoo. For souvenirs, stop in the gift shop, **Mystery Mountain**, or **Mexico's World Import Market Place**. Wonder World is open year-round, 8–8 in summer, 9–5 in winter. For ticket prices, call Wonder World 512/392-3760, or log on to www.wonderworldpark.com.

As you leave the park and head back to I-35, the adults in the car have a choice to make. Do you cross the highway to the **San Marcos Factory Stores**, Texas' largest factory outlet mall (See Chapter 9, Shopping)? Or do you follow up Wonder World with **Aquarena Springs Resort** (open daily, 800/999-9767), with its glass-bottom boat rides over Aquarena Spring, aquariums filled with endangered native species, and archaeological artifacts dating back 12,000 years? Then there's the historic French/Spanish community of San Marcos itself, with its tree-lined historic districts of Victorian mansions, the **Texas Natural Marketplace**, and snorkeling, tubing, and picnicking along the **San Marcos River**.

Good luck keeping everybody happy. For help making up your mind in advance, call the San Marcos Chamber of Commerce at 888/200-5620 (toll-free).

Getting There from San Antonio: *Take I-35 north to the Hwy. 80 exit and follow the signs.*

Day Trip: Laredo, Texas, and Nuevo Laredo, Mexico

Distance from San Antonio: 150 miles or about a 2.5-hour drive

Make a run for the border and Los Dos Laredos—The Two Laredos. On the U.S. side of the bridge is the city of **Laredo, Texas**. Established in 1755, the town is one of the state's first. Today it's filled with historic buildings, palm trees, and shops stocking regional crafts and antiques. Don't miss the gargantuan, late-1700s **St. Augustine Church** and its equally venerable neighbor, **St. Augustine Plaza**.

To learn more about the city's history, stop in at the **Museum of the Republic of the Rio Grande** at 1009 Zaragoza Street, a one-level adobe that was the capitol of a republic that split from Mexico in 1839 and lasted two years. Zaragoza is also home to a collective of wholesalers whose handiwork includes leather, wovens, pottery, and other crafts at very low prices. Young people will enjoy the **Laredo Children's Museum** on Washington Street (210/725-2299), a hands-on collection of fun science activities and other wonders. Before or after, stop in one of the too-many-to-count Mexican restaurants along Zaragoza to sample real border-town cooking.

After lunch, park at the mall on the U.S. end of the bridge and walk into **Nuevo Laredo (New Laredo), Mexico**. You can drive across as well, but walking is easier, and you can take your time looking at the **Rio Grande**. Step off the bridge into Nuevo Laredo's shopping district, **El Mercado** (marketplace), where you'll immediately be spotted by street vendors offering food, clothing, toys, and almost anything else not too big to carry, and be serenaded by strolling mariachis. The shops lining the street vary in the quality of their wares, but prices are always good—sometimes embarrassingly so. Still, don't be afraid to haggle for what you want. None of the shopkeepers expects to get the asking price, with two exceptions:

Marti's, a shop three blocks from the bridge, is N.L.'s finest, and Marti knows it. Expect (relatively) pricey but lovely jewelry, clothing, and homewares. If you're keen to walk on, leave the marketplace and go about a mile on Avenida Reforma to number 3861 (take a cab if you're still shopping). That's **El Cid Glass Factory**, a family-owned business for more than 20 years. Glassware of all types and sizes is found here, most in the brilliant, impossible-to-reproduce colors of Mexican folk art. Also on Reforma, at 624, is a favorite restaurant of Nuevo Laredans, **La Principal**. Try the *cabrito*. Go ahead, try it!

Getting There from San Antonio: *Take I-35 south and follow the signs. As you drive into Laredo (U.S.), stop at the visitors center for a guide brochure.*

Day Trip: Brackettville

Distance from San Antonio: 120 miles or about a two-hour drive
If you haven't had your fill of the Alamo in San Antonio, you might as well see the other one. In the late 1950s, John Wayne was preparing to make his film directorial debut with *The Alamo*. The Duke knew he couldn't get the effect he wanted on San Antonio's Alamo Plaza ("Ya better have that tour bus outta here by sundown, pilgrim"), so he built his own to the west, on a ranch owned by "Happy" Shahan. Shahan was even happier after the film wrapped because it left him with a tourist attraction called **Alamo Village** and a ready-made film set for NBC-TV's *The Alamo: Thirteen Days to Glory*, the IMAX film *Alamo: The Price of Freedom*, and countless other features and commercials.

Wayne was insistent that art director Al Ybarra create a realistic set, and Ybarra did. In fact, since it includes several buildings that no longer exist on Alamo Plaza, the site offers a look back at the Alamo long before it became a tourist attraction. Alamo Village has a slight theme-park feel about it, with frequent shoot-outs staged in front of the working cantina. There's a **John Wayne Museum**, of course, and a blacksmith shop, chapel, bank, and jail. You may recognize one or all of these buildings from your favorite Western. Alamo Village is open daily throughout the year except Christmas. Call the village for its current hours and admission fee (210/563-2580).

Brackettville is also home to **Fort Clark**, an 1852 Army stronghold against the area's native peoples. The fort was decommissioned after serving as a POW camp for Nazi soldiers during WWII, but its impressive stone barracks have been ingeniously reborn as a resort. The stockade remains, too, in its role as the **Old Guardhouse Jail Cavalry Museum**. Open weekends, the jail presents exhibits on the fort and the soldiers who served here (including George S. Patton).

Getting There from San Antonio: *Take U.S. 90 west to Brackettville and follow the signs.*

Day Trip: Space Center Houston

Distance from San Antonio: 197 miles or about a three-hour drive

Sadly, what most people remember about Houston's role in the manned space program is that it gave Tom Hanks a place to call and say, "We have a problem."

Space Center Houston can remedy that. The official visitors center for NASA's Johnson Space Center, SCH will remind young and old Americans that, though it seems space shuttles take to the skies as often as Southwest Airlines, space exploration is the most glorious adventure ever undertaken.

Start your self-guided tour at the indoor **Space Center Plaza**. There you'll find a full-scale mock-up of the flight deck and mid-deck of the **Space Shuttle**, the galaxy's largest collection of **Moon rocks** (next to the Moon itself), and the 20-minute presentation *The Feel of Space*, which shows you what it's like for shuttle astronauts to live and work in space. Then try your hand at landing the 85-ton orbiter on a flight simulator.

Blast off in the IMAX theater with the film *To Be an Astronaut*, which uses breathtaking earthly and otherworldly footage to take you through astronaut training. Then walk through the **Mission Status Center**, a replica of the famous Mission Control that is constantly tuned in to current shuttle missions. Non-astronaut food is available in the **Zero-G Diner**.

Outside, take the **NASA Tram Tour** through the sprawling Johnson Space Center. You'll see the real **Mission Control**, the **Weightless Environment Training Facility**, the **Space Environment Simulation Laboratory**, and other multisyllabic installations that show you why NASA is so fond of acronyms. If you're lucky, you'll see real astronauts training for upcoming missions. On the way back to the plaza, the tram stops at **Rocket Park**, with its massive exhibits of the Saturn V, Mercury Redstone, and other real launch vehicles. Back inside, kids will enjoy the new **Kids' Space Place**, where they'll learn even more while playing in 17 activity areas and zooming down the shuttle escape slide.

Open year-round: Memorial Day to Labor Day daily 9–7; rest of the year Mon–Fri 10–5, Sat and Sun 10–7. Closed Christmas Day. $11.95 adults, $10.95 seniors, $8.95 children 4–11. Parking is $3. The entire center is wheelchair accessible, and chairs are available for rent. Free, air-conditioned pet care is available if you bring your pet's water bowl.

Getting There from San Antonio: *Take I-10 east to downtown Houston. Catch I-45 south. Pass Loop 610, Beltway 8, and Ellington Airport, then turn left on NASA Road 1 to number 1601. During rush hours (or if you don't have any interest in seeing downtown Houston), get off I-10 at Loop 610 east before downtown and follow it to I-45 south. This route is longer, but it's actually faster when the other roads are full.*

APPENDIX: CITY·SMART BASICS

EMERGENCY PHONE NUMBERS

Ambulance, Fire, Police, 911

United Way 24-Hour Helpline
210/227-HELP

Rape Crisis Center 24-Hour Hotline
210/349-7273

HOSPITALS AND EMERGENCY MEDICAL CENTERS

Baptist Health System

Baptist Medical Center
111 Dallas St.
210/297-7000

North Central Baptist Hospital
520 Madison Oak
210/297-4000

Northeast Baptist Hospital
8811 Village Dr.
210/297-2000

Southeast Baptist Hospital
4214 E. Southcross Blvd.
210/297-3000

St. Luke's Baptist Hospital
7930 Floyd Curl Dr.
210/297-5000

Methodist Health System

Methodist Hospital
7700 Floyd Curl Dr.
210/575-4000

Metropolitan Methodist Hospital
1310 McCullough Ave.
210/208-2200

Northeast Methodist Hospital
12412 Judson Rd.
210/650-4949

Santa Rosa Hospital System

Santa Rosa Hospital/Children's Hospital
519 W. Houston St.
210/704-2011

Santa Rosa Northwest Hospital
2827 Babcock Rd.
210/705-6300

University Health System

University Hospital
4502 Medical Dr.
210/358-4000

University Health Center/Downtown
527 N. Leona
210/358-3400

RECORDED INFORMATION

San Antonio Express-News
ExpressLine
(24-hour news/information)
210/554-0500

Time and Temperature
210/226-3232

VIA Metropolitan Transit
Route and Schedule Information
210/362-2020

Weather Forecast
210/225-0404

VISITOR INFORMATION

Alamo Visitors Center
217 Alamo Plaza
210/225-8587

City of San Antonio
Convention & Visitors Bureau
203 S. St. Mary's St.
210/207-6700

Greater San Antonio
Chamber of Commerce
602 E. Commerce St.
210/229-2100

DISABLED ACCESS INFORMATION

Assistance for the Blind
800/252-5204

Region VI Disability Services
of Texas
210/599-1495

Teletype for the Deaf
210/207-7245

CITY TOURS

Local Arrangements Ltd.
Custom Tours
210/224-3061

Lone Star Trolley Tours
210/222-9090

San Antonio City Tours
210/212-5395

CAR RENTAL

Advantage
800/777-5500
www.arac.com

Dollar Rent A Car
800/800-4000
www.dollar.com

Enterprise
800/325-8007

Hertz
800/654-3131
www.hertz.com

National
800/227-7368
www.nationalcar.com

Rent A Wreck
800/535-1391

Thrifty Car Rental
800/367-2277
www.thrifty.com

POST OFFICES

Main Branch
10410 Perrin Beitel Rd. (NE)
210/368-8481

Airport Facility (24-hour service)
10250 John Saunders Dr. (NE)
210/828-9656

Alamo Heights (window service)
4801 Broadway (NE)
210/826-0461

Arsenal Station
1140 S. Laredo St. (DT)
210/227-3535

Beacon Hill Station
1064 Vance Jackson St. (NW)
210/735-9881

Brooks AFB Station
Bldg. 726 (S)
210/534-5979

Cedar Elm Station
5837 De Zavala Rd. (NW)
210/641-7828

Cresthaven Station
3731 West Ave. (NW)
210/342-7281

Dobie Station
4950 E. Houston St. (NE)
210/662-7003

Downtown Station
615 E. Houston St. (DT)
210/227-3399

Ft. Sam Houston Branch
2300 Stanley Rd. (NE)
210/223-4749

Hackberry Station
2000 S. Hackberry St. (NE)
210/534-4022

Harlandale Station
6302 S. Flores St. (S)
210/922-0681

Heritage Station
702 Richland Hills Dr. (NW)
210/523-1261

Highland Hills Station
3918 Clark Ave. (NE)
210/532-8281

Laurel Heights Station
2400 McCullough Ave. (NE)
210/735-1561

Leon Valley Branch
6825 Huebner Rd. (NW)
210/680-5074

Lockhill Station
12951 Huebner Rd. (NW)
210/493-2174

Los Jardines Station
5555 San Fernando St. (NW)
210/433-8551

Nimitz (window service)
10300 Heritage Blvd. (NW)
210/341-0223

North Broadway Station
9211 Broadway (NE)
210/824-6108

Northeast Carrier Annex
11119 Landmark 35 Dr. (NE)
210/590-8163

Serna Station
7503 Harlow St. (NE)
210/655-0151

South San Antonio Station
2612 W. Southcross St. (S)
210/922-1021

South Texas Medical Center Station
4835 Medical Dr. (NW)
210/616-0777

Frank M. Tejeda Branch
7411 Barlite Blvd. (S)
210/923-6081

Terrell Wells Station
2602 Pleasanton Rd. (S)
210/923-6081

Thousand Oaks Station
15610 Henderson Pass (NE)
210/494-9671

University Park Station
914 Bandera Rd. (NW)
210/433-1721

Valley Hi Station
5510 SW Loop 410 (S)
210/674-3153

Wainwright Station
515 Pierce St. (NE)
210/227-3711

RESOURCES FOR NEW RESIDENTS

Bexar County Voter Registration
210/335-6625

Newcomers of San Antonio
210/228-5040

League of Women Voters
210/226-3530

Bexar County Tax Office
210/335-6628

City Public Service (gas
and electricity)
210/353-2222

San Antonio Water System
210/704-7297

San Antonio Library System
210/207-2500

Welcome Wagon International
210/824-6355

MULTICULTURAL RESOURCES

African American Chamber of
Commerce
210/490-1624

Carver Community Cultural Center
210/207-7211

Esperanza Peace and Justice
Center
210/228-0201

Gay and Lesbian Community Center
210/732-4300

Korean American Association of
San Antonio
210/590-9751

Native American Assistance
Program
210/432-6336

San Antonio Hispanic Chamber of
Commerce
210/225-0462

Senior Community Services Inc.
210/227-3146

SIS Women's Resource Center
210/646-7477

BABYSITTING/CHILD CARE

Alamo City Sitters
210/377-1113

Caring Nannies of San Antonio
210/666-2669

Stay 'n' Play Drop-in Child Care
Center
210/945-0410

CITY MEDIA

Newspapers

La Prensa de San Antonio
(bilingual Latino, twice weekly)
210/242-7900

San Antonio Business Journal
(weekly)
210/341-3202

San Antonio Current
(alternative weekly)
210/227-0044

San Antonio Express-News
(major daily)
210/250-2000

San Antonio Informer
(African American weekly)
210/227-8300

San Antonio Register
(African American weekly)
210/222-1721

Magazines

Key
(monthly entertainment calendar)
210/342-0072

Our Kids
(parenting)
210/349-6667

Rio Magazine
(river-centered entertainment)
210/227-4262

San Antonio Food & Leisure
210/655-9342

San Antonio Kids
(parenting)
210/680-3291

South Texas Fitness & Health
210/680-3291

Radio Stations

KPAC-FM 88.3/NPR, classical
KSTX-FM 89.1/NPR, news
KYFS-FM 90.9/Christian
KROM-FM 92.9/Latino
Mix 96.1/pop, contemporary
KJ-97/country
KISS-FM 99.5/hard rock
Y-100 FM/country
KQ-102 FM/pop
KZEP-FM 104.5/classic rock
Magic 105 FM/pop
KCJZ-FM 106.7/light jazz
KXTN-FM 107/Tejano

KCHG-AM 810/Christian
KTSA-AM 550/news, talk
KDRY-AM 1100/Christian
KONO-AM 860 and FM 101/oldies
WOAI-AM 1200/news, talk

Television Stations

KMOL-TV 4 (cable 3)/NBC
KENS-TV 5 (cable 5)/CBS
KLRN-TV 9 (cable 10)/PBS
KSAT-TV 12 (cable 13)/ABC
KABB-TV 29 (cable 11)/WB
KRRT-TV 35 (cable 7)/Fox
KWEX-TV 41 (cable 8)/Univision

BOOKSTORES

B. Dalton Bookseller
Ingram Park Mall
Ingram Rd. and I-410 W.
210/681-9620

North Star Mall
San Pedro Ave. and I-410
210/340-7893

Rolling Oaks Mall
6909 N. Loop 1604 E.
210/651-5649

Windsor Park Mall
7900 I-35 N.
210/657-2256

Barnes & Noble
321 NW Loop 410
210/342-0008

6065 NW Loop 410
210/522-1340

12635 I-10 W.
210/561-0205

Booksmiths of San Antonio
209 Alamo Plaza
210/271-9177

Borders Books & Music
Quarry Market
255 E. Basse Rd.
210/828-9496

11745 I-10 W.
210/561-0022

Brentano's
Rivercenter
849 E. Commerce St.
210/223-3938

The Red Balloon
5009 Broadway
210/826-5087

The Twig Bookshop
5005 Broadway
210/826-6411

Waldenbooks
Ingram Park Mall
Ingram Rd. and I-410 W.
210/681-2955

Rolling Oaks Mall
6909 N. Loop 1604 E.
210/651-5304

Westlakes Mall
1401-124 SW Loop 410
210/673-6510

Windsor Park Mall
7900 I-35 N.
210/655-0591

INDEX

Accommodations: Downtown San Antonio, 37–50; Northeast San Antonio, 50–52; Northwest San Antonio, 52–56; South San Antonio, 56–57
Acequias and aqueduct, 108
African-Americans, 3, 13, 106
Air Force History and Traditions Museum, 116
Alameda Theatre, 86–88, 173
Alamo, 1, 5, 6, 10, 88, 92
Alamo Cenotaph, 88, 92
Alamodome, 3, 11, 88, 156, 157, 173–74
Alamo Dragway, 155
Alamo Heights, 4, 144–45
Alamo Street Restaurant and Theatre, 169
Antiques, 142, 146
Architecture, 31
Armadillos, 2, 123
Arneson River Theatre, 93, 172, 174
Arts and Cultural Affairs, Department of, 171
¡Arts! San Antonio, 170, 171
Austin, Moses, 5, 10
Austin, Stephen, 6
Austin, Texas, 199–200
Ayres, Atlee, 4, 111, 137, 176

Ballet San Antonio, 172
Barbecue, 77
Baseball, professional, 155
Baseball and softball, 158
Basketball, professional, 155–56
Battle of Flowers, 11, 98
Bean, Judge Roy, 93
Beethoven Hall, 174
Bexar County, 2, 23
Bexar County Court House, 31
Bicycling, 32, 108–10, 158
Blue Star Arts Complex, 3, 117–18, 169
Boating/sailing, 158–159
Bowie, Jim, 6, 94, 97
Bowling, 159
Brackenridge Park, 104, 105, 132, 133, 161
Brackettville, Texas, 202
Brooks Air Force Base, 3, 116–17
Bus services, 25–28, 35, 107
Bus tours, 89–91, 93, 97–99, 206

Calaveras Lake, 158–59
Calendar of events, 17–20
Campgrounds, 57
Canary Islanders, 5, 94, 135

Canoeing, 159–60
Canyon Lake, 159
Carver Community Cultural Center, 118, 171, 174–75
Casa Navarro State Historical Park, 88
Cascarones, 2, 96
Chapel of the Miracles, 106
Chili queens, 89
China Grove, 105
Cinco de Mayo, 12
Civil War, 7, 11, 137
Coleto Creek, Battle of, 7
Contemporary Art Month, 117
Convention and Visitors Bureau, 13, 17
Coppini, Pompeo, 88
Crockett, Davy, 7, 94, 97
Crowne Plaza St. Anthony Hotel, 39–40

Daughters of the Republic of Texas, 11, 88, 92
Day of the Dead (Dia de Los Muertos), 12
Dignowity Park, 3
Dining: Downtown San Antonio, 60–66; Northeast San Antonio, 66–76; Northwest San Antonio, 76–84; South San Antonio, 84–85

Edge, The, 89
Eisenhower, Dwight D., 104, 161
Enchanted Rock State Park, 197–98
Enrique de la Peña, José, 6
Esquire Tavern, 189
Europeans, 3, 7, 10, 12, 91–92

Fairmount Hotel, 40, 119
Far West Rodeo, 183
Fiesta, 1, 20, 98, 107
Fiesta Flambeau Parade, 98
Films, 8–9
Fire ants, 135
Firelight Players, 169
Fishing, 158–59
Fitness clubs, 160
Floods, 8–9, 11, 101
Folklorico dance, 171
Fort Sam Houston, 3, 4, 8, 11, 100–04, 117, 169
Fort Sam Houston National Cemetery, 104, 105
Fredericksburg, Texas, 197–98
Freeman Coliseum, 176–77
Friedrich Park, 132–34

Geronimo, 11, 104, 122
Golf courses, 160–65
Golf, professional, 156
Goliad, Texas, 7, 10
Gompers, Samuel, 39, 119
Guadalupe Cultural Arts Center, 120, 172, 177
Guadalupe River, 159–60
Guenther, Carl Hilmar, 91

Harlequin Dinner Theatre, 169
H-E-B Science Treehouse, 116
HemisFair 1968, 9, 11, 99–100, 101, 113
HemisFair Park, 31, 66, 91, 99–100, 108, 113, 122–24, 134
Hertzberg Circus Museum, 31, 113, 127
Hiking, 165
Hill Country, 2, 199
Hockey, 156
Horse racing, 156
Houston, Sam, 7
Hugman, Robert, 94, 101

IMAX Theatre, 91, 126
Institute of Texan Cultures, 113–14, 127–28
Instituto Cultural Mexicano, 91

Japanese Tea Garden, 133, 138
Jazz'SAlive, 138–40
Jim Cullum Jazz Band, 42, 188
Josephine Theatre, 169
Joske's, 147
Jump-Start Performance Company, 169

Kelly Air Force Base, 3
Kiddie Park, 130
King William Historic District, 3, 13, 28, 91–92, 96–97, 98
King William Street Fair, 98

Lady Bird Johnson Wildflower Center, 199–200
Lackland Air Force Base, 3, 116
Lake McQueeny, 159
La Mansión del Rio, 42–43
Laredo, Texas, 201–02
Las Posadas, 12
Latino heritage, 12
Laurie Auditorium, 177
La Villita Historic District, 92–93, 107, 116, 143
Leeper Auditorium, 177–78
Legoretta, Ricardo, 94
Lila Cockrell Theatre, 178
Lindbergh, Charles, 34

Lone Star Buckhorn Museums, 114
López de Santa Anna, Antonio, 6, 10, 92–93
Luminarias, 99
Lyndon B. Johnson National Historic Park, 195–97

Magic Time Machine, 125
Magik Theatre, 126, 169
Majestic Theatre, 37, 175, 178
Market Square (El Mercado), 1, 93, 129–30, 143
Maverick, Samuel, 138
McAllister Auditorium, 178–79
McAllister Park, 134–35
McCombs, "Red," 154–55
McNay Art Museum, 111–12
McNay, Marion Koogler, 111
Menger Hotel, 43–44
Mexican food, ordering, 72–73
Milam Park Playground, 124, 135
Military Plaza (Plaza de Armas), 96
Mill Race Studio, 31, 105
Mission Bridge, 2, 112
Missions, 10: Concepción, 108–10; San José, 95, 110; San Juan Capistrano, 110; San Francisco de la Espada, 110
Movie theaters, 192
Mud Parade, 18, 101
Municipal Auditorium, 4, 176, 179
Murals, 112
Museum of Flight Medicine, 116–17
Mutual UFO Network, 105

Native Americans, 8, 12–13, 92, 137: Apaches, 11, 104, 110, 137; Aztec, 137; Coahuiltecas, 5, 137; Comanches, 5, 110, 137; Payaya, 5, 100, 137
Natural Bridge Caverns and Wildlife Park, 11, 124
Navarro, José Antonio, 88
Nelson A. Rockefeller Center for Latin American Art, 111, 112–13
New Playwright's Theatre, 169
Night in Old San Antonio, 93, 98, 107
North Star Mall, 151–52
Nuevo Laredo, Mexico, 201–02

Olmos Basin/Creek/Park, 4

Parks and Recreation, Department of, 132, 172
Paseo del Rio Association, 2
Perfecto de Cos, Martin, 6, 10, 92–93
Ripley's Believe It or Not!/Plaza Theatre of Wax, 28, 93–94

Quarry Market, 4, 152

Rafting, 159–60
Railroad, 8, 11, 34, 114–15
Randolph Air Force Base, 3
Republic of Texas, 7, 10, 14–15
Retama Park, 156
Rivercenter, 11, 30–32, 94, 100, 151, 152–53;
River Walk (El Paseo del Rio), 2, 3, 9, 11, 16, 63, 94, 99, 101
River Walk Bottom Festival, 18, 101
Rodeo, 156
Roller coasters, 128
Roosevelt, Theodore, 44

Sailing, 158–59
St. Anthony of Padua, 5, 10
St. Mary's School for Boys, 42, 161
St. Paul Square, 3, 104–06
San Antonio Botanical Gardens, 124–25, 136–37
San Antonio Central Library, 94, 128
San Antonio Children's Museum, 128–29
San Antonio International Airport, 24, 32–33
San Antonio Museum of Art, 31, 112–13, 129
San Antonio Opera Company, 170–71
San Antonio Public Theater, 169
San Antonio River, 2, 10, 11
San Antonio Speedway, 155
San Antonio Stock Show and Rodeo, 156–57
San Antonio Symphony, 37, 126–27, 171
San Antonio Zoological Gardens and Aquarium, 104, 125, 133
San Fernando Cathedral, 5, 10, 31, 94
San Jacinto, Battle of, 1, 7, 10
San Marcos, Texas, 200–01
San Pedro Park, 137–38
Scobee Planetarium, 125–26
Sculpture, 115, 119
Sea World of Texas, 106, 130–31
Seguin, Juan, 97
Selena, 148
Six Flags Fiesta Texas, 16, 106–07, 131
Skating, 166
Skeet/target shooting, 166
Skydiving, 166
Sky Ride, 133
Soccer, professional, 157
Southwest School of Art and Craft, 95, 120–21
Space Center Houston, 203–04
Spanish Governor's Palace, 5, 10, 95–96
Splashtown, 104, 131

Sporting District, 54
Steves, Edward, 96–97
Steves Homestead, 96–97
Stinson, Marjorie, 34
Streetcars, 34
Strieber, Whitley, 4
Sunken Garden Amphitheatre, 133, 172, 178, 179
Sunset Station (Sunset Depot), 3, 31, 35, 104–06, 187
Swimming pools, 163, 167

Taxi service, 28–29
Tejano/Conjunto music, 7, 12, 173
Tennis, 167
Texas Adventure, The, 97, 127
Texas Cavaliers River Parade, 98
Texas Folklife Festival, 113–14
Texas Highway Patrol Museum, 97
Texas Open Golf Tournament, 156
Texas Transportation Museum, 114–15, 129
Tower Life Building, 4, 31
Tower of the Americas, 31, 66, 99–100, 134
Train services, 35
TransGuide, 25, 34
Travis Park, 138–40
Travis, William Barrett, 6, 94, 97
Trolleys, 25–27, 100
Tubing/canoeing/rafting, 159–60

Union Stockyards, 107–08
Urban 15, 172–73
U.S. Army Medical Museum, 104, 117

Visitor information, 206
Volleyball, 167

Wildflowers, 136
Witte Museum, 115–16, 129
Women's Army Auxiliary Corps (WAAC), 11, 104
Works Progress Administration, 9, 11, 101

Xeriscaping, 134

Yanaguana, 5, 100
Yanaguana Cruises, 100

You'll Feel like a Local When You Travel with Guides from John Muir Publications

CiTY·SMaRT™ GUIDEBOOKS

Pick one for your favorite city: *Albuquerque, Anchorage, Austin, Calgary, Charlotte, Chicago, Cincinnati, Cleveland, Denver, Indianapolis, Kansas City, Memphis, Milwaukee, Minneapolis/St. Paul, Nashville, Pittsburgh, Portland, Richmond, Salt Lake City, San Antonio, St. Louis, Tampa/St. Petersburg, Tucson*

Guides for kids 6 to 10 years old about what to do, where to go, and how to have fun in: *Atlanta, Austin, Boston, Chicago, Cleveland, Denver, Indianapolis, Kansas City, Miami, Milwaukee, Minneapolis/St. Paul, Nashville, Portland, San Francisco, Seattle, Washington D.C.*

TRAVEL✦SMART®

Trip planners with select recommendations to: *Alaska, American Southwest, Carolinas, Colorado, Deep South, Eastern Canada, Florida Gulf Coast, Hawaii, Illinois/Indiana, Kentucky/Tennessee, Maryland/Delaware, Michigan, Minnesota/Wisconsin, Montana/Wyoming/Idaho, New England, New Mexico, New York State, Northern California, Ohio, Pacific Northwest, Pennsylvania/New Jersey, South Florida and the Keys, Southern California, Texas, Utah, Virginias, Western Canada*

Rick Steves' GUIDES

See *Europe Through the Back Door* and take along guides to: *France, Belgium & the Netherlands; Germany, Austria & Switzerland; Great Britain & Ireland; Italy; Russia & the Baltics; Scandinavia; Spain & Portugal; London; Paris; or the Best of Europe*

ADVENTURES IN NATURE

Plan your next adventure in: *Alaska, Belize, Caribbean, Costa Rica, Guatemala, Honduras, Mexico*

JMP travel guides are available at your favorite bookstores. For a FREE catalog or to place a mail order, call: 800-888-7504.

John Muir Publications P.O. Box 613 ✦ Santa Fe, NM 87504

ABOUT THE AUTHOR

Erik Ketcherside, an 11-year San Antonio resident, is a native of another river city—St. Louis, Missouri. A recovering music teacher and mediocre trombone player, Erik is now a freelance writer who refuses to go anywhere near downtown San Antonio during Fiesta.

This book is for Larry, who introduced the author to critical thinking, human-powered waterskiing, bumblebee badminton, willow swinging, and Frank Zappa. Thanks, my friend. See you at the Eric Dolphy Memorial Barbecue.

JOHN MUIR PUBLICATIONS and its City•Smart Guidebook authors are dedicated to building community awareness within City•Smart cities. We are proud to work with the Benitia Family Center as we publish this guide to San Antonio.

The Benitia Family Center established its Adult Literacy Program in 1995 upon realizing that illiteracy caused much of the distress residents of the San Antonio community encounter. English as a Second Language, high school equivalency (GED), and citizenship classes are offered for free, as well as basic computer literacy classes and a one-on-one tutoring program for students with specific needs. To better serve the students, services are also offered at nine satellite locations throughout San Antonio.

For more information, please contact:
Literacy Coordinator(s)
Benitia Family Center
4650 Eldridge Avenue
San Antonio, TX 78237
210/433-9300
fax: 210/432-6739

The Benitia Family Center